D1297464

John Fitzmaurice

THE POLITICS OF BELGIUM

THE POLITICS OF BELGIUM

Crisis and Compromise in a Plural Society

by
JOHN FITZMAURICE

With a Foreword by
LEO TINDEMANS

C. HURST & COMPANY, LONDON

First published in the United Kingdom by
C. Hurst & Co. (Publishers) Ltd.,
38 King Street, London WC2E 8JT
© John Fitzmaurice, 1983
ISBN 0-905838-89-0
Printed in Great Britain

CONTENTS

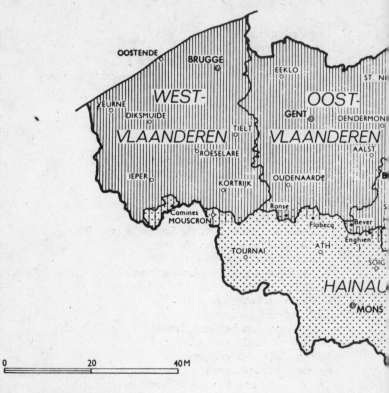

0   20   40 M

⊚ National capital
⊙ Provincial capital
▥ Provincial frontiers
▦ Dutch language region
▨ French language region
▦ German language region
▦ Bilingual district (French - Dutch)
▦ Dutch speaking area with protected
       French-speaking minority
▦ French speaking area with protected
       Dutch-speaking minority
▨ French speaking area with protected
       German speaking minority
▬ German speaking area with protected
       French-speaking minority

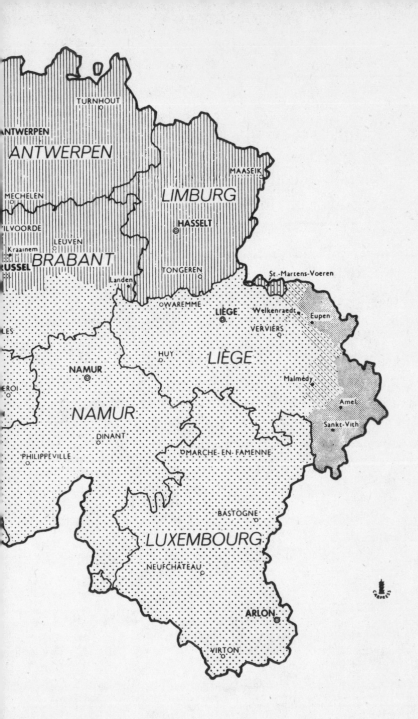

FOREWORD BY LEO TINDEMANS

FORMER PRIME MINISTER OF BELGIUM

I most warmly welcome this timely initiative of publishing a book on Belgian politics aimed at an English language readership. Despite close ties in NATO and the European Communities, Belgium's political problems are little known in Britain or the United States, and reaction is often incomprehension based on over-simplification of the issues involved. The enactment in August 1980 of laws fundamentally restructuring the State in the direction of a so-called 'federalism' has added to the complexity of our political life, as have the deepening economic problems we face.

This work is therefore a most timely effort at increasing knowledge of and sympathy for our difficult and complex political realities. The author, an Englishman living in Brussels, is well placed to undertake this task, which he has approached with the sympathetic but often also critical eye of the detached and informed observer. He both informs and analyses. He has his own views and expresses them, which contributes greatly to the liveliness of the book. Indeed, no Belgian political party or institution will find all his conclusions to their liking or endorse them, but most will agree with a great deal of what he has to say, and that is how it should be.

For my part, I wish every success to this work, which will I hope contribute to a deeper knowledge and insight into our country and its political institutions.

Brussels,
September 1982

Leo Tindemans

ACKNOWLEDGEMENTS

I owe my thanks to a very large number of people, too large to mention them all individually, for guiding me in the complexities of Belgian politics and enriching my own knowledge, experience and analysis in ways which often led me to see various matters in a new light.

I would, however, particularly like to thank Mr Jansens, Director of the Elections Department of the Ministry of the Interior, and his Deputy Mr Pieron for giving me their time and expertise to understand the complexities of the electoral system. The Documentation and Committee Secretariats of the two Houses of Parliament were also most helpful. The political parties responded unstintingly to my requests for their programmes and statutes, and for details about their history and organisation.

Many Belgian political leaders have over the years given me the benefit of their views and experience, which has greatly enriched this book. I would particularly like to mention Mr Tindemans, Mr Van Miert, Mr Oscar Debunne, Mr Ernest Glinne, Mrs Spaak, Mr Gendebien and Mr Deleuze, who together cover a wide range of both Flemish and Walloon opinion.

Thanks are due to many Belgian friends, who have also contributed to my understanding of their political system, though I do not expect them all to agree with what I have written! I would like to mention in particular my friend and colleague Mr Jean Louis Salmon, whom I would like to thank for many hours of stimulating discussion about Belgian political life and socialism, to which we are both attached.

Nor must I forget Mrs A. Gawenda for once again coping so well with my intractable handwriting and disordered method of work. Finally, all opinions expressed in this book are my own responsibility and in no way engage any other person or institution.

Brussels,   J. F.
March 1983

ABBREVIATIONS

Parties

PSC	*Parti Social Chrétien*
CVP	*Christelijke Volkspartij*
PVV	*Partij voor Vrijheid en Vortuitgang*
PRL	*Parti Réformateur Libéral* (1978)
PRLW	*Parti des Réformes et des Libertés Wallones* (1977)
PLP	*Parti de la Liberté et du Progrès* (old Liberal Party)
PL	*Parti Libéral* (Brussels)
POB	*Parti Ouvrier Belge* (1885–1945)
PSB/BSP	*Parti Socialiste Belge/Belgische Socialistische Partij*
PS	*Parti Socialiste* (1978–)
SP	*Socialistische Partij* (1978–)
PCB/KPB	*Parti Communiste Belge/Kommunistische Partij van België*
RW	*Rassemblement Wallon*
FDF	*Front Démocratique des Francophones*
VU	*Volksunie*
VL BLOK	*Vlaams Blok* (splinter from VU)
UDRT/RAD	*Union Démocrate pour le Respect du Travail/ Respekt voor Arbijd en Democratie*
AGALEV	*Anders Gaan Leven* (Flemish Ecologists)
Ecolo	*Walloon Ecologists*

Others

MPW	*Mouvement Populaire Wallon*
MOC	*Mouvement Ouvrier Chrétien*
FGTB	*Fédération du Travail de Belgique*
CSC	*Confédération des Syndicats Chrétiens*
FEB	*Fédération des Entreprises Belges*

INTRODUCTION

Belgium is a small country, but one which has always occupied a central strategic position in Europe. Even before Belgium existed as an independent nation, Britain was constantly alert to ensure that the Low Countries — 'a pistol pointed at the heart of England' — did not fall under the control of the dominant continental power, be it Spain, France, Austria or later Germany. The Low Countries were until 1830 the plaything of the great powers, and purely internal movements failed or succeeded only to the extent that they paralleled great power interests. Britain, for example, had an important — and in the nineteenth century predominant — hand in the working out of the destiny of the Low Countries. She was instrumental in creating the Kingdom of the Greater Netherlands in 1815 and then destroying it to create an independent Belgian state in 1830 which she guaranteed and supported in two World Wars.

Belgium is an ancient civilisation but a recent state, newer than the United States of America: she celebrated her 150th anniversary of statehood only as late as 1980. Doubts about the viability and desirability of the new state are as old as its statehood. For many Belgians who preferred a French or Dutch connection, the new state was an artificial construction of the great powers. The tensions of the two World Wars, with the attraction of the German occupier for some Flemish nationalists, the battle over the future of Leopold III after 1945, the relative economic failure of Wallonia and the rise of a new and democratic economic and political nationalism both in Flanders and Wallonia in the 1960s, have fuelled and indeed exacerbated these persistent doubts, to the point where the celebrations of 1980 were considerably more muted even than those of the '*Cinquantenaire*' (fiftieth anniversary) held in 1880 and the '*Centenaire*' of 1930. These self-doubts of post-colonial and post-industrial Belgium are only too familiar to the British.

As in Britain, the development of a strong regional dimension to political life has at times threatened the integrity and governability of the state; *relatively* calmer waters had been reached in the early 1980s. Regional nationalism was at first a Flemish defensive phenomenon in what, in the century after 1830, was a state created by and for the Francophone bourgeoisie — which, it should be noted, at that time dominated the larger Flemish towns as well as Brussels and the Walloon regions. Reconstituted after the Second World War under the banner of the Volksunie and a number of the Flemish cultural organisations and with firm roots in the Flemish

1

universities, Flemish nationalism became a force to be reckoned with rather than to be ignored or discredited. With the relative economic decline of Wallonia, accelerated by the post-1973 world recession, it was perhaps inevitable that a defensive Walloon nationalism would develop to defend both the privileged status of French, which is now the minority language of the country as a whole, and the economic position of a region in severe decline. Thus, after 1965, federalist Francophone movements emerged in Brussels (FDF) and in Wallonia (RW), and became significant political forces. The presence of these two blocs — often objective allies against the older 'Belgian' or 'national' parties (except in the intractable matter of Brussels) — has forced these traditional parties to become regionalised and to take on board regional issues and demands to an unprecedented degree, to the point where only the CVP aspires, even covertly, to any sort of 'national destiny'. Belgium has thereby come to resemble a supertanker, so cumbersome that the tiniest course correction takes about 5 miles of water. Most practical issues, however minor, become 'regional' disputes. The necessity for com-promise created by such a structure, exacerbated by the plethora of overlapping contradictions between a pyramid of competing and often hostile authorities, means that solutions to problems are mostly not solutions, but rather agreements to differ or let sleeping dogs lie — or, worse, agreements in principle to be implemented, perhaps, at some future date. The key question now must be: is Belgium governable?

It became fashionable in Britain after the 1979 General Election to talk of 'Two Nations': the North, labour and working-class, with problems of severe de-industrialisation; and the South, conserva-tive, more classless and meritocratic, with less severe economic problems. In Belgium, the same syndrome is institutionalised to a dangerous degree, with divergences overlapping rather than cross-cutting. Flanders is more rural, at least in its ethos; more Catholic, more conservative. Wallonia is more urban, more industrial, faces more severe economic decline, is more working-class in ethos, and is more anti-clerical and more left-wing (Socialist, Communist, *Rassemblement Wallon* [RW]). The Regional parties are in the image of their country: the FDF is a broad church; the RW more left-wing and the *Volksunie* more right of centre. In the Walloon Christian Democrats (PSC), the influence of the union-based MOC faction is considerably greater than that of its Flemish counterpart in the CVP.

Severe economic problems, strongly defensive trade unions and a defective political decision-making process have created, as to some degree in Britain, parallel decision-making processes, outside the normal constitutional framework. This 'sidelining' process has applied in a wide variety of areas, on both an *ad hoc* and a more institutionalised basis. The classic process is for extra-parliamentary actors — be they 'the social partners', a group of political parties with or without relevant interest groups, or a conclave of political parties and experts — to agree on a solution, which is then rubber-stamped *en bloc* as a package deal by the Cabinet and Parliament, both so as to respect the forms and to give the agreement a binding legal character. This process has been applied to such diverse issues as the school subsidy question (*Le pacte scolaire*), state financing of the television networks, 'regionalisation' (devolution), prices and incomes policy, and conditions of service in the medical and para-medical professions. It can be argued that these 'displacement' procedures have been justified because they alone have produced results. However, it is increasingly argued, especially on the political right and by employers' organisations, that an over-mighty corpo-ratism has been created, in which organisations wield too much power, downgrading normal democratically-responsible bodies to the role of spectator and rubber-stamp and above all providing for no arbitration machinery between interests where no agreement can be arrived at. Once again, the question about ungovernability is appropriate.

Belgium was, at a very early stage, an urban country. Industry and trade were highly developed in the Middle Ages. After Britain, Belgium was the first country to undertake an industrial revolution. Her economy was dominated by the classic heavy industries located in the Sambre-Meuse basin on the Liège–Namur–Charleroi–Mons axis: coal, iron and steel, metallurgy, chemicals, glass, textiles. These industries are now in severe decline, with heavy de-industriali-sation and job losses. Belgium, at the time of writing, has the highest rate of unemployment in the EEC and that despite the relative success of Flanders in attracting new industrial growth-points: electronics, service industries, food-processing, oil-refining and petro-chemicals. It follows, therefore, that economic forces are creating divergent trends in Flanders and Wallonia. Belgium well knows the familiar debate about job preservation versus com-petitiveness in an international environment; she knows the weary round of half-successful government salvage operations of firms in difficulties, followed by restructuring proposals, coupled with job losses, compromise and further salvage operations. Since these operations take place predominantly in Wallonia, they rapidly become the cause of inter-regional conflict. The recession has greatly accelerated and made more publicly evident the economic diver-gences between the two regions. The political repercussions of these

economic developments are hard to assess and possibly contradic-
to·y; they have without dc·.bt exacerbated conflict between the
Regions and accentuated the more interventionist tendencies already
observable in Wallonia and the equally clear rejection of such
approaches by the majority of Flemish political opinion. In short,
the 'ideological stereotyping' of each Region is reinforced in a
manner which may increase the difficulties of any dialogue between
the two regions.

The dominance of the regional problem, with its frequent need for
special parliamentary majorities, the deepening recession with its
regional undertones, the regionalisation of the political parties, and
the complexity of the institutional structure have led to a consensual
style of government. Coalitions are often composed of five or six
parties, covering an impossibly broad span of opinion. Within each
Region the need for internal solidarity has, particularly in the two
Francophone Regions (Brussels and Wallonia) led to a high degree
of non-ideological cooperation between Socialist and non-Socialist
parties, which has prevented the Walloon left from playing the
oppositional role which it alone might play. The political parties are
pragmatic and consensus-seeking, avoiding sharp ideological
conflict. Oppositions are usually weak and divided, even when
governments are cumbersome and immobile.

Belgium was among the first countries to recognise the need for
European integration. As early as 1944, her wartime government-
in-exile signed the Benelux Treaty with Luxembourg and the
Netherlands, establishing an Economic Union, which was in many
ways the precursor of the European Communities. As a small
country which had frequently been the theatre and victim of great
power rivalries, Belgium, even while still an important colonial
power, readily saw the need to put an end to the intermittant and
indeed increasingly frequent 'European civil wars' and was prepared
to make the necessary concessions of sovereignty to that end.
Belgium was an enthusiastic founder member of the Council of
Europe, Western European Union and then the European Coal and
Steel Community and the European Economic Community and
Euratom. Through such statesmen as Paul-Henri Spaak, she was
always a champion of the European idea, a believer in further and
more rapid integration and a firm supporter of British entry to the
EEC, despite the brake that this undoubtedly put on integration.

This book will therefore seek to explain how Belgium is governed,
and to set out and analyse, in a comparative perspective, recent
trends in Belgian politics and society which are influencing her
development and where possible seeking to extrapolate these trends
into the medium term.

1
A SHORT HISTORY OF BELGIUM[1]

The Belgian state of today is not only, as we have seen, a very modern creation, but it was also to a considerable extent an artificial one. Paradoxically, it came into existence both as a reaction against its arbitrary fate resulting from historical accident and the machinations of the great powers, and at the same time as the direct result of those very machinations.

Belgium, then, has a long 'pre-history' stretching far back before the Revolution of 1830. The various influences which flowed across this narrow but strategic strip of the North European plain have all chaotically left their mark on the social, political and religious culture of the area. Above all — and this is an important factor in understanding the origins of many of the difficulties of modern Belgium — these various influences created more diversity than unity, more basis for conflict than for a folk memory of common historical experience, lived together as Belgians.

Between 57 and 52 BC, Julius Caesar conquered Belgium, which was previously inhabited by six different Celtic tribes, related to the Gauls,[2] and established Roman rule, which was to last until the fifth century AD. Initially the administrative division of Gallia Belgica covered what is today Belgium, but this was later split into three provinces. The Romans established order and government as well as good communications and trade. The third century saw the coming of Christianity. However, the Belgian provinces were on the marches of the Empire and as early as 275 came under Frankish attack. In order to defend the outlying areas, the Romans permitted allied peoples, such as the Rhenish Franks, to move north, which rapidly adulterated Roman civilisation and soon led to degeneration and breakdown of any kind of overall control, except in isolated areas. The Franks settled in the north and west, leaving the Gallo-Roman people in the south, creating already the linguistic boundary which still exists to this day.

The next period is confused and chaotic. The Huns were repulsed in 451 by the energetic leadership of Merovée and Clovis (481–511), creating a large Frankish kingdom stretching from the Danube to the Pyrenees, but after his death there followed a long period of disorder, which was partly broken by the reigns of Clothaire (613–28), Dagobert (629–39), Charles Martel, who won the crucial battle of Poitiers against the Arabs in 732, and Pépin le Bref

(741–68). These kings attempted a strong policy of centralisation within defensible frontiers.

It was only with Charlemagne (born in 742 near Liège) that this policy was fully successful. This vast empire (around 800) recreated the old Pax Romana and re-established a beginning of law, culture and trade. However, after his death, his heritage was slowly dissipated by his son Louis le Pieux (814–40), whose sons divided the Empire at the fateful Treaty of Verdun (843). This Treaty created three kingdoms: a Frankish kingdom stretching into what is now Flanders (modern France), Francia Orientalis (a German state) and between these strong, compact and rival kingdoms, the weak, but strategically vital Francia media which soon itself split again (855). One kingdom was created in Italy, a second in Provence and Burgundy and a third between the sea, the Rhine and the Meuse covering most of what is today Wallonia (Lotharinga). Thus by 843 and certainly by 855 the die was cast for the history of the next millenium: a secular rivalry between the two large Frankish successor-states, later France and Germany, of which the 'Middle Kingdom' would be the principal victim.

Belgium had already acquired several of its salient characteristics.[3] The cultural and linguistic division was established; she had already acquired her position as 'the cockpit of Europe' and she had become the object rather than the subject of history. All these characteristics acted as a *leitmotiv* down the ages of Belgian history.

Ninth-century Flanders developed in a more favourable way than the southern part of Belgium which, as we have seen, belonged to Lotharinga. The Counts of Flanders, especially Baudouin I and Baudouin II, were able to maintain considerable independence within the Frankish state. During the tenth century, trade and industry, drainage and the building of polders developed rapidly in Flanders.

In Lotharinga, schism and barbarism were the order of the day. The *Regnum Lotharii*, which resulted from the division of the Middle Kingdom in 855, was again divided in 959 after intensive struggles, into Lower Lotharinga (Wallonia) and Upper Lotharinga. There too, though in the tenth century — economic conditions constantly improved.

By the tenth century feudalism had become the dominant form of political and social organisation in both Flanders and lower Lotharinga, as elsewhere in Europe. The system provided effective military protection against the Muslims in Spain, the Norsemen, Slavs and Hungarians, who in turn threatened Western Europe, but at the same time it diluted and parcelled out political and economic power to such an extent that it tended to create anarchy, chaos and inefficiency, quite apart from its gradually more and more repressive nature, although in theory it was a system of both rights and obligations.

Over the next century Flanders was to blossom to a much greater degree than Lotharinga. Baudouin V considerably expanded it both to the west (Artois) and into Zeeland in the north and east.

Lotharinga was part of the Holy Roman Empire and in 1012 was given by the Emperor Henry II to Godefroi I, who sought to break the power of local barons. His successor attempted to raise the whole of the Low Countries in an alliance against the Empire, but failed. Nevertheless, after 1100, central authority was considerably eroded in favour of a number of more local dukedoms — Brabant, the *comtés* of Hainaut, Luxembourg and Limburg, and the independent principality of Liège (its prince being the Bishop of Liège), which was able to expand into the lower Meuse valley. Godefroi III (1190–1235) attempted to redress the situation by means of a delicate balancing act, the main purpose of which was to weaken Flanders. Jean I was able to gain Luxembourg after his victory over Imperial troops at the battle of Worringen (1288). Hainaut, however, was united with Flanders as early as 1180.

The rise of urban democracy

By 1250 important social changes had occurred, which were to be of vital importance in the next period. The Crusades and considerable inflation had seen the decline of feudalism, with the weakening of the large feudal landowners. Many smaller lords had been reduced to the level of the peasantry and many serfs had been able to purchase their liberation from feudal obligations. This led to the establishment of a more secure and prosperous agriculture.

However, there was a parallel development of even more significance, namely the development of vigorous and self-confident urban centres, especially based on the wool trade: Bruges (70,000 inhabitants), Ypres (40,000) and Ghent (45,000). These towns were able to obtain charters which guaranteed them and their citizens important economic rights, such as freedom from feudal obligations, the right to levy taxes and later virtual self-government under complicated systems of guilds and corporations, in which power was in the hands of the richer merchants.

At the same time, the state was modernising its institutions with a consequent gain in central authority. Philippe d'Alsace set up a new non-hereditary body of royal officers (*baillis*), who were responsible for justice, order and taxation. Law was codified (Code of 1292) and more questions were removed from feudal to royal jurisdiction.

At the opening of the fourteenth century Flanders was once again, as in the early thirteenth century, embroiled in the secular Anglo-French wars. As in 1226 (Treaty of Mélun) it was an Anglo-Flemish Treaty (the Treaty of Lierre of 1294) which provoked the crisis. Above all, the autonomy of the Count of Flanders and his tendency to ally with England was unacceptable to Philippe le Bel who in 1301 surpressed Flemish autonomy.

Now the towns[4] were to show their new-found power. A revolt led by Pierre de Coninck, leader of the Bruges weavers, broke out and led to the massacre of non-Flemish elements. An army of 20,000 men was raised, mostly from among the townspeople of Flanders, which defeated the French forces at the battle of the Epérons d'Or near Courtrai on 11 July 1302. An attempt to expand Flemish influence into Zeeland failed, but 'French Flanders' was occupied. Peace negotiations were exceedingly long-drawn-out, only being concluded in 1320. Flemish autonomy was re-established, but Lille and Douai had to be abandoned.

The rest of the century was dominated by serious social conflict and civil war, from which however international rivalries, especially the spill-over of the Hundred Years War, were rarely absent. The heavy fines imposed under the 1320 Treaty led to a tax revolt by the coastal dwellers which even spread to Bruges. Only intervention by the sovereign, King Charles IV of France, saved the Count who had been captured at Courtrai by the rebels. This French intervention followed a new pattern which was to be repeated on several occasions.

In 1337 another revolt of the proletarian weavers broke out in Ghent as a result of the loyal support of the Count to the anti-English foreign policy of France, which led to the closing of the English market and severe consequential economic distress. In Jan van Artevelde the rebels found an energetic and effective leader. He organised an alliance of the three dominant Flemish towns — Ghent, Bruges and Ypres — and this alliance, called 'the Three Members of Flanders', worked in close alliance with England, especially under Edward III. At the same time, in 1339, defensive and free trade treaties were concluded with Luxembourg, Brabant, Hainaut, Holland and Zeeland. These external alliances were directed against France. However, the dominance and repression exercised by the weavers against other classes provoked a severe reaction, and van Artevelde was seriously challenged and then assassinated in 1345.

The policy of consolidation continued, albeit in a more confused manner. Under the Treaty of Ath (1357) Flanders obtained Antwerp and Malines. In return for a pledge of neutrality, Gallican Flanders was returned by the French King.

Severe social unrest was to dominate the next twenty years. This took the form of a struggle between a primitive type of urban proletarian democracy, of which the weavers were the vanguard, and the other social classes led by the Count of Flanders, sometimes supported by the King of France. The weaver Yoens seized power in Ghent in 1379 and the city was subject to three severe sieges. At the battle of Beverhout near Bruges (1382), Philippe van Artevelde (son of Jan van Artevelde) led the forces of Ghent to a crushing victory, but their triumph was to be short-lived. King Charles VI intervened to support the Count and won the decisive battle of West Rozebeke in which van Artevelde was killed. Ackerman continued the struggle with English support, and with general war weariness on both sides, a compromise peace was concluded at Tournai in 1385 which saw the confirmation of both the sovereignty of the Count and the privileges of the cities.

During the same period in Brabant, there were important constitutional innovations, many of which were to last until the end of the *ancien régime* in the 1790s. The democratic split arrived much later in Brabant than in Flanders, but its conquest was more serene and durable, finding expression more in constitution-building than in violence and social revolution.

Much as in England, it was the perennial indebtedness of the rulers and nobles which led to reform. Creditors took to sequestering the property of merchants to meet the debts of rulers. This situation was intolerable, and thus in return for adequate revenues the rulers were forced to concede a series of charters which guaranteed the rights of citizens and ensured some participation in government. The Charter of Cortenberg (1312) established rights for the citizens and set up a Council of four nobles and ten burghers to ensure respect for those rights. After Jean III attempted to break the Charter, two new Charters confirming the previous one and imposing severe limitations on the Duke were adopted in 1314 (the *Chartes Romanes*). In 1356 the '*Joyeuse Entrée*', a codification of earlier Customary Rights and Charters, was adopted and was to remain in force until the 1790s. Citizens were assured important individual civil rights and equality before the law. The powers of taxation and legislation of the Rules were limited in favour of the three orders (nobles, clergy, burghers). This did not prevent disorders, similar to those in Ghent, breaking out in Louvain in 1360, though they never reached the same proportions. The same struggle for democratic rights was also going on in Liège, leading to the creation of a Legislative Assembly of the three orders (Paix de Fexhe), and an arbitral tribunal to consider alleged violations of citizens rights by the Prince-Bishop (Paix des XXII).

The Burgundian period

The early Burgundian period down to the reign of Philippe le Bon (1419–1467)[5] was marked by quiet and unspectacular consolidation of the new equality. Marguerite de Male, the Burgundian inheritor of Flanders, Artois, Burgundy and Franche-Comté married Philip the Bold (1384–1404), who made peace with England and remained neutral in the Anglo-French conflict. His successor, Jean Sans Peur (1404–19) continued this work of consolidation.

With Philippe le Bon[6] a new era opened. He sought to unify under him as many as possible of the diverse states making up the Low Countries, giving them a certain degree of unity and centralisation, to limit their particularism. Many factors, such as increasing trade and the absence of barriers to trade between the various states of the Low Countries, were favourable to these designs, not least because a strong Flanders faced a weakened France and a disparate group of small states to the south which the English had not been able to group together. By a series of dynastic marriages, he was able successively to incorporate Zeeland (1432), Holland (1432) and Hainaut (1432) after the Concordat of Delft. He had already obtained Namur (1429) and Brabant (1430). He was able to purchase the Duchy of Luxembourg in 1441. Now the whole of the Low Countries was under one ruler, except for Liège over which he was nevertheless able to extend a protectorate.

If this work of unification was to be durable, it was necessary to provide the new realm with more solid political institutions. Philippe sought to pursue a certain degree of centralisation without breaking his obligations under earlier Charters and Customary Rights. He established two *Chambres du Conseil* at Lille and in The Hague, which were for the times models of financial organisation. The Estates were reorganised or reactivated in each Province, and a *Grand Conseil* under a Chancellor was established which prepared and administered legislation and justice. Despite a high degree of pragmatism and prudence, Philippe inevitably came into conflict with those seeking to defend their rights and privileges, in particular the urban merchants involved in the wool trade, who were facing extinction from English competition. There were insurrections in both Bruges (1437) and Ghent (1451). In both towns radical elements took control. Both revolts were put down severely.

The successor to Philippe le Bon, Charles le Téméraire (1467–77), was not a great success. However, despite several internal revolts, conflict with the Estates General (1476) and an unsuccessful foreign policy aimed at securing Lorraine, he was able to continue and complete the centralisation policy of his predecessor. He created the *Conseil d'Etat*, responsible for drafting laws and decrees, and the *Parlement* of Malines which acted as an Appeal Court, by dividing the *Grand Conseil*. Both his attempted imposition of French as the exclusive administrative language and a severe taxation policy made necessary by his largely unsuccessful military adventures provoked conflict with the Estates, and saw the loss of the territories so-called '*par delà*' lying in Lorraine, and the Jura. Charles himself was killed at Nancy in January 1477.

The Habsburg period

Charles was succeeded by his only daughter Marie, who ruled until her death in 1482. Following a revolt in Ghent, the Estates seized their chance of recovering their privileges and undoing the centralisation of the last century as did the Flemish towns of the *Membres de Flandres* (Ghent, Bruges and Ypres). Under the *Grand Privilège* (1477) their ancient privileges were recovered. The Estates furthermore had to approve declarations of law, taxation etc. A *Grand Conseil* was set up to supervise the Sovereign, and if in a certain sense this represented a step backwards, it in no way called into question the territorial unification undertaken by the Burgundians. On the contrary, it provided the whole of the Netherlands with a Constitution and political institutions.

Assailed from the south by Louis IX of France, the Low Countries needed the protection of a powerful leader, and so the Estates pressed Marie to marry Maximilian of Austria, which she did in August 1477. The French army was defeated at Lunegatte near St Omer in 1479 and the English Alliance was restored in 1481.

When Marie died, her son Philippe was only four years old and the Regency was assumed by Maximilian. This Regency saw more serious disorders resulting from conflicts with the Estates and the *Trois Membres*. In a first phase Maximilian was forced to make serious concessions, but in 1483 he dismissed the Regency Council and in 1485 forced the capitulation of Ghent and Bruges. In 1487 civil war broke out again and Maximilian was held prisoner by the city of Bruges. He was forced to accept the reintroduction of the *Grand Privilège*, but once freed led an unsuccessful assault with imperial troops. Under Philippe de Clèves, Marie's son, the Netherlands found both leadership and a clear nationalistic political programme.

However, the civil war was a mere corollary to the wider European struggle between Maximilian and Charles VIII of France. The cities of Flanders were gradually worn down, and with the Peace of Cadzand on 30 June 1494 they lost their privileges for ever. With them Flemish pre-eminence in the Netherlands was to disappear: it was the end of a long era.

In late 1493 Maximilian became Holy Roman Emperor and left the government of the Netherlands to his son Philippe, who reigned from 1494 till 1506. In the first period of his reign he distanced himself from his father's expansionist policy, remaining neutral and concluding an important trade treaty with England in 1496. When the death of Don Juan, son of Ferdinand and Isabella of Spain, opened to him the succession to the throne of Spain and possibly in time the Imperial crown itself, he moved closer to his father's line, but died before the likely effects of this new line could be felt in the Low Countries. In domestic policies he had sought to co-operate with the Estates.

His successor, Charles of Luxembourg, was only six years old. The regency was assumed by Marguerite of Austria whose policy was one of reconciliation in domestic affairs and neutrality in foreign policy. In 1515 Charles (later Charles V) came of age and in 1517 inherited the Spanish Habsburg possessions (Spain, Naples, Sardinia, Sicily and the Empire in the Americas); in 1542 he was elected Holy Roman Emperor. The safe and effective Burgundian foreign policy was now replaced by Imperial considerations, and the rich Low Countries were thrown into the maelstrom of a generalised European conflict between France and the Emperor and the religious strife which swept Europe after 1517.

In domestic policy — except, as we shall see, in religious matters — Charles V was conciliatory and tolerant. He largely respected the rights and privileges of what was more or less a confederation of states. He undertook some limited reorganisation of the machinery of government by creating three Councils with advisory functions: the *Conseil d'Etat* (foreign policy, religious matters, etc.); the *Conseil Privé* (drafting legislation, justice), the *Conseil des Finances* (taxation, expenditure). He was however extremely severe in repressing the various new religious movements arising from the Reformation — Lutheranism, Calvinism and Anabaptism — which were in any case marginal in the Low Countries.

In economic life there were important changes. The decline of Bruges was irreversible, and Antwerp took its place as the most important trading centre. New industries replaced the old Flanders wool trade, now in mortal decline, and agriculture too was developed considerably in this period.

However, the Low Countries were more and more drawn into the wars resulting from Habsburg dynastic ambitions.[7] They were able to remain almost untouched by the first two wars, of 1524–6 and 1526–9, which ended with respectively the Treaties of Madrid and Cambrai, under which France abandoned her suzerainty over Flanders; but they were devastated by the ebb and flow of armies in the third (1536–8), fourth (1542–44) and, especially, the fifth (1551–6) wars. By the end of the period she was freed of French sovereignty, and Gelderland, Utrecht and Friesland had been added. An Alliance had been concluded in 1518 with Liège. In 1548 the Imperial Diet adopted an Act (the Augsburg Transaction) whereby the Low Countries became independent within the Empire, their sole obligation being to provide troops for common defence against the Turks, which was balanced by a guarantee of Imperial assistance in the event of French invasion. In 1549 the Diet also approved the Pragmatic Sanction, which unified the inheritance of all the Seventeen Provinces (see below) under one prince in an indissoluble 'package'. By the mid 1550s, the Low Countries had reached their full territorial extent and independence of arbitrary dynastic changes. From this period the name 'Seventeen Provinces' came into use to designate what today constitutes Belgium, the Netherlands and Luxembourg.

On the abdication of Charles V in 1555, Philip II of Spain became ruler of the Low Countries. He was rarely there, and ruled through a series of governors general, to whom he unfortunately allowed only a very limited latitude. He imposed on them two priorities, which were bound to provoke resistance: first, the imposition of absolutism and 'hispanisation' of the Provinces, and secondly, vigorous measures against heresy, imposing counter-Reformation Catholicism. Philip II was to follow a much harder line than his predecessor in his dealings with the Netherlands, and his reign is remembered as one of the unhappiest periods in Belgian history.

The first of Philip's governors, Margaret of Parma, was 'controlled' by the Secret Council (*Consuela*) of three, which was dominated by Antoine de Granvelle, who was entirely an instrument of Philip's policy. The Governor could take no important decision without the approval of this body. The State Council (*Conseil d'Etat*) now had virtual power, and several patriotic noblemen who were members of it, e.g. the Counts of Egmont and Horn and William of Nassau, organised opposition to Granvelle's policy in alliance with the clergy, who saw the reform of the diocesan structure of the Netherlands (1559) as an attack on their privileges and influence. This alliance demanded and obtained the withdrawal of Spanish troops (1561) and Granvelle's recall (1563).

However, these concessions in no way involved a more moderate line on the part of Philip II, but merely a tactical retreat. The ever more open and provocative behaviour of the now numerous Calvinists in such towns as Tournai, Mons and Valenciennes could hardly fail to evoke a reaction. Heavy repression imposed by Philip caused considerable emigration by skilled Calvinist workers. The *Conseil d'Etat* was extremely concerned by this development and sought to moderate Philip's line — without success. Even Margaret was appalled by his instructions which would have required the execution of 60,000 people. Emigration inevitably increased considerably.

In the face of this situation, a group of nobles led by Jean Marnix and Louis de Nassau met at Spa in 1565 to found a league, later named the *Compromis des Nobles*, based on a text which both Protestants and moderate Catholics could support, calling for recognition of ancient privileges and an end to the work of the Inquisition in the Low Countries. With 2,000 signatures, it was decided in April 1566 that a petition should be presented to Margaret, who agreed, while awaiting the King's response, to moderate the application of the religious measures, especially against those who made no public display of their reformist beliefs. This was a considerable victory. However, the more extreme reformers broke the fragile compromise and set in train a movement which, incited by open-air preachers, quickly spread from Armentières all over Flanders, Holland, Zeeland and Friesland. Deceived by Philip's apparent moderation, the nobility themselves organised the suppression of the iconoclasts and dissolved their alliance. Margaret had possibly gone too far in concession to the Calvinist wing. Under pressure from moderate Catholics she demanded a new oath of allegiance to the King, which split the ranks of the nobility. This led to civil war.

The King then dispatched the Duke of Alba, officially as a military commander, although as the King's confidant he held all real power. The Calvinists were holding the Tournai area and Southern Hainaut. Marnix's attack on Antwerp (January 1567) failed. Alba soon imposed his authority over the country. Margaret was increasingly powerless and left her post in December 1567. The Council never met, and moderate Catholics were excluded from influence. Alba established a *Conseil des Troubles*, which inflicted a reign of terror, with some 8,000 victims, of whom the counts of Egmont and Horn were the most famous.

The Prince of Orange, with some Protestant allies, organised the first campaign of liberation. However, at this stage the alliance was insufficiently strong to break Spanish control. All that was left to the people was passive resistance against the ever-increasing repression and against taxation imposed without respect for ancient rights. In the spring of 1572, preceded by guerrilla activity in the woods and on the coast by *corsaires*, Zeeland and Holland went over to open rebellion. William of Orange invaded Gelderland and Brabant; French Huguenots occupied Valenciennes and Mons. Alba seemed lost, but faced with a divided enemy, recovered and soon only Holland and Zeeland remained in arms against him. The winter campaign of 1572–3 was extremely severe, but he was able to take Haarlem and only Alkmaar resisted. However, by early 1573, the war was at virtual stalemate and after a short interlude when the moderate Medina was governor (1572–3), Alba left in December 1573, to be replaced by Requessens, who was able to defeat the rebels at Mook (near Nijmegen), but a mutiny of his troops (unpaid for twenty-eight months) prevented him from exploiting this victory.

At the same time, in line with Philip's new tactics, he issued an amnesty, withdrew some taxes and limited the powers of the *Conseil des Troubles*. However, these concessions were too small and too late to pacify the Estates General of 1574, and the rebels in Holland and Zeeland merely ignored them and continued the struggle. In 1576 Requessens died and Spain was virtually bankrupt.

The 1576 Estates General were both constructive and hopeful. Faced with the pressing danger of mutiny among the unpaid troops of Spain, the States of Brabant and Hainaut imposed their authority on the *Conseil d'Etat* and sought a rapprochement with Holland and Zeeland. Reviving the Transaction of Augsburg of 1548, they summoned the Estates General which set up an independent government for the Southern Provinces and opened negotiations with Holland and Zeeland in October 1587 at Ghent. This led to the Pacification of Ghent, an agreement which created a federation of the Seventeen Provinces; decreed a general amnesty; and adopted a compromise on the religious issue, whereby Catholicism was to be the main religion in fifteen provinces, with considerable tolerance for Protestants, and two provinces (Holland and Zeeland) were to be Protestant. This compromise was the weakest link in the arrangement and was to lead to its failure, but it had been necessary to ensure the conclusion of the pact at all.

Philip nominated Don Juan of Austria as the new Governor. His position seemed impossible, but the unresolved divisions among the signatories of the Pacification of Ghent were an important card in his hands. The moderate Catholics and nobles still sought a reconciliation with Spain, and the Estates entered into negotiations and concluded a 'package deal' with Don Juan. The Estates voted the First Union of Brussels (1577), which imposed the Catholic religion as the sole religion for all the Seventeen Provinces. Don Juan issued the Edict of Marche–en–Famenne which confirmed ancient privileges and pledged moderation, but not content with this compromise, he recalled the Spanish army to the Netherlands and tore up the Edict the same year. This provoked a violent reaction. Rebels took control in Brussels and called in Prince William of Nassau, known as William the Silent, who was elected Regent of Brabant; however, his tolerance and moderation made enemies in both the Catholic and Calvinist camps. The noble faction brought in the nineteen-year-old Archduke Mathias, brother of the Emperor, as sovereign of the Low Countries. Real power remained in the hands of William, who imposed a second Union of Brussels, annulling the first. Thus on 18 January 1578 Mathias was inaugurated as King of the Low Countries and William was appointed Lieutenant-General.

Meanwhile, Don Juan had concentrated his forces in Luxembourg, and from there counter-attacked, winning the important battle of Gembloux on 31 January 1578, forcing Mathias to withdraw on Antwerp. The constant internal disputes between Catholics and extremist Calvinists, such as those of Ghent who had established a republic in that city, prevented any effective military organisation. William was once more forced to seek outside help. He forged an alliance with a Catholic moderate, the ambitious Duke of Anjou, a younger son of the King of France, whom the Estates named 'Defender of the Freedom of the Low Countries'. The military help brought by this new ally created a breathing space. The rebels won the battle of Rymenan on the Dyle near Malines and forced Don Juan to withdraw to Namur, where he died in October 1578.

Once more internal divisions prevented this new respite from being put to use. Extreme Calvinist elements and discontented soldiers organised the Malcontents' Revolt. Anjou was forced to crush the Calvinists in the Arras, Lille and Valenciennes triangle. The new and moderate governor, Prince Farnese, found that his overtures fell on fertile ground only among the Catholics in terror of Calvinist extremism. This was not enough. Artois, Hainaut and Gallican Flanders reacted by signing the Confederation of Arras and the Peace of Arras, which established the primacy of the Catholic religion and the powers of the Estates, and banned foreign (i.e. Spanish) troops. Farnese's tactics had met with cool success.

The response was rapid. In January 1579 the seven provinces (Holland, Zeeland, Utrecht, Gelderland, Overyssel, Friesland, Groningen and some Flemish towns signed the Union of Utrecht, which consecrated the separation of the Low Countries into what were to become Belgium and the Netherlands. The Union readopted the religious provisions of the Pacification of Ghent. By the Treaty of Plessis-lez-Tars, William, in a gesture of openness and moderation, accorded the title of Hereditary Sovereign of the Union to the Duke of Anjou. However, his attempts to impose a religious compromise on the lines of the religious Peace of Augsburg (1555), which applied in the Empire, failed almost everywhere. The battle lines were now tightly drawn. No compromise was possible and the issue would be settled by force of arms. The struggle began in earnest in late 1581.

Apart from the Flemish towns, the Union constituted a compact and defensible mass of territory. In its defensive strategy, the towns in their forward positions were largely abandoned to the siege warfare of Farnese. Anjou had proved a poor choice. He sought first to marry Elizabeth I of England, and then, having been repulsed, to establish an absolute monarchy, with the aid of French and Swiss mercenaries. He failed and was forced to flee (1583). William was assassinated on 10 July 1584, a fact which increased the impossibility of any reconciliation. The Calvinist towns fell one by one — Dunquerque, Ypres, Bruges (1584), Brussels (1585), and finally Antwerp in August 1585. Farnese was the complete master of the southern Low Countries and the division was complete and irrevocable. The war moved to the frontiers of Brabant, Gelderland and Zeeland, without either side gaining any decisive advantage. Spanish priorities were elsewhere: the Armada (1588) and France (1590–2), which drained off forces from the 'side-show' in the Low Countries. In 1595 Henry IV of France invaded the Spanish Low Countries and was only ejected after a heroic struggle which made possible the compromise peace of Verviers (1598) whereby Calais and much of Picardy was ceded to France. This marked the end of a phase. Spanish power was weakening and the situation had reached a *de facto* stalemate.

During this long period of confusion, the principality of Liège was able to remain largely neutral. Its internal constitution, the Peace of St Jacques (1507), held up and the few heretics and Protestants in the principality were treated with toleration. Despite its largely fictive position as an Imperial city, Liège turned less and less to either Spain or Germany, but looked increasingly to France.

Before his death in 1598, having secured the territorial, military and internal security of the Spanish Netherlands, Philip II created an independent state, which he made over to his daughter Isabella and her husband Albert; if they died without issue, the territory would revert to the Spanish Crown and in the meantime Spanish troops remained in the major cities. The new monarchs were moderate and restricted any 'hispanising' tendencies. However, they rejected attempts by the Estates General of 1600 to open peace negotiations. The war intensified and entered a new phase with attacks on the coast and the battle of Nieuwpoort (1600), where the Spaniards suffered a heavy defeat. However, in 1604 they took Ostend after a three-year siege.

The time was ripe for a general truce which was concluded in 1609 and lasted twelve years (1609–21). The Seven Provinces were thus recognised by Spain, as an independent state, whereas the acession of the Spanish Netherlands to semi-independence had proved more and more illusory. The period of the Truce, after forty-two years of war, enabled a few minimal economic and social measures to be taken.

By 1621 the Thirty Years War had broken out and hostilities with the Dutch were renewed. The 'foreign war' and the loss of Maastricht led to the search for a solution which would enable peace to be restored. Some negotiated with the Dutch for a partition of the Spanish Netherlands between France and the Netherlands; others sought to expel the Spaniards with the aid of France to found an independent Belgian state. The Estates General of 1632–4, the last to be called before the Brabançonne Revolution of 1787, were however loyalist and patriotic, but ordered the despatch of a peace delegation to The Hague, but no arrangement proved possible.

In 1633 Isabella died. The Spanish Netherlands, without Antwerp reduced to ten Provinces, was in a difficult position; its fortunes, linked to Spain, were in serious decline. The Spanish Netherlands became the victim of all blows aimed at her by other powers, since Spain still refused to abandon her 'world role'.

She was now to be the victim of a Franco-Dutch alliance organised by Cardinal Richelieu. In 1634 these powers agreed to offer the Spanish Netherlands alternatives: partition or the creation of a smaller Catholic federal republic. In 1635 they concluded a formal alliance and their forces marched on Brussels. Cardinal Mazarin, after 1642, was even more radical: he sought to give France 'natural frontiers'. However, his Dutch ally went on the defensive, content with its sea power and secure frontiers, and was increasingly concerned over rising French power rather than with Spain.

The diplomatic settlements of the Thirty Years War which concern us here are the Treaty of Münster (1648) whereby Spain recognised the independence of the United Provinces and ceded Breda, the southern portions of Maastricht and Northern Flanders (Hulst and Axel), and the Treaty of the Pyrennees (1659) between France and Spain whereby Spain ceded Artois and several fortresses in the Sambre-Meuse valley to France.

With the decline of Spain, hegemony in Europe was within the grasp of Louis XIV.[8] In this he was opposed during the period 1667–1713 by a series of *ad hoc* alliances which usually involved Spain and the United Provinces, the two old enemies now reunited against rising French power. Five wars were fought across the Spanish Netherlands. The fortunes of war oscillated between Louis XIV and the allies, whose lack of unity, especially after their series of victories during the War of Spanish Succession prevented Louis' total defeat. However, the net result was that maritime Flanders (Dunkerque) and Gallican Flanders (Valenciennes), Morlenbourg, Philippeville, Thionville were added to the earlier losses to France by the Treaty of Utrecht (1713). By a complex series of treaties — Utrecht, Rastadt (1714), Bade (1714) and Antwerp (1715) — the Spanish Netherlands were added to the United Provinces 'in favour of the House of Austria', and a series of 'barrier' fortresses, garrisoned by the Dutch, was set up against the French.

Eighty years of intermittent war and religious persecution had led to considerable Protestant emigration and the general depopulation of all towns except Brussels (up to 70,000 inhabitants). Agricultural production fell so low that food had even to be purchased from the Netherlands, officially an enemy country. Trade was also considerably affected but some industries, especially lighter textile production, did prosper in the war years.

Austrian rule

Although the fate of what had been the Spanish, and now were the Austrian, Netherlands was still determined by outside forces, the Austrian period[9] was more tranquil, and favourable to a degree of economic reconstruction. It saw the repopulation of the smaller towns, important development of transport infrastructure, considerable prosperity for the port of Ostend and semi-industrialisation in the south: coal mining, slate, metallurgy, textiles. The economic situation of the principality of Liège was even more favourable. The Austrian regime was, on the whole, much more relaxed and benevolent than its predecessor. However, it was still foreign; even the progressive Joseph II (1780–7) was unpopular precisely because his reforms took no account of the conditions of the country (1715–40).

The first Emperor, Charles VI, pursued a moderate domestic policy. He respected the form of the Ancient Privileges, but hardly their spirit. He never summoned the Estates General, nominated few Belgians to senior posts in the administration, divided the *Conseil d'Etat* into three separate sections and established a supreme Council for the Low Countries in Vienna, whose four members included only two Belgians. Coupled with additional taxation, these measures provoked a revolt led by Anneessens (1719): this was severely put down, and Anneessens was executed, becoming a martyr. The death of Charles VI in 1740 provoked the War of Austrian Succession, with the position of his heir Maria Theresa being contested by Spain, Poland, Prussia, Saxony and France, which placed the Austrian Netherlands in an exposed position. Only the support of Britain and Hungary enabled the Empress to survive. Ostend was the scene of fighting between France and Britain in 1742–3 and France defeated the Austro-British army at Fontenay in 1745. Brussels and Liège fell in 1746 and the Netherlands were incorporated into France. The peace of Aix-la-Chapelle (1748) ended the war in an honourable draw. The Netherlands were returned to Austria. The reversal of alliances in the Seven Years War of 1756–63 (Britain and Prussia opposed Austria and France) spared the Netherlands from involvement in this conflict.

Reform and counter-revolution

In much of Western Europe, political life entered a new and more hectic phase in the 1770s, and this was to establish the outline of Belgian politics for the next century. As early as 1736 Pierre Rousseau in Brussels had started to issue his *Journal Encyclopédique* and in 1785 the *Journal Général de l'Europe* appeared. These publications were the sum of the new progressive thought of the Enlightenment, as manifested in Belgium.

However, the reform movement[10] came less from below than from the 'enlightened despotism' of the Austrian Emperor, who introduced a series of important religious and secular reforms in 1781–2. Catholicism was no longer to be the official state religion, civil marriage was introduced, and episcopal seminaries were closed; new administrative and judicial bodies were created, and the authority of traditional feudal assemblies was reduced. But, far from being welcomed, these reforms provoked wide-ranging opposition which, though temporarily unified, was composed of two factions, of which the *Statistes* under Van der Noot and Van der Eupen were dominant. They were mostly an aristocratic and clerical group seeking to defend privilege. The 'Vonckists', led by Vonck, Verlooy and Van der Meersch, were politically more progressive, seeking the introduction of a broader franchise, at least within the Third Estate, but they were not for the most part anti-clerical. However, a small part of this group, led by the Liège lawyer Doutrepont, was more radical and anti-clerical: its influence was small, but its very existence created an irrevocable tension between the *Statistes* and the Vonckists which was to prove fatal.

A successful revolt was organised from Breda led by Van der Meersch. The imperial forces were defeated at Turnhout, and Brussels was captured in December 1789. The Estates General met in Brussels on 10 January 1790 for the first time since 1632 and a United States of Belgium was proclaimed. The power of the Church and the Estates was restored. Limited power was in the hands of central government led by Van der Noot and Van der Eupen with a Sovereign Congress of ninety members. The *Statiste* faction was dominant. The unity of the rebels was short-lived. Both Verlooy and Vonck published projects for a more progressive constitution, and Cardinal Franckenberg attacked the Vonckists as anti-clericals, which led to their banishment or imprisonment as early as April 1790.

Joseph II died in February 1790, and his successor Leopold II offered the new rebel state autonomy within the Empire. The offer was not accepted, and alliances were sought with both Prussia and France. A French alliance implied a rapprochement with the Vonckists, but this was made impossible by the agitation of the more reactionary *Statistes*. So it was, that undermined from within, the new state was rapidly captured by Austrian forces, with Brussels falling on 3 December 1790. Meanwhile in the independent Prince-Bishopric of Liège, which covered much of modern Wallonia, a progressive rebellion had brought down the *ancien régime* in 1790.

In this period are already to be seen the lines of force of the liberal-Catholic struggle in the nineteenth century.

The French period

The French Revolution spilled over into Belgium, and the fate of the country was totally dependent on the ups and downs of the revolutionary and Napoleonic wars[11] until, once again without any consideration, the great powers created the United Netherlands as a buffer between France and Prussia as part of the 'reconstruction' of Europe undertaken by the Congress of Vienna. Indeed, it was because of Austrian hostility to the Revolutionary régime in France that Belgian territory first became involved in the conflagration. After the battle of Jemappes on 6 November 1792, where the French defeated the Austrian army and occupied Belgium, the victorious General Dumouriez proclaimed Belgium a republic and appointed '*Représentants provisoires*' until a National Convention could be elected. The French were not welcomed as liberators, except by a small *Comité Revolutionnaire des Belges et Liègeois* led by Dumonceau. Even the *Comité Revolutionnaire* sought to ensure control by Belgian revolutionary elements.

Austrian control was restored in March 1793 and the *ancien régime* was re-established; however, this last Austrian restoration was short-lived and ended with the second French occupation in June 1794, when the Austrian armies were defeated at Fleurus. After a period of military government, Liège, the former Austrian Netherlands and the duchy of Bouillon were incorporated within France and as such were given representation in the Revolutionary Assemblies (successively less revolutionary) which succeeded after Napoleon Bonaparte became First Consul in 1799 and then Emperor in 1804. Belgian voters largely boycotted elections to these Assemblies, and were in any case a small minority in a sea of French. Nevertheless, some political figures who were to play an important role in the struggle for independence began their political and parliamentary careers here (Gendebien, Mérode, de Brouckère). As the Napoléonic '*gloire*' became more and more costly in men and matériel, French rule became correspondingly unpopular, except among industrialists in textiles and iron-working to whom it brought considerable prosperity.

The United Netherlands

The future of Belgium after the Napoleonic era was in the hands of the dominant great powers. As early as 1814, it was decided, largely under British pressure, that a greater United Netherlands should be created as a buffer state on the borders of France, and into it the whole of modern Belgium and Luxembourg, with the exception of the Eupen-Malmédy area, was incorporated. What is today Luxembourg was at the same time to be a member of the German Confederation. The great powers gave full approval to this new arrangement in the Second Treaty of Paris (1815), which gave life to the decisions of the Congress of Vienna.[12]

The 1814 Dutch constitution was to be applied with minor adjustments worked out by a twenty-four member commission (eleven Belgian, eleven Dutch and two Luxembourg members). Under this constitution royal power was strong and centralised, and the role of the 110-member Estates-General (fifty-five Belgian members) was limited, especially in budgetary questions. The basic liberal-Catholic division, which was to dominate Belgian political life throughout the century, was well in evidence. The dominant Catholic faction among the fifty-five Belgian members of the States General was strongly opposed to the royal government, especially its policy of reducing the role of the Catholic Church in public life, which led to severe conflict over the application of the Dutch constitution to the new territories and over education policy in the years 1814–17 and later in 1825–7.

Liberal opinion — though in substance also opposed to Catholic claims — was sensitive to the issue of religious freedom involved. From 1827, a 'national' coalition of Catholics and Liberals, with the liberal-Catholic group acting as a bridge, came into being. It was the 'Unionist' coalition which was to make the Revolution of 1830 not only possible but all but inevitable. It was Paul Devaux (Liberal) who in 1827 first argued the case for national reconciliation between Liberals and Catholics. Beginning in progressive Liège, this Unionist movement spread rapidly to Brussels and Ghent. Initially only a small disparate group of doctrinaire anti-clericals, officials and industrialists, who profited from the Orange regime, remained to support the United Netherlands.

The concessions of the Dutch King William I on religious and linguistic issues were too little and too late. The 1830 July Revolution in France was the necessary catalyst to move the Unionist coalition from mere opposition into action, resulting to open revolt. Severe social and economic unrest, above all in Brussels, also fuelled the flames of revolt. The 'September Days' saw open revolt in the streets of Brussels. Attempts at mediation and compromise around the idea of an 'administrative separation' failed, when William I broke off negotiations. A large volunteer force streamed in from Wallonia to defend Brussels — successfully — against the Dutch army. On 24 September, a nine-member provisional government was set up. It considered its task to be limited and transitional, but in its short life it took several political decisions of vital importance.

The new state

The most urgent tasks of the new government were to obtain international recognition by the powers which had underwritten the 1815 settlement, in particular Britain. Closely linked to that aim, since the new state's credibility would thus be enhanced, was the enactment of a constitution which would give the new state a basis of popular support.

The provisional government proclaimed Belgium's independence on 4 October 1830,[13] and the decision was confirmed by the newly-elected National Congress on 24 November 1830, while the London conference on the Belgian question which had opened 4 November 1830, was sitting. Most of the powers (Russia, Austria, Prussia) were opposed to Belgian independence; only France, and to a limited extent England, were sympathetic. It was the simultaneous outbreak of revolution in Poland that prevented a concerted Russian-

Austrian-Prussian military intervention in support of 'legitimate' authority represented by William I and against the rebellious Provinces. A change of government in England, with Lord Palmerston replacing the Tory Lord Aberdeen, was also opportune in that the new Government supported recognition: a Franco-British coalition imposed exactly such a reversal on the conference which approved Belgian independence in January 1831. That decision provided that Luxembourg should go to the Netherlands while remaining in the German Confederation (it did so until 1866) and that the powers would guarantee the permanent neutrality of Belgium and its independence. A second protocol settled the division of the national debt of the old state.

The National Congress,[14] in an understandable but dangerous show of independence, almost wrecked the settlement on Belgium's frontiers, adopting an over-optimistic interpretation of the London protocol in respect of Limburg. However, it was able to obtain satisfaction on enough of the territorial exchanges proposed, and those were enshrined in the Treaty of the 18 Articles (June 1831) which the National Congress ratified on 9 July 1831 by 126 votes to 70.

The Treaty was not accepted by the Netherlands, and on 2 August Dutch troops invaded the country and, after several easy victories at Hasselt and Louvain, reached the outskirts of Brussels on 12 August. Only the intervention of the French at Wavre, forcing the Dutch army to withdraw, prevented total defeat. This was the 'Ten Day Campaign'. A new Treaty, the 24 Articles, was signed in London, whereby Maastricht, the mouth of the Schelde and southern Luxembourg were to go to the Netherlands. For eight years the Netherlands refused to accept the Treaty, and Belgium retained *de facto* control over those areas. Both the original Treaty (ratified by only 59–38 votes with two abstentions) and its final execution in 1839 (58 votes to 42) provoked serious opposition in Belgium and in 1832 led to conflict between the King and his Cabinet, which resigned *en bloc* in protest against the moderate royal policy towards the Netherlands which was largely dictated by British pressure.

A much more serious issue, in that it brought Belgium into collision with its most important protector, without which it could not survive, was the choice of a monarch. The constitution had been adopted on 7 February 1831, and the system of hereditary constitutional monarchy had been voted for by an overwhelming majority (174 to 13). On 24 November 1830, the National Congress had formally declared that William of Orange was no longer King of Belgium. After the decision of the London conference to support Belgian independence, the Duke of Nemours, second son of King

Louis Philippe of France, was elected King of Belgium by the Congress — by only 97 votes, as against 74 votes for the Duke of Leuchtenberg (a member of the Beauharnais family, connected with Napoleon I) and 21 for Archduke Charles of Austria. However, coming up against British opposition, Louis-Philippe refused this offer, and the President of the Congress, Surlet de Chockier, was elected Regent until a king could be elected. After consultation with the powers, the choice fell, with 152 votes in favour, on Leopold of Saxe-Coburg (uncle of Queen Victoria and widower of Princess Charlotte of Great Britain, only child of George IV). Leopold only accepted after the Congress had ratified the Treaty of the 28 Articles, and took the oath on 21 July 1831, ending a five-month regency. Belgium was thus established in late August 1831, both internally and internationally.

The 1830 Constitution

Parallel to the workings of great power diplomacy and Belgian efforts to influence it in favour of their cause, the internal process of constitution-making was set in train. No doubt in part due to great power sensibilities, but also because the majority of Belgians were ardent traditionalists, the few republicans among the revolutionaries of 1830 had little chance of carrying the day. As we have seen, the choice of monarch fell upon Leopold I largely for international reasons, which forced the leaders of the new state to accept the rather more 'monarchical reading' of their constitution desired by Leopold himself.

The 1830 constitution[15] stood in its time as a model of 'modern' liberal constitutions, despite the fact that it had been drawn up and adopted with great rapidity. Such speed was of course in part dictated by the need to present the great powers with a *fait accompli*. The provisional government which came into being during the 'September days' quickly set about establishing an elected National Congress which was able to meet by November. In the meantime an *ad hoc* committee had prepared a draft of a constitution on which the Congress would work. This draft was ready by 23 October and was approved without amendment by the provisional government and transmitted to the Congress when it opened on 10 November 1830.

The basis of the franchise for the Congress, though a slight improvement on the Dutch franchise, was in reality extremely strict being based on age, payment of a minimum amount in taxes and academic qualifications. There were only 46,099 voters (a mere 0.11 per cent of the population) of whom only some 30,000 (0.075 per cent of the population) in fact voted to elect the 200 members of the National Congress. The Congress contained ninety-eight members elected in Flanders, seventy-five in Wallonia and twenty-seven in Brabant. The middle class was overwhelmingly represented, but there were some fifty nobles and thirteen priests. There were no organised parties in the modern sense, but most belonged to the 'Unionist' tendency with either liberal or Catholic leanings. There was a small group of militant Liberals and at most some fifteen Republicans. There was a group of about twenty Orangists (supporters of William) and an equal group of supporters of joining France.

In appearance the constitution was most advanced in that it enshrined certain important progressive principles:

— Executive power was to be in the hands of a government responsible to Parliament and not in the hands of the monarch, whose role was reduced to that of a constitutional head of state.

— Unity of the nation in the national interest. Members of Parliament represented the nation as a whole and not Provinces or other local entities.

— Legislative power was invested in two elected Houses of Parliament.

— Government was democratic, at least in the bourgeois-liberal sense, in that it was responsible to the middle class, who were therefore given the right to vote.

— Individual rights were constitutionally guaranteed.

However, there were important restrictions. The King 'appoints and dismisses his ministers', a provision which Leopold I insisted on taking at its face value. The Senate, which was to have equal powers with the Chamber of Representatives, was elected by voters with the same qualifications as for the Chamber, but only those over forty years old. The tax qualification for eligibility for the Senate was so high that no more than 400 were in fact eligible; and even the electorate for it remained very restricted. No one in the Congress proposed universal suffrage. An annual tax obligation ranging, according to place of residence, from 20 to 80 florins was required, giving a total electorate in 1831 of some 55,000. The constitution was drafted in a French version only, and the high qualifications for election ensured that the political class would be drawn almost exclusively from the Francophone bourgeoisie, which had made the 1830 Revolution. Indeed, despite the popular character of the early revolts in September and initial strong reservations felt concerning the national movement by the Francophone bourgeoisie, it was the latter which rapidly took control of the Revolution, converting it into purely national channels rather than social ones which might then have challenged bourgeois interests. The result was a state made in the image of the liberal, Francophone bourgeoisie. At least two groups, the Walloon industrial workers and the Flemish masses, were outsiders in the new state and remained alienated from it, and indeed were not to be involved in political life until late in the nineteenth century.

Political life in the nineteenth century

In the first ten years after independence, the dominant political issues related to the establishing of the new state and education. Laws were passed setting up local government (the Provinces Act 1836 and the Local Government Act 1836); two free (non-Catholic) universities were established (1835) in Brussels and Mechelen (Malines) and a new law on higher education was passed. The first railway between Brussels and Mechelen was opened in 1834, and in 1858 the Maas-Scheldt Canal was completed. Customs treaties liberalising trade were concluded with France and the German *Zollverein*.

It is difficult to talk of party politics at this period, but Catholic and liberal tendencies are clearly identifiable. However, until 1847 the 'Unionist' alliance, which after 1828 had made the Revolution possible, remained in existence, although after 1840 it was in decline. In this Unionist period Belgium was ruled by nine governments of which that of Count de Theux lasted for longest — over five years.

The period 1847–57 can be considered transitional. After the first Liberal Party Congress in 1846, party government began to develop,[16] and during this period Belgium had a succession of Liberal governments, with the exception of the two-year Unionist government under Deckers. This return to Unionism was in part a personal attempt by Leopold I to block the advance towards party government — which proved unsuccessful. Over the period 1857–70, a series of moderate Liberal governments held office to be followed by two years (1870–2) of Catholic government. From 1878 a radical Liberal government under Frère Orban held office and introduced controversial measures in the minefield of education policy. These measures were reversed after the Catholic election victory of 1884, which ushered in a period of Catholic rule which was to last without a break until the First World War. After 1893, and even more so with the introduction of proportional representation in 1899, the Liberals lost their position as the major opposition party. In several elections the Socialists, who had first entered the Chamber in 1894 with twenty-eight seats out of 152, overtook the Liberals.

The election system was an important issue throughout the period

between Independence and the First World War. The first reforms
were made in response to the 'events' of 1848 throughout Europe.
The qualification was reduced to its constitutional minimum —
20 florins in annual taxes — which increased the electorate to
79,000, or by 71 per cent. Only small minority groups supported the
introduction of universal suffrage, but they did so with growing
insistence. The first bill was introduced in 1870, but failed even to
be debated. After 1885 the Belgian Workers' Party (Socialists)
demanded the introduction of universal suffrage. Initially they were
not supported even by the breakaway progressive wing of the
Liberals under Janson, whose founding congress in 1887 rejected
universal suffrage, demanding the vote only for those who were
literate. After the strikes of 1886 an active group of Socialists,
Progressives (Liberals) and Social Catholics began to mount a
concerted campaign for some degree of reform. Under pressure, the
Catholic Cabinet accepted a proposal, presented by Janson, that the
constitution should be amended. The Chamber which was elected in
1892 to carry out that amendment no longer contained the Catholic
two-thirds majority necessary to carry the amendment sought by the
Catholics (a householder qualification). There was also the extra-
parliamentary pressure of the Socialists. A compromise was reached
and approved by 119 to 14 votes. Universal suffrage was introduced,
but it was tempered by plural voting for the more highly qualified
electors who would have up to three votes. 853,628 voters would
have one vote, 293,678 two votes and 223,381 three votes. Thus the
electorate was enlarged from 136,755 to 1,370,687, and at the same
time voting was made compulsory. The secret ballot had been
ensured by an Act of 1877. Despite continued activity by the
Socialists on the issue, it was only after the sacrifices of the First
World War and under strong pressure from King Albert that in 1919
universal male suffrage was introduced by the Delacroix government
which was constituted immediately after the war.

The development of political parties was another important theme
in the period up to the First World War. As we have seen, there were
already distinct liberal and Catholic political tendencies in evidence
at the foundation of Belgium, but, it was not until 1846 that the first
political party was founded. On 14 June 1846 a Congress of 384
delegates of the Liberal Electoral Associations was held in Brussels,
under the chairmanship of E.E. Defacqz. This Congress established
the *Confédération Générale du Libéralisme en Belgique* and adopted
a six-point programme: reduction of electoral qualifications as far as
was permitted by the constitution; independence of the civil power
from the Church; organisation of a state system of education at all
levels; increase in the number of senators; repeal of reactionary laws;

and immediate improvements in the condition of the working class. But already at the time of this Congress, the divergences within the Liberal movement were visible. The 'Alliance', the Brussels branch of the Liberal Party and the radical *Union Libérale* from Liège, were pressing for more radical and social positions, some of which indeed found their way into the programme. In Brussels, the Alliance split, when the doctrinaire Liberals' proposal on the suffrage was rejected and a moderate group under Verhagen was set up for the 1847 elections. These early battles prefigured the Liberal splits of the 1880s. With the greater modernisation of Belgian society in the 1860s and 1870s and the development of scientific positivism in the mid-nineteenth century, the radicals in the Liberal Party gained ground, especially on the issues of clericalism and the suffrage. After the Liberal election defeat of 1884, the Liberals were in opposition for thirty years. The traditional 'doctrinaire-bourgeois' Liberal group showed no indication that they were prepared to accept the Radicals' proposals on the suffrage issue and on social questions. In 1887, a new Progressive Party came into being under Paul Janson. This party, although rejecting universal suffrage, had many points of convergence with the *Parti Ouvrier Belge* (POB). The Liberals were reunited in 1900, with many concessions to the Radicals.

The Catholics were much slower in creating a party. The need for some organisation was recognised, but there were divergences about the validity of linking the fate of the Catholic cause to any one particular party. A centre or conservative party seemed preferable. Only the later 'provocations' of the Liberals on the schools issue ensured the creation of a Catholic party. Meanwhile Catholic conferences,[17] such as those at Mechelen in 1863–4 and 1867, and organisations such as the *Société de St Vincent de Paul* created the ideological basis for the Catholic movement and enabled difficulties between moderates and ultra-montanes to be resolved. Both the Flemish movement and local *Antwerp Meeting Partij* (anti-militarist, Flemish nationalist) reinforced pressure for a more organised Catholic opposition. From the 1850s, Catholic election committees were set up in the constituencies under the title of *Union Constitutionelle et Conservatrice* — forged into a national federation in 1864. At the same time, some fifty *Cercles Catholiques* were formed, again with a federal committee: these were more actively involved in policy-making, whereas the former were merely electoral agencies.

Throughout the 1870s the political battle became more bitter. The ultra-montane group under Charles Périn went as far as to reject the Liberal constitution and criticised the Catholic governments of the period 1870–8 as excessively moderate. The internal debate was swept aside by the Liberals' educational legislation after 1878, and in

1889 a Catholic party was formed by the fusion of the *Fédération des Cercles Catholiques* and the *Fédération des Unions Constitutionelles et Conservatrices*. Within the new body under Beernaert (prime minister 1884–94), the main issue was about social questions in the light of the Papal encyclical '*Rerum Novarum*' (1891). The Christian Social tendency began to emerge, and by means of such umbrella bodies as the *Ligue du Suffrage Universel*, made common cause with Radicals and Socialists.

Belgian Socialism[18] was also in process of entering the arena. The *Association du Peuple* of César De Paepe joined the First International in 1865. The severe internal tensions between Socialists and Anarchists, which marked the First International, were mirrored in Belgium. In Wallonia the Anarchist tendency was dominant, whereas in Brussels and Ghent the less radical Socialists, such as De Paepe and Anseele, were in control. The Flemish Socialists supported the reformist Gotha Programme of the German SDP (1875), and after negotiations with the Walloons, the Flemish Socialist party and the Brabant Socialist parties were founded in 1877. These fused in 1879 into the Belgian Socialist Party. Practical support by the new party for the Borinage strikers in 1884 created the conditions for a genuinely national party. Sixty-nine delegates met to found the party at '*De Zwaan*' in Brussels in April 1885, and the first Congress was held in Antwerp in August 1885. The new party, the Belgian Workers' Party (POB) joined the second International on its formation in Paris in 1889. The basic programme for the party, the so-called *Déclaration de Quaregnon*, was adopted in March 1894. Its basic philosophy was all that material riches should belong to all citizens. As a practical political programme, it was to strive for universal suffrage and proportional representation, and a number of social measures. The POB first entered Parliament in 1894 with twenty-eight members.

One of the main political battles of the nineteenth century was over education and the role in it of the Church. The *Convention Nationale* had already had to come to terms with Catholic demands for freedom of religion and education. However, when the Vicar-General Sterckx, as required by the Vatican, reported on some aspects of the 1830 constitution, it only just avoided papal condemnation. As we have seen, it was this issue which provoked the formation of the Liberal Party in 1846 and the later formation of a Catholic party. Until the First World War it also meant that, unlike today, the Liberals and Socialists stood closer than the Socialists and the Christian Democratic wing of the Catholic party. Frequent clashes arose over such issues as the maintenance of churches and churchyards, scholarships, the work of charitable institutions, and

the organisation of the school system, culminating in the contro-
versies of the years 1879–84, which saw the adoption of strongly
anti-clerical school legislation by the doctrinal Liberal Cabinet of
Frère Orban and its reversal after the Catholic election victory in
1884.

Another important issue, which emerged from time to time, was
that of the Flemish language. As we have seen, the Revolution and
the state which it created were in a real sense appropriated by the
Francophone bourgeoisie. The Flemish people were outsiders. Laws
of 1831 and 1845 stipulated that the French-language versions of
Acts of Parliament and of royal decrees were to be the only official
texts. Flemish could be used neither in Parliament nor in the courts,
and was not used in the school system.

Gradually, in the period down to the First World War, the
growing Flemish movement[19] won important concessions. An *Arrêté
royal* (royal decree) on the correct spelling of Dutch in Flanders was
issued in 1844, and in 1851 a Royal Commission was set up to
examine the Flemish question. This was a clear response to the
nascent Flemish movement which had found expression through
actions such as the 1840 General Petition to Parliament. The
Commission proposed, in Flanders, the exclusive use of Flemish in
primary education, equality with French in secondary schools, and
the use of Flemish in administrative and legal procedures. The
government of Charles Rogier totally rejected this report. After 1859
more Flemish activists entered Parliament, and a series of court
cases, in which Flemish-speaking defendants were even sentenced to
death in French, moved opinion. The *Antwerp Meeting Partij* was
also Flemish-minded and in 1866 declared Flemish to be the official
language of Antwerp; in 1863 Jan de Laet, one of its Deputies, had
taken the oath in Flemish. From 1879 parliamentary proceedings
were printed in both languages, and from 1888 speeches could be
made in Flemish.

Considerable progress was made over the use of Flemish in the
courts. An Act of 1873 provided for the use of Flemish in criminal
assizes; in 1893 the problem of the appeal courts in Brussels and
Liège was settled, but only in 1908 was a Flemish assize court set up
in Brussels for Brabant. In 1878 a law was passed providing for the
use of Flemish in administrative correspondence and documents,
where the citizen opted for that language. However, it was only after
the reform of the suffrage in 1893, when the Flemish people were at
last enfranchised, that real pressure built up for equality between the
languages. The 1894 Congress of the *Katholieke Vlaamse Bond*
came out for such equality. The 1894 election, the first under the new
law, saw the entry into Parliament of a considerable number of

Flemish activists such as Corremans, Daens and de Vriendt, who finally in 1898 obtained the passage of a law guaranteeing the equality of the two languages. However, the Flemish version of the Civil Code only appeared in 1961. A 1913 law went some way toward giving Flemish its proper status in the army, but orders had still to be given exclusively in French, which was to become a serious issue during the 1914–18 war.

Another area of pressure was that of education and literature. A series of laws in 1883, 1890 and 1914 gradually extended the use of Dutch in schools in Flanders. The 1913 language law adopted the 'mother-tongue' principle, but the amendments of Flemish activists in favour of the 'territorial principle' were rejected by Parliament. The Royal Flemish Academy for language and literature had been set up in 1886, and with other Flemish cultural bodies and societies (*Willemsfonds, Davidsfonds*) was a permanent source of ideas and pressure. In the period immediately before First World War, the key issue was that of a Flemish university and its 'Flemishisation'. A mass movement related to this issue led by politicians from the three parties — Van Cauwelaert (Catholic), Huysmans (Socialist) and Franck (Liberal) — and a petition with 100,000 signatures maintained pressure after 1910. However, no positive results had been obtained that year. The last victory came in another area with the use of Flemish being introduced in Catholic schools under a law of 1910.

There was by that time a certain backlash in Walloon opinion, especially in the Senate, which made each successive step in any area increasingly difficult. The Senate had caused major problems over the law on the equality of the two languages. On the university question the episcopate added its opposition to that of others.

Due to the personal initiative of Leopold II, Belgium became a major colonial power in Africa.[20] The King was recognised as the sovereign ruler of the Independent Congo State by the Berlin Conference of 1884, and the Belgian Parliament authorised this by the necessary two-thirds majority. However, the Congo was still not a Belgian colony. In 1886, 1887 and 1890 laws were passed authorising loans to the Congo State, both for railways (Matadi-Stanley Pool) and so as to enable Leopold to meet his obligations under the 1890 Brussels anti-slavery convention. This loan of 25 million francs was backed by the right of the Belgian state to take over the Congo in the event of default after ten years. When new private loans became necessary in 1895, the government sought to take over the territory immediately, but met too strong opposition both in Conservative circles, which feared the financial consequences, and in Radical Liberal and Socialist circles which were opposed to the colonial ethic. A second and more serious attempt by the Catholic Cabinet to take over the Congo occurred in 1901 when the ten-year loan expired. Under strong Socialist, Liberal and international attack (Britain, France and Germany), Leopold reacted strongly, posing unacceptable conditions for the take-over. A compromise was difficult but was finally reached in 1907 after the affair had caused Leopold considerable unpopularity. After a controversial election campaign in which the Catholic Party lost two seats, the bill for the annexation of the Congo was passed in August 1908.

Social questions came increasingly to the fore at the end of the period. The serious economic crisis of the mid-1880s, unlike earlier crises, met an active trade union and labour movement. In 1866 the previous legal prohibition on 'combinations', as trade unions were designated, was partly removed, although the right to strike remained severely limited by restrictions on necessary secondary activity such as picketing. In the spring of 1886 there were a greater number of serious strikes than there had been earlier, although severe strikes had already taken place as early as 1839, 1849, 1857 and 1861 in the Ghent textile industry, and in 1861, 1868 and 1869 in the coal mines in the Charleroi area. Immediately after the 1886 strikes, a series of laws (1887–9) was passed following the recommendation of a royal commission on the condition of workers. These laws regulated — at long last, after many years of pressure — wages and the working conditions of women and children, and established conciliation machinery to deal with disputes. The doctrinaire Liberals and conservative Catholics opposed — perhaps for different reasons — such state intervention in economic matters.

In 1907–9 a new ideological battle broke out over the right to regulate working hours. In legislation on the mines, amendments were passed, against the wishes of the conservative Catholic government, by a coalition of Socialists, Radicals and Social Christians. The doctrinaire Liberals remained opposed. The fall of the government interrupted the passage of the Bill, which was later passed in a milder form but still contained important measures of social progress: underground work for women and for boys under fourteen was forbidden, the working day was limited to nine hours, and miners were to receive a pension at the age of sixty.

After Independence, foreign policy assumed less political importance than domestic issues. Exceptions were perhaps the drive for free trade (largely attained by 1860), the colonial question, and defence policy, with its obvious foreign policy implications. The status of Belgium had been regulated by the great powers, which guaranteed its neutrality and territorial integrity. Gradually her relations with the Netherlands were normalised, although throughout the nineteenth century there was a tendency — sometimes criticised in Flanders — to lean towards France. Only the ill-advised support given by Leopold II to Maximilian of Austria's Mexican adventure; the pressures from Napoleon III and later Bismarck to control agitators operating from Belgian soil; the future of Luxembourg when the North German Confederation was dissolved in 1866; and the ideologically motivated support of the Liberal governments for Italian unification against the Vatican, which led to a short breach of diplomatic relations with the latter, troubled the serenity of Belgium's foreign relations before 1914.

Belgium in the First World War

When war broke out in the Balkans in July 1914, Belgium expected to remain neutral, and indeed the powers initially indicated their acceptance of her neutrality. However, the long-prepared German plan for the invasion of France — the Schlieffen plan — required passage through Belgium. As a precaution the Belgian Government ordered mobilisation on 31 July; on 2 August Germany presented an ultimatum to Belgium and on 4 August invaded.

It falls outside our scope to consider the course of the war in any detail;[21] suffice it to say that, despite Allied aid, the greater part of the country was rapidly overrun and was occupied by the Germans. Brussels fell on 20 August, by mid-September the country south of the Meuse was in German hands, and Antwerp fell on 20 October. After the great German offensive on the Ijzer river from 18 to 30 October, which failed, the war of movement was over. Only a small strip of territory in the north-west, bounded by the coast and the Leie river, the Ijzer and the French frontier, containing the town of Ypres, remained in Belgian hands and was to do so throughout the four long years of trench warfare on the Western front. The Belgian front became part of the vast Allied front stretching from the Swiss frontier to the Channel coast. It remained relatively calm, and an army of 170,000 men was built up which took part in the offensive of September 1918. However, by the Armistice in November the line had only moved east as far as Ghent and Mons.

During the war the government of de Brocqueville, formed in 1911, remained in office, operating from Sainte-Adresse near Le Havre in France; in June 1918 de Brocqueville was replaced by Corremans. At the outbreak of war, the Socialist Emil Vandervelde and the Liberals Paul Hymans and Goblet d'Alviella were brought into the government, initially as ministers without portfolio. The most important question which exercised the government during the war years related to foreign policy — whether the pre-War neutrality of Belgium should be preserved, as the King and some ministers sought, or abandoned in favour of a frankly pro-Allied stand with territorial demands on Germany. This last viewpoint largely prevailed after various attempts to test German peace terms had shown that these were unacceptable to Belgium. The other important question related to the attitude to be adopted towards the growing Flemish movement. In March 1918 commissions were set up to study the closely related issues of the Flemish movement, universal suffrage and the schools question.

The War itself and developments in occupied Belgium were to have important post-war consequences. The War had seen the Socialists integrated into government, and had created pressures for universal suffrage which could no longer be ignored. The occupation had also led to developments in Flanders which strengthened the Flemish movement,[22] but at the same time it had set off hostility at a new and hitherto unknown level against it in Brussels and Wallonia. Much as many Irish nationalists, such as Roger Casement, supported the German cause in the First World War in their own national interest, so to varying degrees the Flemish nationalists saw the German occupation as an opportunity for themselves. The most radical group, *Jong Vlaanderen* (its main leaders were Nieuwenhuis and Borms), based in Ghent with its newspaper *De Vlaamse Post*, worked for an independent Flemish state. The Unionists supported a federalist solution. Within this group, the exiles in Amsterdam (mostly 'Monarchists', i.e. supporters of a monarchical union between Flanders and Wallonia, such as Anton Jacob and Frans van Cauwelaert), though radicalised after 1915, feared that excessive reliance on German support would damage the Flemish cause. However, some important results were obtained. In March 1916 a German decree made the University of Ghent a Flemish 'institution', and the 'Quisling' Ministry of Arts and Science was split in the same year. In February 1917 the *Vlaams Nationale Landdag* (Flemish National Assembly) set up a *Vlaamse Raad*, representatives of which went to Berlin and obtained the total administrative separation of Flanders (capital Brussels) and Wallonia (capital Namur). In November 1917 the *Vlaamse Raad* declared the Le Havre government removed from office and on 22 December 1917 declared Flanders independent. This last move caused the resignation of moderates and led to a radical second *Raad van Vlaanderen* whose representatives sat in a German administrative commission, responsible only to the Governor and in reality established to control the nationalists. The Le Havre government naturally condemned all these measures and declared them void, but it was forced to promise a Flemish university.

Economic and political conditions under the occupation became more and more severe. Basic freedoms were suspended, unemployment rose to 500,000; food was extremely scarce; and 120,000 workers were deported to Germany in addition to 90,000 who went more or less voluntarily. This situation provoked resistance and a flourishing illegal press, such as *La Libre Belgique*. Many personalities such as Cardinal Mercier of Leuven, Burgomaster Adolphe Max of Brussels and the Supreme Court judges who resigned *en bloc* in 1918 set an example. A number of people who took action against the occupiers, such as Edith Cavell, were shot. Not unnaturally, relations between such circles and the Flemish movement deteriorated to the point of no return.

Between the World Wars

With the introduction of universal suffrage the Socialists definitively eclipsed the Liberals as the second largest party and became the largest party in Wallonia. However, the expectations of the Socialists were not to be fulfilled insofar as their steady rise was not sustained. They gained thirty seats in 1919, achieving a total of seventy, and reached a peak of seventy-eight seats, equal to the Catholics, in 1925; but their representation then declined throughout the 1930s, to a low point of sixty-four seats in 1939. The 1925 election had seemed, with the creation of the Poullet-Vandervelde Socialist progressive Catholic Cabinet, to offer the Socialists the springboard to majority status. This was not to be. The period was one of considerable instability. Between 1830 and 1918 there were twenty-seven governments, and in the inter-war years there were eighteen. Despite previous co-operation and affinities on the schools question, there were no Liberal-Socialist governments.

The first period (1919–21) saw a series of historic reforms carried out by three tripartite progressive '*Union Sacrée*' governments. As we have seen, governments in which the Socialists played a major role introduced universal suffrage, reformed the Senate, brought in the eight-hour working day and obtained at Versailles the abolition of the compulsory neutrality imposed by the 1831 Treaty and the incorporation of the Eupen-Malmédy area into Belgium, thus creating a German-speaking community alongside the Flemish and Francophone ones. Belgium failed to obtain Luxembourg (or Maastricht) as she had hoped, but entered an economic union with the Grand-Duchy.

All the political parties underwent some reorganisation and

internal turmoil[23] between the wars. The Catholic party took the name *Union Catholique Belge* and organised itself as more clearly representative of various 'estates' in society. The old *Fédération des Cercles Catholiques* was joined by the *Boerenbond* (farmers' organisation), ACW (Catholic trade union) and the *Fédération Chrétienne des Classes Moyennes*. The General Council was made up of six representatives of each body. After the 1935 elections, at which the Flemish nationalists did well, separate Walloon and Flemish wings — the *Parti Catholique Social* and the *Katholieke Vlaamse Volkspartij* (KVV) — joined in the *Bloc des Catholiques Belges*.

The Socialists (POB) became increasingly reformist, at least until 1931. In that year a radical group formed around Paul-Henri Spaak and Henrik De Man which favoured planning and a generally more radical stand. A split was avoided by De Man's compromise *Plan de Travail*; however, it led to Emil Vandervelde's resignation in 1939. In 1933 the post of Party President had officially been created and Vandervelde elected as its first occupant. The Socialist trade unions, which since 1898 had merely been a *'Commission syndicale'*, gained some minimal autonomy when they became the *Confédération générale du Travail de Belgique* in 1938.

The Liberals strengthened their organisation. Although they now clearly occupied the third place in Parliament, their influence in this period was greater than numbers alone would suggest. The National Council was the leading body, which elected the Party Chairman and Bureau. Here the Party's parliamentary Deputies played a dominant role. There were continual divergences on doctrinal purity. Some, such as Devèze, wanted to moderate the Party's economic liberalism, and Heymans and Janson wanted to moderate its anti-clericalism. Despite the efforts of figures such as Louis Franck, the Party remained hostile to Flemish demands.

Some smaller new parties developed in this period. The *Frontbeweging* gave rise to the *Frontpartij*, a small Flemish party which supported Flemish self-government and was anti-militarist. It won five seats in 1919, four in 1921 and six in 1925. The party later developed into the *Vlaams National Verbond* (VNV), which won seventeen seats in 1939 (8.27 per cent of the national vote). Throughout the period important divisions remained within the ranks of the Flemish nationalists, making it difficult to present a united front.

The depression, the falling prestige of Belgian parliamentary democracy and the rise of Adolf Hitler in neighbouring Germany created the conditions for Rexism led by Léon Degrelle (later a SS volunteer). This movement, which began as a Catholic rightist-populist movement, inclined more and more towards Fascism as the 1930s advanced. It brought to Belgian politics the personal abuse, crude propagandistic lies, verbal and physical violence and open contempt for democracy which characterised National Socialism in Germany. The Rexist Party won 11.49 per cent of the vote and twenty-one seats (in the 202-member Chamber) at its first election in 1936. In the Walloon Provinces and Brussels its vote rose to 21 per cent, and in parts of Wallonia was nearer 30 per cent. However, a common front against Rexism by the traditional parties was symbolised in the 1937 by-election in Brussels, when the prime minister Paul van Zeeland defeated Degrelle with the support of all the main parties, receiving 76 per cent of the vote against 19 per cent for Degrelle. At the 1939 election, the Rexists suffered a sharp decline to 4.43 per cent and a mere four seats (two in Brussels against five in 1936 and two in Wallonia against thirteen and no seats in Flanders).

In 1920 a left-wing group in the *Parti Ouvrier Belge* (POB) called *Les Amis de l'Exploité* was excluded from the Party and went on to form a separate party under F. Jacquemot. Under pressure from the International, it fused in December 1921 with a pre-existing party led by Van Overstraeten to form the Belgian Communist party (PCB). It first entered the Chamber in 1925 with two seats and 1.64 per cent of the vote. At the 1936 election it gained 6.05 per cent and nine seats, a figure which it held in 1939.

As we have seen, the Flemish question became more and more important, and conflict over it sharper. A new climate had developed. Flemish demands could no longer be ignored, but on the other hand they were not easily accepted. As early as 1921, a new law was passed, after considerable resistance in the Senate, on the use of languages in local government administration. Despite concessions on Brussels — a bilingual area — which was extended to cover seventeen as against fourteen Communes, the principle of territoriality and therefore the exclusive use of Flemish in Flanders was established.

The issue of a Flemish university in Ghent remained very much alive. Of course, the creation of such a university by a German decree in March 1916, which had in any case divided the Flemish movement, could not be accepted. The speech from the throne in 1918 promised the establishment of such a university, but gave no details. Divisions in all parties ensured that no rapid action ensued. The parliamentary commission set up to examine the matter proposed in late 1922, by a very small majority, the gradual transformation of the existing university into a Flemish institution (*Vervlaamsing*). Opponents of this proposal saw that they could not reject the principle of a Flemish university and so argued for the retention of a French university in Ghent as well. The Chamber passed the proposal by a majority of four, but it was rejected by the Senate. The government was forced to introduce a compromise proposal. Ghent University would be essentially Flemish, but would have Flemish and Francophone sections within it. This compromise passed both Houses and became law in August 1923.

Another serious issue which reached a climax in 1928 was that of an amnesty for the so-called 'Activists', which had become an insistent Flemish demand going well beyond the extremists. The most celebrated case was that of August Borms who, from prison, won a by-election in Antwerp against a Liberal, with the Catholics and Socialists calling for a spoiled ballot. This gave the issue an altogether greater impact than in earlier years (1924–6) when amnesty bills were heavily rejected. A compromise was reached. In the case of sentences of less than ten years imprisonment a special review commission was established. For others, including Borms, the sentences were considered to be irrevocable (i.e. not subject to further review) but also to have become null, a very strange judicial conception.

The Christian trade unions (ACW) and the Socialists declared themselves in favour of a linguistic frontier defined by law, each region then being unilingual, possibly with a special regime for Brussels. The gains of the Flemish nationalists in the 1929 elections made action even more urgent. As a result, the Government pledged itself to propose solutions. An immediate response was a bill making Ghent University fully Flemish (with some transitional provisions), which became law in April 1930. The Liberals still wanted to retain some concessions for the French-speaking minorities in Flanders, but this was now almost impossible to achieve on any permanent basis.

Progress continued towards the complete application of the 'territorial' principle, with a minimum of exceptions. In 1932, after a false start in 1930, a new law was passed covering both private and state schools. Under this law, the 'mother-tongue principle' was limited exclusively to Brussels. In 1932 a unilingual administrative regime in each of the two Regions was enacted, with concessions to minorities of 30 per cent in *Communes* (urban administrative units) in Brussels. In 1935 a new law was passed on the language to be used in legal proceedings. From then on, with minor exceptions (still contested), Flemish was to be used exclusively in Flanders. In 1937, a new amnesty law was passed, but did not give civic rights back to those who had been convicted.

This was where the 'Flemish question' rested at the outbreak of the Second World War: the movement had made important

advances along the road to complete equality in the eighty years that
it had been campaigning. But the collaboration of some Flemish
nationalists with the Nazi occupiers was to set the movement back
considerably, and the line of advance was only fully resumed in the
late 1950s.

Social and economic problems were increasingly important in this
period. As we have seen, the post-war governments *de l'Union
Sacrée* (a 'government of national unity' is the closest Anglo-Saxon
equivalent of this peculiarly Gallic conception) were progressive in
character and introduced important social reforms. After 1921,
apart from the short-lived Socialist-Catholic progressive government of 1925–6 and the second Van Zeeland government in 1936–7,
which took office after the serious strikes in June 1936, the various
successive governments were mostly concerned to reduce public
expenditure and maintain confidence in the franc. The measures of
the post-war National Unity Cabinets — the eight-hour day,
universal suffrage, a reform of the 'reactionary' character of the
Senate and some improvement in the rights of trade unions were to
remain as almost the only significant social achievements.

The 1925–6 Poullet-Vandervelde government intended to introduce wide-ranging social reforms, but was overtaken by a financial
crisis arising out of the escalating national debt, which led to a
serious weakening of the franc from 107 against the pound sterling
to 162 in early 1926. The government was forced to resign on 8 May
1926. The next government was able to stabilise the franc by issuing
shares in Belgian railways to reduce the public debt. The period
1927–30 saw considerable economic progress. External trade went
from 15 billion francs in 1925 to 32 billion in 1932. Despite important public works such as the Albert Canal, the national debt fell
from 52 billion francs in 1926 to 32 billion at the end of 1930. Laws
of 1928 and 1930 introduced and extended a system of family allowances for workers.

Between 1930 and 1932 the world recession made its impact in
Belgium. Trade fell back to 15 billion francs in 1932; the budget
deficit rose to 1 billion, share values fell by one-third and the cost
of unemployment relief rose by eight times. The number of
unemployed reached 225,000. Action was required, but the parties
failed, despite elections in both 1932 and 1933, to agree on any solution, and faced a series of strikes by workers whose wages were being
actually reduced, especially in the Charleroi industrial area. The
government obtained from Parliament a delegation of full power to
act. Wages and pensions were reduced, taxes were increased,
measures were taken to split up large banks and thereby improve

credit facilities, and public works were planned. Price and production controls were imposed.

These measures were largely ineffective.[24] The Socialist opposition put forward its '*Plan du Travail*', produced by Hendrik De Man and Paul Henri Spaak, who soon came into conflict with the traditionalist Vandervelde, who resigned as leader in 1937. The plan departed from both the Marxist notion of class struggle and that of proletarian internationalism. It sought national solutions to economic problems by 'Keynesian' means: more public spending and state intervention, an active and enlarged public sector alongside the private sector — in short a mixed economy with the state setting basic macro-economic targets. The plan failed to gain the support of the Catholic unions, which reduced its immediate practical importance. However, it was prescient as a coherent alternative economic strategy to neo-classical orthodoxy.

By 1935 it was clear that the measures of the Catholic-Liberal government were inadequate to meet the increasingly serious economic situation, with unemployment, bankruptcies, financial scandals, falling exports and an overvalued currency. Serious strikes were in prospect. Without Socialist support the royal commission on employment failed to produce viable results. In the classic manner, the response was a tripartite (Catholic-Socialist-Liberal) government, the first led by Van Zeeland (1935–6). Rapid measures were taken to devalue the franc by 28 per cent, balance the budget, control interest rates and set in train measures for public works on a limited scale under the *Office de Redressement Economique*. Unemployment fell to 100,000, a considerable success which, however, far from satisfied the Socialists, who sought a more complete application of the De Man plan.

After the 1936 election, as we have seen, the country became increasingly ungovernable. The formation of a new Van Zeeland tripartite government coincided with a serious wave of strikes, which developed into a general strike with 320,000 workers out. On the model of the 'Matignon Agreement' in France, a national conference of unions, employers and government was held. Only when a comprehensive social programme backed by the employers and government had emerged did the strikes come to an end. The programme stipulated a forty-hour week and seven-hour day in heavy industries, six days paid holiday a year, increases in wages and family allowances, and compulsory sickness and invalidity insurance. Political agreements sought to improve the working of Parliament and to ensure greater stability for the Executive. A study centre for the reform of the state was set up to act as a 'think tank'. The social measures were all enacted by the end of July and a rapid start was made on the political measures, but these were on the whole not realised before the government fell in October 1937 after unfounded but damaging allegations of financial impropriety had been made against Van Zeeland, from which the Rexists and VNV derived important propaganda advantage in their campaign against the 'rottenness' of the parliamentary system. It then became increasingly difficult to form a government, and internal strains in all parties increased. As a result, no effective measures were taken against the renewed economic crisis resulting from increasing world protectionism after 1938. The only response of the first (21–27 February 1939) and second (April–September 1939) Pierlot governments was to propose a 5 per cent reduction in public expenditure and a vague promise to improve the unemployment benefit system.

A major issue throughout the inter-war period was foreign policy.[25] As we have seen, Belgium was only relatively successful at Versailles. Her demands on Allied Luxembourg and neutral Holland were not accepted. She did however obtain the *'Cantons de l'Est'* (Eupen-Malmédy), trusteeship over the African Territories of Rwanda and Burundi, reparations from Germany and the removal of the neutrality clauses of the 1839 Treaty. However, the victory of the anti-neutrality party by no means in itself solved the problem of Belgium's future foreign policy orientation, although for many the implication was clear: an alliance with France, if possible supported by Britain. This orientation was strongly contested by the Flemish movement.

This was to play a considerable role in the controversy about the secret Franco-Belgian military agreement of 1920, whereby the parties were pledged to assist each other in the event of aggression. This Pact made possible the conclusion of the economic union with Luxembourg, and rejected the Luxembourg referendum in favour of union with France, in the interest of the Franco-Belgian Alliance. The projected military union between Belgium and Luxembourg failed to materialise. The pact made Belgian participation in the occupation of the Ruhr in 1923 morally obligatory. The related increase in the length of national service provoked serious domestic controversy, as did the ratification of the Franco-Belgian agreement; the latter was made an issue of confidence by the Theunis government, which fell when the Chamber rejected it.

Belgium was forced to accept the Dawes plan which limited reparations to BF 400–500 million, which hardly exceeded the renegotiated (and reduced) Belgian debt to the United States of some 300 million. The plan ended the occupation of the Ruhr and improved the political climate. In this new atmosphere the Locarno pact (1925) was signed. Italy, Germany, France, Britain and Belgium guaranteed, among other things, the Franco-German and Belgian-German frontiers. Over and above the guarantee itself, Belgian foreign policy was placed in a wider multilateral framework, which could more easily attain consensus in Belgium. The Kellogg-Briand Pact and the disarmament conference which began in Geneva in 1932 were hopeful signs that the post-Locarno spirit was bearing fruit. However, the world depression and above all the accession of Hitler to power in Germany in 1933 shattered these hopes and led to a new troubled period which culminated in the outbreak of war in 1939.

This new situation was underlined by the patent failure of the League of Nations to act against the re-occupation of the Rhineland and the Italian intervention in Abyssinia (Ethiopia). Belgium, like other small nations which had placed their faith in the League and the 'Locarno spirit', adopted a suicidal position. In 1936, in solemn statements, Leopold III and Paul-Henri Spaak, the Foreign Minister, postulated a sort of new neutrality. The 1920 military agreement with France was virtually abandoned, and Belgium declared that she would defend herself against any threat from any quarter. This was tantamount to refusing any effective co-ordinated action against Germany, which in the conditions of modern *Blitzkrieg* was to make the Franco-British aid promised in April 1937 largely ineffective. When war broke out in September 1939, the government was obliged to include the Socialists, previously in opposition. A declaration of neutrality was issued and the army mobilised.

Belgium in the Second World War

Methods of waging war had changed since 1914, but the strategic and tactical conceptions of Germany's enemies, including Belgium, had stood still. Belgium lasted for a mere eighteen days after the German invasion of the Low Countries on 10 May 1940. Germany immediately obtained a decisive advantage, and Allied help was too little, too late and misconceived. The German *Panzer* divisions broke through the French positions at Sedan and by 20 May reached the Somme at Abbeville. By 27 May the British evacuation from Dunquerque had begun, and on that day Belgium sued for peace.[26]

In wartime, according to Belgian custom, the King assumes effective command of the army, and it was in that capacity that Leopold III, personally and *without* consulting his government, which was in France, ordered the surrender. The government had requested the King to leave with them, but he had refused to do so. From Poitiers the government condemned the King's action and assumed his executive power. After the fall of France the majority of the

Cabinet, Deputies and Senators abandoned any active role and returned to Belgium or remained in the Unoccupied zone of France, having resigned. Only Pierlot, Spaak, Gutt, De Vleeschauwer and later Delfosse, De Schryver and Balthazar went to London and constituted an exile government. The government only gradually broke with all the German satellites and Italy, and not till 1942 did the government become a full ally of Britain, the United States and the Soviet Union by signing the Atlantic Charter. It also signed the Benelux economic union agreement with the Dutch and Luxembourg exile governments in September 1944. Belgians outside Belgium and in the Congo played an important economic and military role in the war.

Internally there were many parallels with 1914–18, but the reality was much more severe. Nazi Germany was a barbarian state obsessed with its evil racist totalitarian ideology which would tolerate no dissent or opposition. Its main aim was to weld the conquered territories into a 'New Order' in the service of Germany. Any apparent concession or co-operation, for example with Flemish movements, was based on the most total cynicism and opportunism. In contrast to 1914, the trauma of such rapid defeat and the subsequent defeat of all Germany's enemies except Britain, whose survival hung by the thread of the indomitable 'Few' of the Royal Air Force Fighter Command, the events of May 1940 induced a state of shock, disorientation and passivity, which served the German cause well. Many thousands of Belgians had left their homes, the economy was in chaos and the army was in German prisoner-of-war camps; all internal leadership had gone and the dispute between King and government increased the general confusion.

At first, as in 1914–18, the Germans established a military government under General von Falkenhausen, with a civil administration under his command. In addition, of course, the various 'ideological' agencies such as the Gestapo and SS operated in Belgium against the Resistance and the Jews. The secretaries-general of the Belgian ministries remained in office and constituted a subordinate Belgian administration, which established numerous special agencies in the field of food supply and control of industry. A corporatist type of organisation was introduced for many key economic sectors (coal, metallurgy and textiles) and by the replacement of the trade unions with the *Union des Travailleurs Manuels et Intellectuels*. At the same time Hendrik De Man dissolved the *Parti Ouvrier Belge* (POB).

As the initial stupefaction wore off, reaction to the occupation developed along three main lines. The majority of the population accepted, unwillingly, the new situation as a necessary evil, seeking merely to survive. No doubt in the early war years, with the memory of the failures of the parliamentary system fresh in their minds, and presented with the apparent invincibility of German arms and, for some after June 1941, the attraction of the assault on Communism, a few leaned towards support for the 'New Order' rather than mere acquiescence in it. However, as the war progressed, rationing bit deeper, German barbarism revealed its real face, and the battles of Stalingrad and El Alamein and the 1,000-bomber raids offered a glimmer of hope, the vast majority leaned increasingly towards the Allied cause.

However, a small group both in Flanders and Wallonia openly embraced collaboration. In Flanders two groups, the nationalist but fascistic *Vlaams National Verbond* (VNV) under Staf De Clercq and later Elias saw collaboration as a means of realising their dream of a *Groot Nederland*, embracing Flanders, Northern France and Holland as part of the 'New Order'. Germany certainly encouraged these aims, but took much less concrete action than in 1914–18. The Nazis preferred the less nationalist and more clearly National-Socialist *De Vlag* under Vandewiele. Both groups provided contingents for the German armies on the Russian front. As elsewhere in Europe, German tactics towards such movements lacked any subtlety and led to a crisis within the VNV. In Wallonia *Rex* under Léon Dégrelle, was the main collaborationist organisation. The VNV had 86,000 members. In all over 340,000 persons were accused of collaboration after the war, of whom 58,000 were found guilty and 241 were executed. That excludes 60,000 who volunteered to work in Germany, and who were not brought to trial.

Resistance rapidly grew. By the liberation six major organisations had some 120,000 men under arms, and double that number of other active members. The most important were the *Armée Secrète*, the military organisation run by the exile government (about 50,000 members), the left-wing *Front de l'Indépendance* (40,000) and the *Mouvement National Belge* (20,000). Belgium was liberated rapidly. British troops crossed the frontier on 2 September 1944 and liberated Brussels on 4 September. By 3 November all German troops had left Belgian territory. However, the country had to suffer two more trials: 'V1' and 'V2' rockets fell in Liège and Antwerp and the Ardennes counter-offensive between 16 December 1944 and the end of January 1945 almost brought the Nazis back to the Meuse.

Belgium after the War

The events which have marked post-war Belgian history have been varied and controversial: the repression of collaboration to which we have already referred; the '*Question royale*'; the remarkable economic recovery; Belgian membership of NATO and the European Communities; the decolonisation of the Congo in 1960; and the rise of the language and 'community' issue, especially after 1965: Many of these issues will be discussed later in this book, particularly the 'regional' question and the major changes in the party system which occurred during the 1960s.

Compared with earlier periods, political stability has been as elusive as ever. There have been twenty-eight governments since the liberation up to the time of writing. Of these only four lasted longer than three years and only one the full four years of the legislature. There have been twelve elections since the first post-war election in 1946, giving the average legislature a life of barely three years. Almost all possible types of government have been formed: homogeneous CVP/PSC; homogeneous Socialist; CVP/PSC-Socialist; CVP/PSC-Liberal; Socialist-Liberal; classic tripartite PSC/CVP-Socialist-Liberal; governments including all the regional parties (RW, FDF, RU) or only some of them (FDF or RW) and between 1944–7 four governments including Communists, and a few governments without the Catholic party in 1945–7. However after 1947, the Catholic party has only been in opposition for four years (1954–8). There have been governments headed by both Socialists (eight) and CVP/PSC (twenty), but no Liberals. Most governments have fallen as a result of their internal dissensions rather than by defeat in Parliament.

Between 1945–51 three questions dominated political life: the '*Question royale*,'[27] reconstruction, and the reorientation of Belgian foreign policy in response to the onset of the Cold War after 1947. When Belgium was liberated in September 1944, the Germans removed Leopold III to Germany and he was only freed by American forces in May 1945. Parliament, therefore, elected his brother Prince Charles as Regent on 20 September 1944. Statements of that time gave no hint of the animosity that was to develop against the King when he was freed, but in the face of Socialist, Communist and some Liberal reservations, he was asked by the government not to return to Belgium but to stay in Switzerland.

In June 1945, a law was passed to the effect that the Regency could only be ended by a vote of both Houses of Parliament in joint session. A CVP/PSC proposal for a referendum was not then accepted. The Spaak-Eyskens government (PS-PSC/CVP) agreed to disagree on the issue. The 1949 election — the first at which women could vote and the first to take place after the Prague coup — saw a significant rightward swing, which greatly modified the situation. The PSC/CVP almost had an absolute majority in the

Senate. Logically, a Liberal-CVP/PSC government was formed, which agreed on a referendum on the future of Leopold III. This was held on 12 March 1950. Overall, 57.6 per cent voted 'yes' (in favour of the King's return), but in Brussels only 48 per cent did so, and in Wallonia only 42 per cent, whereas in Flanders the 'yes' vote was 72 per cent. After the 1950 election, in which the CVP/PSC alone gained a secure absolute majority in both Houses, Parliament voted for the end of the Regency as prescribed by Article 82 of the constitution and the law of June 1945.

The referendum result was not accepted in Wallonia, and the opposition — Socialists, Communists and others — organised meetings and demonstrations, including a march on the royal palace at Laeken, just outside Brussels. On 15 August 1950, in order to avoid further violence, unrest and division, Leopold abdicated in favour of his son Baudouin. So the *Question royale* ended, but the bitterness it had generated lived on, not least in Flanders, where it was felt that a minority had gained its will by the use of violence and civil disorder in the face of a clear vote of the people.

In defence of the opponents of King Leopold, the very strong emotions aroused by the *Question royale* should be understood. This substantial minority considered their action justified on the grounds of Leopold's behaviour during the war. In the first place, he had taken it upon himself to surrender the Belgian army without the approval of the government, and had refused to follow his ministers into exile. His remarriage (his first wife, the popular Queen Astrid, had been killed in a car accident in 1935) also fuelled controversy, because it seemed inconsistent with his declared intention of sharing the lot of his troops as a prisoner-of-war, and because of the Flemish and Catholic origins of his second wife Liliane Baels. A more serious ground might seem to be his relatively extensive dealings with exponents of the 'New Order' — only now coming fully to light, but which were already at that time exemplified by his meeting with Hitler at which he purported to discuss the future of Belgium within a Europe dominated by Nazi Germany. Perhaps not surprisingly, his opponents, mostly from the ranks of the Walloon Resistance, considered that he had disqualified himself from the right to reign.

Post-war reconstruction was also a key issue. Housing was an immediate priority: 200,000 new houses were needed. Laws of 1947 and 1948 made grants up to BF 22,000 and loans at the low interest rates of 2 and 2¾ per cent for house building. The law on the National Bank (6 October 1944) 'sterilised' a considerable part of the inflationary money supply, coupled with tight controls on prices and incomes. The economic measures taken initially by the returning Pierlot government were ill-adapted to the actual situation and were only partially successful. The Van Acker government gave priority to the immediate reopening of the coal mines which was the best available source of export revenue. With the liberalisation of world trade and the inflow of Marshall aid, Belgium benefited from the general view of growth which began in the early 1950s. The resulting prosperity made possible a relatively painless solution of major structural problems brought about by technological change. The Sambre-Meuse coal mines were almost all closed, causing almost 200,000 jobs to be lost, directly or indirectly. Even in Flanders considerable numbers of jobs disappeared. But apart from the strikes against mine closures in early 1959 and the very severe but almost totally, unsuccessful strike of the winter 1960–1 in protest against the so-called '*Loi unique*', which reduced public expenditure and social benefits, the 1950s and early 1960s were a period of social peace.

In the period 1945–60, foreign and colonial policy was a major preoccupation. With the Brussels Treaty directed at Germany and then with the onset of the Cold War after 1947–8, Belgium for the first time committed herself to a system of preventive alliance by becoming a founder-member of NATO in 1949. Belgium was an early supporter of European integration, joining the Council of Europe (1949) and becoming one of 'the Six' to join the European Coal and Steel Community in 1952 and later playing a major role in the establishment of Euratom and the European Economic Community (1957). On a wider plane, she was a founder-member of the United Nations, and joined the IMF, GATT and OEEC established under the Marshall plan.[28]

Towards the end of the 1950s, with many former colonies of Britain and France in the process of achieving independence, the anti-colonial movement began to gather strength. In the Congo itself an urban proletariat had come into existence and was increasingly unionised. The educated Africans began to organise nationalist movements such as UNISCO. A triumphant visit of King Baudouin in May-June 1955 served to conceal the growing nationalist reality. Parties were formed by such figures as Kasavubu (ABAKO) and Lumumba (*Mouvement National Congolais*). Events moved extremely rapidly, perhaps too rapidly. As late as November 1958, when the Eyskens-Lilar government was formed, there was still no clear policy towards the Congo.

A timid beginning was made with a mission to the Congo by a group of Belgian politicians in late 1958. A statement on future policy was promised, but this was overtaken by the riots in Leopoldville in January 1959. These events led indirectly to the resignation in September 1959 of the minister for the colonies, van

Hemmelrijck, who was replaced by the more decisive August De Schrijver. The latter accelerated the trend towards re-evaluation already in train, and organised the famous '*Table Ronde*' between Belgian and Congolese political leaders in January-February 1960. The conclusion was that the Congo should become independent on 30 June 1960. The rapidity of the move towards independence probably contributed to the later tragic events, which led to the need for several military interventions by the Belgians and the UN both to save lives and to safeguard the still enormous Belgian economic interests, which became further threatened in the civil war caused by the breakaway of the copper-rich Katanga province.[29]

In the 1950s the old 'school question',[30] which had proved so divisive in the 1880s, returned to the forefront of actuality. In 1947 and 1950 problems arose over state subsidies to 'free' (Catholic) technical education and general secondary schooling. Until 1954 the PSC/CVP was in power either as the major component in coalitions or, between 1950-4, with an absolute majority; and during these years it regulated the problem in a way which could not be acceptable to the opposition — involving considerable increases in subsidies to Catholic schools (more than BF 300 million under a law of 1951). The Education Minister Pierre Harmel sought a permanent solution: by the law of 17 December 1952 permanent increased subsidies were introduced, together with full freedom of choice of parents between 'free' and state education. On educational methods and curricula these laws also increased the influence of the Catholic education sector by means of 'mixed advisory committees', which thus gained a right of intervention in the State sector.

In the elections of 1954, the PSC/CVP lost its absolute majority, and the school question was a major factor in the formation of the unusual coalition of Socialists and Liberals, under A. Van Acker (Soc.), which resulted. A new law was prepared which would both reduce subsidies and increase the number of state schools. Subsidies were also to be subject to greater control of curricula and the qualifications of teachers in Catholic schools. Despite vast demonstrations, a petition with two million signatures and episcopal condemnation, the law was approved by both Houses in July 1955.

The 1958 election showed that such an extreme policy was not desired by the electorate. The outgoing coalition lost its majority, and a CVP/PSC minority government came to power. The new situation required a peace or at least a truce in the 'school war'. The National School Committee, composed of the Presidents of the three major parties was formed, and a compromise, incorporated in the 'School Pact', was concluded for twelve years, later renewed. A *Commission du Pacte scolaire* was set up to monitor its operation.

This was an early example of Parliament being bypassed by 'corporate' *ad hoc* bodies, since Parliament's role was limited to approval — unanimous except for the Communists — of the results of the negotiations. However, peace was restored and has barely been disturbed since.

Although considerable ill feeling was aroused in Flanders when '*Incivisme*' (a latter-day euphemism for collaboration with the Nazi's) was repressed with particular severity there, 'the Community question' was not a major political issue in the 1950s. However, it was to become the dominant political issue of the 1960s and 1970s, breaking up the old party structure and making the state almost ungovernable. We shall look at this issue in greater detail in chapter 4, so suffice it here to point to the main milestones along the way.

With the recession of the post-war Communist tide (twenty-three parliamentary seats in 1946 and only five in 1961), the three traditional parties dominated political life. The new *Volksunie* appeared in 1954 with one seat; by 1961 it had five. The first Deputies from the Brussels based *Front Démocratique Francophone* (FDF) and *Front Wallon* — three FDF and two *Front Wallon* — were elected in 1965. Until then the 'Community' parties had been totally marginal, but the years 1960–1 saw a general radicalisation which was to change the picture totally. The strikes of 1960–1 were midwife to a new Walloon consciousness. Wallonia was now on the defensive economically; this created a new situation and new nationalist reflexes, which found expression in the *Mouvement Populaire Wallon* and the *Front Wallon*, which later fused into the *Rassemblement Wallon*. The same defensive reaction in Brussels led to the formation of the FDF in 1964. By 1968 the 'federalist' parties (*Volksunie*, RW and FDF) had made a decisive breakthrough gaining respectively twenty (9.79 per cent of the vote), seven and five (5.90 per cent of the vote) seats.

At the same time, the three 'national' parties were feeling the pressures of community problems, which in time led to each dividing into two; the 'pairs' of ideologically similar parties on either side of the community divide having different positions from each other. As early as 1968, the PSC and the CVP were clearly two separate parties. The Liberal 'family' soon followed, and in 1978 the PSB-BSP became the PS and SP.

The Community issue[31] could no longer be ignored. Palliatives such as discussions about the linguistic frontier (fixed in 1932) — arising out of the language census of 1960, especially in relation to the *Communes* in the suburbs of Brussels — were no longer enough. Attempts to alter the status of several *Randgemeenten*

(Flemish *Communes* near Brussels) during 1961–3, basically to include new *Communes* in the bilingual capital area and create facilities for French speakers in otherwise Flemish areas, led to increased conflict. At the same time, no change in the distribution of seats in Parliament had taken place since 1947 due to Walloon opposition, but the distortions had become so flagrant (Wallonia deserved to lose four seats) that action was now inevitable.

More radical measures required changes in the country's political structure, which presupposed a constitutional reform. After a round table conference in January 1964, agreement was reached on limited changes, and the Parliament elected in 1965 was *'Constituant'*. However, the agreement was not implemented as the situation worsened. The Harmel-Spinoy (1965–6) and Vanden Boeynants–De Clercq governments fell without being able to steer any amendment through Parliament, in the case of the latter, it was over the issue of the creation of a French section at Leuven University. So the 1965 Parliament was dissolved. The federalist parties made large gains in north and south. The problem of regionalisation had now forced itself on to the political agenda. However, the forces in favour of a unitary state, especially the CVP and certain economic groups, remained very strong.

A CVP/PSC-PSB/BSP government was formed under Mr Eyskens (1968–71) with the revision of the constitution as its main task. An initial proposal met so much opposition that it was withdrawn, and a 'Committee of Twenty-Eight', including opposition members, was set up in September 1969. Although it achieved no results, it had cleared the ground, and led to a compromise proposal from the government in February 1970. Some articles were passed with the aid of the *Volksunie*, giving the necessary 142 votes, which the coalition lacked (128 seats). Just before Christmas 1970, the last major amendments were approved by both Houses. The basis was now laid for a 'semi-federal system':

— Article 59 *bis* established two (Flemish and Francophone Cultural Councils and a council for the German-speaking Community, with law-making powers in cultural matters;

— Article 107 *quater* established Regional Councils for Wallonia, Flanders and Brussels with important powers in the socio-economic field;

— A *'Sonnette d'alarme'* (alarm-bell) system (Article 38 and 38 *bis*) giving two-thirds of a linguistic group the right temporarily to suspend the adoption of certain language laws.

— It was required that laws implementing articles 59 *bis* and 107 *quater* be approved by two-thirds majority *and* a majority in each linguistic group in Parliament.

The following election in 1971 saw even more drastic gains for the federalist parties: FDF/RW gained twelve, and *Volksunie* gained one. These gains were consolidated, but not expanded at the following elections (1974, 1977, 1978, 1981). The Community problem thus remained a permanent feature of the political landscape, not least because the solutions of 1970 created new problems and required considerable implementing legislation. Some of the least controversial of this legislation, such as the laws on the functioning of the Community Councils (1971 and 1973) and the reform of local government, creating five '*Agglomerations*' (Brussels, Liège, Charleroi, Ghent, Antwerp), were passed.

However, the elections of 1971 and the election to the Council of the new Brussels *Agglomeration*, of which the FDF seized control, sharpened conflict and made progress on the implementation of the key article 107 *quater* on the Regions impossible. Neither the second Eyskens government (January-November 1972) nor the Leburton government composed of the three traditional parties (1973–4) was able to make any significant progress.

After the 1974 election Mr Tindemans formed a PSC/CVP-PLP/PVV government, while attempting to find a broader based solution to the Community problem. 'Provisional' regionalisation laws, falling short of the degree of devolution required by article 107 *quater* but representing a degree of decentralisation, were envisaged, and for the first time the inclusion of the 'federalist' parties in government was a serious option. The conclave held at Steenokkerzeel failed to reach a global solution, and in any case excluded the Socialists, but narrowed down disagreement and led to the entry of the RW into the government. This coalition was divided — as the RW moved leftwards in 1976 and lacked the 'special majorities' needed to execute 107 *quater*. It fell in April 1977. However, the 'inter-Community dialogue' had started, and the ground was prepared for the Egmont-Stuyvenberg pact, which was the basis of the second Tindemans government in which the community parties (PSC/CVP-BSP/PSB-FDF-VU) were included.

The continued resistance to reorganisation inside the CVP sabotaged this brave effort at an elegant, coherent global solution (see Chapter 4.) and led to a new election and a prolonged crisis in 1978–9. The four governments of Wilfried Martens (CVP), who personally enjoyed the confidence of the other parties, fell in turn between 1979 and 1981 because of the suspicion of the CVP engendered in the other parties both on Community questions and on its economic policy aims, especially reductions in public expediture.

However, the 1978 legislature was, unlike that of 1977, *Constituant*, and the Martens III government, made up of the three traditional parties, succeeded in the summer of 1980 in passing a package which — apart from the Brussels issue and the reform of the Senate — completed the programme embodied in the Egmont pact. Although the final result was more patchy and less coherent than the Egmont Pact intended, the Community issue could nevertheless at long last go on to the back burner.

In 1980 and 1981 the main economic and social issues (and sources of controversy were unemployment, public expenditure, the indexing of wages to the cost of living, issues relating to the role of the police and the maintenance of public order against private militias, mostly of the extreme right, and 'cruise' missiles. With eight governments since 1973, Belgium had become increasingly ungovernable. The recession has created a vicious circle: coalition governments 'across the middle' (i.e. PSC/CVP-PS/SP) have become ever more necessary to ensure social peace, but have become ever more unwieldy and immobile at a time when divisions between right and left were being exacerbated by the crisis and a whole range of issues among which the indexing of wages, public expenditure and defence policy are the most visible.

Despite the best efforts of the FDF and the upheavals in the RW, leading to a breakaway by its historic leader P.H. Gendebien, Community issues were in the background at the election in November 1981 but they have since returned to the centre stage. New small parties — the Ecologists and the UDRT (the anti-tax party), appeared to have some impact in a general 'anti-politician' mood, but in the end their electoral impact remained modest. While the electorate largely resigned itself once again to its relative powerlessness to provoke change, returning a parliament whose basic structure differed but little from that elected in 1978 and offered few new possibilities, it would be wrong to conclude that there was no change, at least in the mood of the electorate. This mood is quite unequivocally autonomist in both Flanders and Wallonia, and generally pessimistic and resigned.

NOTES

1. The aim of this chapter is to provide a short and easily comprehensible account of Belgian history, as it bears on the characteristics of the country, its people and political culture; accordingly footnotes and unnecessary detail have been kept to a minimum. The main sources on which the chapter draws are, for the period before 1790, Frans Van Kalken, *Histoire de la Belgique et de son Expansion Coloniale*, Office de Publicité, Brussels, 1954, and, for the period after 1790, F. Van Kalken, *op. cit.*, and Th. Luykx, *Politieke Geschiedenis van Belgie*, Elsevier, Amsterdam/Brussels, 1977. In two vols with through pagination.

2. For the pre-Roman and Roman period, see Van Kalken, op. cit., 5–17 and 18–30, and F. Cumont, *Comment la Belgique fut Romanisée*, 2nd edn, Lamartin, Brussels, 1920.

3. Van Kalken, op. cit., 49–50 and 51–4.

4. On the role of the towns see Van Kalken, op. cit., 110–12, and H. Pirenne, *Les Villes et Institutions Urbaines*, vol. 2, Nouvelle Société d'Edition, Brussels 1939, and V. Friis, *Histoire de Gand*, De Tavernier, Ghent, 1930.

5. Van Kalken, op. cit., 168–74.

6. Ibid., 175–83 and P. Bonaufont, *Philippe le Bon*, Collection notre passé, Renaissance du Livre, Brussels, 1943.

7. For the Spanish period and the revolt of the Low Countries, see Van Kalken, op. cit., 152–356; A. Henne, *Histoire du Règne de Charles V en Belgique*, 10 vols, Flautan, Brussels, 1858–60; and L. Pfandl, *Philippe II*, Hachette, Paris, 1942.

8. Van Kalken, op. cit., 375–86.

9. For the Austrian period, ibid., 422–55, and Luykx, op. cit., for the first Brabançonne revolution (1788), 31–6.

10. Van Kalken, op. cit., 450–64.

11. For the French period, ibid., 477–510.

12. For the Dutch period, ibid., 512–28, and Luykx, op. cit., 40–5.

13. For the Belgian revolution, Luykx, op. cit., 46–60.

14. For the work of the National Congress, Th. Fuste, *Le Congrès National*, Brussels 1880; and for the international context see R. Steinmetz, *Englands Anteil an der Trennung der Niederlande 1830*, The Hague 1930, and R. Rollot, *Les Origines de la Neutralité Belge*, Paris 1902.

15. See Luykx, 52–62.

16. Ibid., 94–7 and 100–7.

17. Ibid., 124–30.

18. Ibid., 182–4 and 205–9, for the origins of the Socialist Party.

19. Ibid., 113–20, 160–2, 163–4 and 167–8, for progress in improving the rights of Dutch speakers.

20. Ibid., 239–43; E.D. Morel, *King Leopold's Rule in Africa*, London, 1904; and E. Van der Velde, *Les Derniers Jours de l'Etat Indépendant du Congo*, Mons, 1911.

21. See Van Kalken, op. cit., 662–701, for the 1914–18 war, and 704–6 for the Versailles settlement.

22. On the Flemish question in the war and after, see Luykx, 254–66 and 329–30.

23. Van Kalken, op. cit., 724–7 and Luykx, op. cit., 283–9.

24. For inter-war domestic policy, see Van Kalken, 707–35 and Luykx, 298–367.

25. Van Kalken, op. cit., 718–20.

26. Luykx, op. cit., 383–400 for Belgium in the War.

27. Ibid., 441–52, on the '*Question royale*'.

28. Ibid., 460–9, 478–9 and 483–4.

29. For developments after 1960, see ibid., 498–500 and 516–19.

30. Ibid., 484–87 and 509–11.

31. See Chapter 4 and Luykx, op. cit., 585–602, 606–10 and 619–21, and A. Allen and P. Van Speybroek, *Le Réforme de l'Etat Belge de 1974 jusqu'au Pacte Communautaire*, CEPESS 1977, and *Dossiers du CRISP*, no. 893–4, 'La Réforme de l'Etat', 1980.

2
THE ECONOMY AND SOCIETY

In Belgium more than in most countries, political issues are ultimately linked to economic cleavages. Her economy is exceptionally open and therefore vulnerable. Trade links, cost structures, comparative competitiveness and the value of the franc are all of such importance that they dominate politics, except when the 'intra-community' question is dominant. Relations between the two communities are also largely connected with economic problems, although this is not to deny the importance of linguistic and cultural differences. The history of Belgium has been a continuous see-saw of economic predominance between north and south, which does much to explain their difficult political co-existence within the Belgian state. And when one adds the fact that the predominant ideological approach to economic problems — liberalism or state intervention — has also been 'regionalised', some sense of the extreme sensitivity and complication of the issue begins to emerge.

It is not our purpose here to present a detailed economic geography or economic history of Belgium, but some indication of the country's vital statistics, of the trend of economic development over the past 300 years, and of the present structure of the economy — its strengths and weaknesses and medium-term problems — is essential before we can analyse economic policy-making and current economic policies.

The country and people

Belgium is a relatively small country, but it is one of the most densely populated in Western Europe. It is in essence part of the north European plain, wedged between France and Germany, and crossed by a major river, the Meuse. It has therefore always been of strategic importance and a vital economic crossroads. In terms of its physical and human geography, the country can be divided into two zones. In the north, from the coast to the Sambre-Meuse valley, is the Flemish plain, crossed by several smaller rivers, as well as the Scheldt with its mouth at Antwerp, the country's major port. The Sambre-Meuse valley, crossing the country from west to east, is the major industrial basin, with the towns of Mons, Charleroi, Namur and Liège. To the south and east lies the Ardennes region, rugged and thinly populated.

The greatest length (north-south) of the country is about 290 km and the greatest width about 145 km. The total area of the country is 30,519 square km, slightly larger than Wales. Some 60 per cent of the land area is in Wallonia and 40 per cent in Flanders. The total population is 9,848,000, a density of 760 per square km. This is only exceeded in Europe by the Netherlands, and is considerable by any standards. Were it not for the Ardennes, the density would be greater than the Netherlands. This compares with 530 per square mile (137 per square km) for the United Kingdom; however, the population density in England is higher than that in Belgium.

As to the distribution of the population,[1] 56.12 per cent live in the Flemish provinces, 32.73 per cent in the Walloon provinces and 11.15 per cent in the Brussels region. The major cities in the country are Brussels (1,015,700), Antwerp (197,305), Liège (224,136), Charleroi (224,229), Namur (100,647), Mons (87,216) and Ghent (243,523). The German-speaking population of the *Cantons de l'Est* (Eupen-Malmedy area) near the German border is very small, numbering only about 70,000, but it does benefit from a special political status.[2]

It is difficult to say that the population is homogeneous, but there are no evident 'ethnic' minorities. There are two distinct cultural communities and, if the small German-speaking community is included, there is a third one. However, there are in each community important minorities and anomalies. Ghent was long an enclave of French culture in Flanders. Brussels, which is physically in Flanders, is now over 80 per cent French-speaking with variation between boroughs from 72 to 92 per cent, but retains a significant Flemish minority. In the Flemish *Communes* surrounding Brussels, a French-speaking population of commuters, typical 'suburbanites', has grown up, 'drowning' the Flemish population, and in some *Communes* — Kraainem and Tervuren, for example — increasingly represents the majority.

In the last decade a large number of immigrant workers have come to Belgium, mostly from the Mediterranean and North Africa. At present these immigrants number about 850,000. In some Brussels boroughs they represent close to one third of the population.

Belgium never had any other overseas territories besides the Congo (now Zaïre) and the two League of Nation Mandates Rwanda and Burundi. The Congo became independent in 1960, and the two Mandates in 1962.

The economy

As we saw in Chapter 1, there has been a perpetual see-saw between the northern (Flemish) and southern (Walloon) provinces in terms of economic development. In the Middle Ages, thanks to the wool trade, a flourishing urban civilisation grew up in Flanders,[3] which ranked as one of the richest areas in all Europe. English competition, political complications, internal strife and the silting up of the port of Bruges led to the decline of the Flemish economy and with it the political power of the quasi-independent Flemish towns by the end of the Austrian period.

Early industrialisation

The first step towards the Belgian industrial revolution came with the French occupation in the 1790s; Belgium was thus the second industrialised country after Britain. The concept of economic liberalism was gradually introduced, in place of the semi-feudalistic corporations which had hitherto characterised the Belgian economy. More flexible and efficient legal, fiscal and administrative structures were put in place, which encouraged capitalist development. At the same time the needs of the French war economy encouraged production and modernisation. Three main industrial centres developed in this period: Liège, Charleroi and Ghent. It was the steam machines of the Englishman William Cockerill which modernised both the weaving industry in Verviers and the metal industry in Liège, based on nearby coal supplies and abundant high-quality labour. The mines of Hainaut, with steam pumps, produced one million tons of coal, a quarter of the total continental European production in this period.

In the 1820s important improvements in canal communications were undertaken (Charleroi-Brussels) and in 1835 railway expansion began. With these advantages, heavy industry in both the Liège and the Charleroi-Mons areas developed considerably in the period 1830–50. Only one industrial growth-point developed in Flanders, based on mechanised cotton-spinning in Ghent (10,000 workers in 1810), but after 1815 it suffered a severe setback in the face of competition.[4]

The golden age of Wallonia

The Revolution of 1830 by which Belgium gained her independence left the new state severe economic problems. It now had only a small internal market, having lost the Dutch colonial markets in Asia, while the loss of control of the Schelde river limited the value of Antwerp as a major transit port. The new government reacted energetically to meet these challenges, and a major part of this policy was the creation of a railway network (593 km in 1843, 1,730 km in

1860 and 3,350 km in 1870). This construction in itself stimulated industry and provided major benefits in terms of transport of raw materials and finished goods.[5]

Another important advantage was the policy of the Société Générale de Banque, which soon initiated long-term loans to finance industrial investment. The Walloon metal industry grew by 3 per cent annually in the 1830–45 period, but had doubled that rate of growth in the next fifteen years to 1860. There was a considerable industrial concentration in Liège and Charleroi to take advantage of economies of scale and the transport network.

The depressions of the late nineteenth century slowed down growth and increased concentration (in 1895 there were only twenty-nine large furnaces operating as against fifty-six in the 1840s). The home market too became saturated, and export opportunities were reduced. However, increases in productivity and control of costs, which caused severe labour unrest, enabled Belgian industry to remain internationally competitive in the difficult period 1875–90. The spearhead of Belgian industry was coal mining, which quadrupled its production between 1850 and 1895. It employed 116,000 workers in 1896, more than the textile, metal-working and machinery industries combined. Other major industries besides coal, steel and textiles were zinc and glass-working (glass exports grew at 9 per cent yearly between 1840–73).

Meanwhile, the Flemish economy[6] was relatively in a state of stagnation or worse. Between 1830 and 1880 the cloth industry and agriculture, the mainstays of the Flemish rural population, suffered severe setbacks. The traditional linen industry collapsed in the 1850s creating much unemployment and misery. And bad rye harvests and potato blight (as in Ireland) had a severe effect on Flemish agriculture. Many unemployed or under-employed Flemish workers or evicted peasant farmers were forced into emigration, either to seek work in Walloon industry or, in the case of 30–40,000 of them, in America.

In the 1870s, the opening up of the American and Canadian West and falling transport costs saw serious falls in cereal prices; this made Flemish agriculture, which still employed well over half the population, uncompetitive. Already by now industrial concerns dominated government; protectionist measures were rejected for fear of reprisals against Belgian (Walloon) industrial exports. From the 1890s, reconversion to less labour-intensive animal husbandry began to gather pace.

For industry the only light in the tunnel was the relative success of the more modern textile industry based on Ghent and St. Niklaas. However, Antwerp's port became the main growth-point in

Flanders. Registered tonnage handled grew from 159,999 tons in 1840 to 457,000 in 1860 and 2,623,000 in 1880, placing Antwerp at the head of the European ports, ahead of Rotterdam and Hamburg. Growth continued more slowly, reaching 6,720,000 tons in 1900 and 14,140,000 in 1913. This expansion attracted many associated industries: food processing, sugar refining, and some technologically innovatory industries, such as Bell telephones and the Minerva motor company (co-production). Already by 1913 these 'futuristic' activities in Antwerp were employing some 6,000 workers.

The later part of the nineteenth century and the early twentieth saw overall industrial employment growing faster in Flanders than Wallonia, and in 1901 coal mines were opened in Limburg. Flanders had an industrial future, even if her experience before 1913 had been very difficult.

Taking the 1880 level as 100, industrial production in Belgium reached 163 by 1900 and 257 by 1913 on the eve of the war. Cereal agricultural production, already standing at 79 in 1845 (against 21 for industrial production) reached only 114 by 1900 and 122 by 1913. Belgium had — due to the Walloon industrial revolution — become an industrial nation well before 1914. Whatever the continued importance of agriculture, industrial policy would henceforth be the dominant political consideration of all governments.

The economic loss from the First World War was very large: 16–20 per cent of the nation's assets. Production only reached 1913 levels by 1924. In 1920 the price index had risen to 455 (1913 = 100), and it continued to rise. However, especially with the aid of raw materials from the Congo, and a major and well-organised national effort, recovery was remarkably rapid. The main problem remained the inflationary spiral caused by the over-abundant money supply. In 1926 drastic deflationary measures were necessary, and were carried out successfully. Production continued to rise, reaching 130 (1913 = 100) in 1929. It seems with hindsight that this growth was too rapid and uncontrolled.[7]

Structural change was also taking place.[8] Coal production soon recovered and reached a peak in 1925, but the Walloon mining regions were no longer expanding. Hopes were now pinned on the (Flemish) Limburg mines. The apparently unbounded growth in other key sectors — steel, textiles, glass — hid important structural and cost problems, which the 1926 devaluation partly and temporarily resolved, at least in restoring international competitiveness. Now industries such as electricity, represented by ACEC of Charleroi, and specialised metallurgical industries based on metals from the Congo (copper, gold, radium) were also gaining in importance. However, no significant Belgian motor industry was able to survive even in the 1920s.

This then was the state of the Belgian economy at the onset of the great depression which in effect lasted until the Second World War. With competitive devaluations, falling demand, generalised cutbacks and protectionism, Belgian industry, with its over-expansion and high cost structure, was in a poor position to meet the crisis and ride it out. This was particularly problematical for the older Walloon industrial areas. Between 1929 and 1933 Belgian exports fell by half. Textile and steel production fell by 60 per cent. In agriculture herd sizes and cereal production also fell after 1930. Unemployment rose massively from a mere 9,000 in 1929 to 22,000 in 1930 and 79,000 in 1931, peaking at an annual average of 165,000 in 1935. The highest recorded figure was 223,000 in the winter of 1934/5. By 1939, the yearly average figure was still 160,000. At times, as many as 40 per cent of the workforce were unemployed. Bankruptcies and bank failures were numerous. The Van Zeeland National Unity government held the line with a 28 per cent devaluation and some 'semi-Keynesian' measures inspired by the Socialist *'Plan de Travail'* (the *'Plan de Man'*).

Flemish industry had, as we have already seen, already begun to catch up before the First World War, and the process continued between the wars. The Flemish share in total national industrial employment rose from 31.05 per cent in 1910 to 38.7 per cent in 1937. The advance of Flemish industry was spread over a broad front. In Wallonia, what limited growth there was fell below the national average and many traditional industries suffered decline. This was partly because wage costs were 25–30 per cent lower in Flanders. Transport costs were also vital. Thus by 1937, 16 per cent of mine workers were in Flanders as against 0.2 per cent in 1910; and the share in metallurgy was 26 per cent (18.5) and in glass 18 per cent (2.0). Of all the workers in Flanders 37 per cent now worked in industry as against 31.51 per cent in 1910.

Contrary to almost all expectations, the thirty years after the Second World War saw continuous expansion and optimism.[9] By 1948 production had reached its 1938 level. In the early post-war years average growth at 2.5 per cent was lower than the OECD average (5 per cent), but in 1960–73 real growth was up to 5.1 per cent and throughout the 1970s was up to 5.4 per cent. Unemployment fell steadily to reach a low point of 1.6 per cent in 1965, but showed some relatively high temporary increases.

The movement out of agriculture continued apace, as the accompanying table shows. This has meant a total loss of 300,000 jobs in the primary sector (209,000 in Flanders and 100,000 in Wallonia), which the industrial growth of the 1950s, 1960s and early 1970s could readily absorb, either in manufacturing industry (+ 70,000 jobs in Flanders by 1960) or in the tertiary sector (Flanders + 59,000 jobs, Wallonia + 34,000 jobs 1953–60). Regional policy measures have created 375,000 jobs since 1959.[10]

WORK FORCE IN AGRICULTURE (%)

	Flanders	Wallonia
1947	19.8	11.8
1960	10.7	9.2
1970	5.1	5.0
1978	3.6	3.3
1980	3.0	3.0

Source: *Annuaire Statistique*, 1980.

Other significant structural changes have taken place. Walloon industry has faced serious difficulties. Coal mining in Wallonia is in severe decline (103,000 jobs in 1950; 39,000 in 1960). In the same period, there has been a net global loss of 76,000 jobs in Walloon manufacturing industry.[11] In Flanders the reverse has been true. There has been a significant move away from commuting to work, with the creation of jobs in the localities — Ghent, Antwerp, Bruges and many smaller towns — where labour was available on a much more decentralised basis. The Flemish industrial revolution is based on 'new' industries: electronics, petrochemicals, with highly skilled labour, foreign investment and diversification. Like all new industry it has shown some initial vulnerability to the world economic situation. The increasing involvement of multinationals both in Flanders and Wallonia has brought investment, but at the high price of seeing control of sensitive investment and employment decisions pass out of Belgium.

This period has seen Flanders catch up with and overtake Wallonia economically.[12] In 1955–60 its GDP grew spectacularly faster — + 16.5 per cent (Wallonia + 5.5 per cent). In 1966–71 GDP in Flanders grew by 6.1 per cent per year and only by 3.9 in Wallonia. The Flemish share in national GDP rose from 47 per cent in 1955 to 49 per cent in 1965 and 55 in 1974. *Per capita* income in Flanders overtook Wallonia in 1966.

Unemployment in Flanders remained more significant than in Wallonia until 1970; indeed as late as 1961, 64 per cent of all Belgian unemployment was in Flanders. In 1959 for example, it was 8.3 per cent, as against a national average of 6.7.

The crisis

Since 1975, Belgium has felt the impact of the crisis. Problems of the rural exodus, high wage costs, outmoded declining heavy industry, — earlier masked by the beneficient effects of steady growth, which created new jobs to replace those lost — could be masked no longer. The uninterrupted rise in production after 1958 was brutally broken in 1975, to recover slightly in 1976–7. From 1975 there was a fall in the absolute number employed in industry. Real growth in GDP was negative in 1975 (–2 per cent) and marginally positive in 1976, 1977 and 1978. Unemployment rose to 6.7 per cent in 1975, reaching 7.0 per cent in 1976 and 11.6 per cent in 1981. Closures of businesses rose from 305 in 1974 to 671 in 1975 and 1,127 in 1977. 17,879 jobs were lost in 1974; there were dramatic rises to 21,123 in 1975 and 32,898 in 1977. The largest losses were in metallurgy (18.8 per cent), construction (17.5), clothing (12.9) and textiles (10.8). Belgium's budget deficit rose to 15 per cent of her GDP in 1980 and her external indebtedness was 1,419 ECU in 1979, with a rise to 3,714 ECU in 1980.[13]

The structure of the economy

Here we shall look at the structure of the economy as it is today, in regard to the main sources of production, employment and trade.

Agriculture now only accounts for 3.0 per cent[14] of the total workforce (1980), with Britain (2.6 per cent) the lowest in the European Community. There are, however, important regional variations. Agriculture, forestry and fishing only constitute some 2.5 per cent of gross value added in the whole economy. Taking 1970 as 100, agricultural output has grown slowly to reach 113 in 1979. Yet agriculture exports did represent 8.9 per cent of all Belgian exports (by value) in 1980,[15] whereas imports of agricultural products represented 10.1 per cent of imports. In absolute terms Belgium had therefore a 1,094 billion ECU net deficit in this sector. Of all usable agricultural land, 53.6 per cent is in arable and 46.4 per cent in grassland,[16] which is close to the EEC average but varies considerably from the British pattern (only 38.1 per cent arable land). Of all usable agricultural land some 25.6 per cent is under cereals (mainly wheat and rye); 6.4 per cent is under sugar beet and 2 per cent under potatoes. About 0.7 per cent is under horticultural production. Belgium produces only about 1.6 per cent of all EEC cereal production, mostly wheat, barley, rye and mixed oats. As for livestock, Belgium had (1979) 3.7 per cent of all EEC cattle and 3.9 per cent of all dairy cattle. She had 6.5 per cent of all EEC pigs and 1.8 per cent of sheep and goats. Only in sugar has Belgium contributed a sizeable proportion of EEC total production — 6.8 per cent of EEC production of sugar beet. For meat in general (but not beef) Belgium was in 1979 a net exporter; she contributed 5.1 per

cent of total EEC meat production and only a very small percentage
of milk, butter, cheese and egg production.

Belgium is only self-sufficient in sugar (self-sufficiency 100) at 245
on the index, and in vegetables (115), butter (115), pork (162) and all
meat (119), but for cereals, potatoes, cheese and fats she has a
serious deficit.

The structure of Belgian agriculture is somewhat different from
British farming. Of all holdings 29.1 per cent are below 5 hectares in
size; 76.5 per cent are under 20 hectares and only 3.8 per cent are
more than 510 hectares. In Britain only 14.5 per cent are below 5
hectares and 31.5 per cent are more than 50 hectares. Belgium has
however fewer than the EEC average of marginal farms (1–5
hectares holdings). Only 19.2 per cent of all land area is used in the
larger holdings of 50 hectares and more. There is rough equality
between the amount of land which is owner-farmed and that which is
tenant-farmed.

Industry (and energy) is though now a far more important factor
in the Belgian economy. Belgium has a serious primary energy
deficit, in spite of having a significant but declining coal production.
Belgium produced 21,539,000 tonnes in 1961 but only 6,324,000 in
1980. There has since 1970 been a significant increase in her net
imports from 35.92 million tonnes oil equivalent (MTOE) to 44.85
MTOE in 1979, but with a fall to 41.39 MTOE in 1980,[17] whereas
for the United Kingdom there was a radical fall in net imports for
the same period. Belgium produces no natural gas, oil or primary
electricity, but does produce 4 MTOE of coal and lignite (2.3 per cent
of Community production) and 2.8 MTOE of nuclear energy, more
than all but France, Germany and Britain representing 7.5 per cent
of EEC production.[18] Oil remains, at 49.7 per cent, the most
important source of energy, but Belgium's oil dependence is lower
than that of France, Italy, Denmark, Ireland and Greece.

Belgium has few raw materials other than coal. She produces no
iron ore, copper, lead, zinc, bauxite or potash, which constitute the
basic industrial raw materials. However, 34.8 per cent of the workforce is employed in industry,[19] less than in France, Germany or
Britain, but still significant. Looking at the distribution of industrial
employment in 1977, with 1963 figures in brackets, we have the
following picture:

	%	
Machinery	32.8	(35.6)
Metallurgy	10.5	(8.3)
Textiles	15.6	(24.5)
non-metallic minerals	4.1	(4.5)

Almost all other categories are very small and show only small changes.[20]

When one looks at more recent changes in industrial employment, we may note a steady tendency for jobs to be lost since the 1960s. 12,324 jobs were lost in industry in 1978, which was the same as the average for the period 1968–73 and lower than for 1966–8. Only in the early 1960s were annual job losses in the industrial sector as low as 6,000 (1964). After 1975 they became more serious: 17,879 in 1974 and 32,898 in 1977. The most significant losses occurred in textiles (10.8 per cent of the total loss in 1977, 20.9 per cent in 1970), clothing (12.9 per cent), metallurgy (18.8 per cent in 1977, 26.9 per cent in 1976, only 12.0 per cent in 1964) and building (27.5 per cent in 1977).[21]

The structure of Belgian industry has been changing fast, with 62.2 per cent of the workforce employed in the service sector by 1979[22] (compared with 58.4 per cent in Britain). What are now the main sectors of industrial activity in Belgium? We shall seek to identify those sectors which are significant in relation to the whole Belgian economy and in terms of total EEC[23] production. Belgium is an important producer of iron and steel products. In 1980 she produced 11.09 per cent of total EEC pig iron production, 9.58 per cent of crude steel and 9.52 per cent of finished and rolled products. She produced more crude steel in 1980 than Britain, though traditionally she has produced between one-third and a half of British production. In 1961 she produced 7,002,000 tonnes (7.27 per cent of EEC — and UK — production) and in 1981 12,445,000 tonnes (9.7 per cent). Her peak production was 16,225,000 tonnes in 1974, with severe falls in 1975 and 1976. In other metals, she has no natural resources, but in copper processing (39.4 per cent of EEC production) she is only rivalled by Germany, the Soviet Union, the United States, Japan and Canada. The source of the raw copper is the Katanga province of Zaïre, the former Belgian Congo. For lead (7.4 per cent of EEC production), zinc (19.83 per cent) and tin (11.58 per cent) she also has considerable processing capacity.

She has a significant production of basic chemicals (especially sulphuric acid and caustic soda), fertilisers and plastics (small compared with Britain, but 6.15 per cent of EEC production). She also has a significant output of cement and bricks. Belgium has no national motor vehicle company, but an important assembly output, largely in Flanders and close to Brussels. Her actual production of cars is negligible (283,000 in 1979), being only 2.67 per cent of the EEC total. As for the assembling of cars not locally manufactured (in any case only 795,000 for the whole EEC), Belgium contributed 94.46 per cent of the EEC total. For commercial vehicles the situation is similar: 2.30 per cent of EEC production.

Belgium has some significant shipbuilding capacity, although since the early 1970s this sector has been in severe decline. For the whole EEC 2,495,000 tonnes gross was under construction in 1979, and of shipping launched in that year Belgium contributed 224,000 tonnes gross (8.98 per cent). She contributed 121,000 tonnes gross of the entire EEC production of 840,000 tonnes gross. Her maritime fleet constituted a mere 0.4 per cent of the world total in 1979 (EEC total 26.7 per cent, including Greece), as against 6.8 per cent for Britain. Her share of EEC maritime traffic was also very small.

As we have seen, textiles — cotton, wool, man-made fibres — are also important to the Belgian economy, constituting about 10 per cent of EEC production in each category, but these sectors have suffered severe decline since 1975.

Especially under the influence of multinational companies which have established themselves in Belgium in large numbers since 1965, and especially in Flanders, there has been an important expansion of the technologically advanced industries, such as petrochemicals and electronics. On the other hand, small and medium-sized undertakings (SMUs) have continued to provide a significant proportion of employment in the private sector:[24]

Type of employment	SMUs	%	Large undertakings	%
Industrial	297,090	30.6	560,865	69.4
Non-industrial	651,775	47.6	718,880	52.4

External trade[25] is a vital element in the Belgian economy. In 1980 her imports represented 3.7 per cent and her exports 3.4 per cent of world trade. Taking 1975 = 100, her imports in volume terms stood at 74 in 1970; at 117 in 1978 and 129 in 1980. On the other hand her exports stood at 77 in 1970, 124 in 1978 and 132 in 1980, showing an even faster growth. However, a severe balance of trade deficit is endemic. The best surplus year was 1973 (+ 293 million ECUs), but by 1975 the deficit had reached 1,626 million ECUs, and by 1980 5,173 million ECUs. Trade represents 51.8 per cent of Belgian GDP.[26]

For imports, the EEC provided the lion's share with 64.5 per cent in 1979 and 63.1 per cent in 1980. Likewise for exports, the EEC took 73.3 per cent in 1979, with a slight fall to 71.8 per cent in 1980. The main customers in the EEC were Germany (31.19 per cent), France (25.92 per cent), the Netherlands (20.19 per cent) and Britain (12.65 per cent). France and Germany together take 56 per cent of Belgian intra-EEC exports and 40.21 per cent of all Belgian exports, and of the latter the Netherlands takes a further 14.93 per cent. The only other trading partners of any significance were, for imports, the

United States (7.7 per cent), Japan (2.0 per cent), and ACP (associated African, Caribbean and Pacific) states (3.3 per cent) and for exports the United States (3.4 per cent) and ACP states (2.2 per cent). The main components of Belgian trade in 1980 were:

	Imports (%)	Exports (%)
Food, etc.	10.1	18.7
Mineral oils	17.3	22.2
Crude materials	7.1	6.1
Machinery and transport equipment	22.4	17.0
Other	42.2	35.9

Standard of living

Taking 1975 = 100, inflation[27] has been relatively moderate, but in the most recent years has accelerated. The consumer price index stood at 83 in 1973, but had risen to 121 by 1978 and 134 by 1980 compared with the German figures of 88 in 1973, 111 in 1978 and 129 in 1980, and the British figures of 69 in 1973, 146 in 1978 and 196 in 1980. For food the Belgian index stood at 125 in 1980 (Britain 193). Wages in industry (1975 = 100) give the following comparison:[28]

	1978	1979	1980
Total	125.6	134.4	146.9
Men	123.0	134.7	146.7
Women	125.5	132.4	144.4

Women's earnings therefore progressed slightly less rapidly than those for men. Belgian wages grew more rapidly than in her main markets, except France. Average hourly earnings in Belgian industry were 220BF against £2.23 in Britain (April 1980). At the then market rate of exchange (£1 = 90BF) the Belgian hourly earnings represented approximately £2.60. Hourly earnings in Belgium ranked second only to Denmark, which represented an important relative improvement because in 1975 they had ranked fifth. Hourly labour costs in manual and non-manual industry (1979) represented 10.20 ECU, the highest in the EEC (Germany 9.30 ECU and Britain 5.90 ECU). The structure of costs also showed some variation from the pattern in other countries. Direct costs represented 76.1 per cent in 1978 (1975, 79.22 per cent). Social security was 21.9 per cent (Britain 14.3 per cent; Denmark 4.2 per cent, the Netherlands 23.8 per cent). Agricultural wages were on average 155BF in 1979 which compared reasonably well with industrial wages. Only stockmen on large farms could expect much higher earnings (170BF per hour). In 1980, the average hours worked per week in industry were 36.9 (Germany 41.8, France 40.9, Britain 41.3).[29]

If we look at various indicators of the standard of living,[30] it is clear that Belgium has one of the highest standards of living in western Europe. The GDP per head is US$8,300 (1979) exceeded only by Germany and Denmark in the EEC and by the United States, Canada and Sweden in the rest of the world. For meat consumption she is third in the EEC, for energy per head second only to Luxembourg (4925 MTOE in 1979), for steel second only to Germany (402 kg per year crude steel equivalent); and third in motor vehicles in use per 1,000 of the population (312 in 1979). With only 486 telephones per 1,000 she lies above average for the EEC (413 per 1,000) but only in seventh place in the Community.

Her health and social services are good, but patchy. They have proved extremely expensive and have come under severe criticism. Medicine is private, with public health insurance, and doctors and the other paramedical professions are a powerful and at times reactionary lobby. Belgium's ratios of 225 doctors and 93.4 pharmacists per 100,000 of population are the highest in the EEC, the figure for pharmacists being higher than in the United States.[31] But her 893 hospital beds per 100,000 is only in seventh place in the EEC. Sickness (37 per cent) and pensions (38 per cent) are the most important charges on the social security system, but unemployment benefit is now one-tenth of total costs. Belgium spends 27.1 per cent of her GDP on social expenditure (1979),[32] which places her second only to the Netherlands in the EEC (31.2 per cent), a large share of this burden falls on employers. Taxes and social contributions (in 1979) took 43 per cent of GDP, distributed between indirect taxes (25.9 per cent), direct taxes (43.1), capital taxes (0.9) and social contributions (30.1). Britain relies less on direct taxation and social contributions.[33]

What overall impression of the Belgian economy emerges from even this limited sample of statistics? Belgium is clearly an advanced industrial country with a very high standard of living, with all the characteristics of a post-industrial economy; agricultural employment has fallen to negligible proportions although there is some important intensive production (milk and sugar beet); the industries of the first industrial revolution are in decline, especially in Wallonia (steel, coal, glass, textiles, basic chemicals); but there is a new and hopeful expansion of the services sector, and technologically-based industries are developing, spearheaded by foreign multinational capital.

Problems of the economy and economic policy

In the course of our examination of recent Belgian economic history and of the present structure of the economy, we have touched on many of the weaknesses and problems of the economy, but here we shall attempt to look at the present problems of the Belgian economy in a more systematic manner and set out briefly the consequences that these problems have had for economic policy-making and for the political process in general. The main issues can best be examined under five general headings: the openness of the economy; cost structure; institutional rigidities; structural problems; and regional divergences.

As we have seen, the Belgian economy is one of the most open in the world, and openness also means vulnerability in times of crisis. Over half of GDP is involved in trade. With the exception of her coal and her growing nuclear power capacity, Belgium is still largely dependent on imported oil (some 18 per cent of all imports). Lacking in raw materials, she is a processor and exporter, which requires free access to raw materials sources and subsequently to markets. More specially she is almost totally dependent on intra-EEC trade and within the EEC on trade with Germany, France and the Netherlands. Belgium has therefore always opposed protectionism and supported the greatest possible degree of free trade, strongly supporting European economic and political integration since such developments are vital to her trade. Monetary stability, too, has been a major Belgian concern. She has enthusiastically supported schemes for monetary integration in Western Europe — the early EPU (ensuring covertibility), the 'Werner plan' for an Economic and Monetary Union (EMU), the later 'snakes' of related currencies and most recently the European Monetary System (EMS), launched in 1980. With this has gone the need to defend the value of the franc and avoid devaluation, which has often taken priority over other economic policy objectives to an extent which would otherwise be difficult to explain and justify. In February 1982, the pressure proved too much and an 8.5 per cent devaluation was necessary.

Closely related to the openness of the Belgian economy is the difficult question of cost structure.[34] For a country which lives by trade, in highly competitive markets, it is evident that costs, which effect the country's competitive position in these markets, are a vital matter. However, despite broad agreement on the need to control costs, political consensus breaks down over the question of which elements in the cost structure are most important and how these should be controlled. Certainly wages, taxes and social security contributions are, as we have seen, major elements in the cost structure. Wages are very closely and automatically linked to the index of consumer prices. Hence, for example, devaluation and increases in oil prices both affect the cost of basic raw materials *and* lead via indexation to increased wage costs. This has been yet another argument against devaluation. For several years, and with increasing insistence, the Treasury and the political parties of the right have argued for a break in automatic indexation of wages, whereas the Socialist parties and the '*Front commun*' (united front of all trade unions, both Socialist and Christian) have obdurately refused to countenance any break in the principle. The new Martens V PVV/PRL-CVP/PSC coalition excluding the Socialists, formed in late 1981, obtained 'special powers' which it used to carry through a partial 'de-indexation' for one year, an 8.5 per cent devaluation, price controls until June 1982 and public expenditure cuts. These measures provoked severe trade union reaction and their success is not yet clear.

Institutional rigidities concern both government, business and trade union structures, inhibiting rapid and radical decision-making in any direction. Governments are always coalitions, often spanning the political centre, which inhibits any clear-cut cohesive economic strategy. All decisions on crucial matters, such as taxation, public spending, social security and structural policy are taken essentially on the basis of political compromise. The divergences in needs, objectives and economic structure in the north and south of the country add an extra dimension of difficulty. Whether the new regional system of government will alleviate these problems by decentralisation or aggravate them by conflicts of competences remains to be seen.

The complex structure of interest groups in Belgium, with its highly corporatist and consensus-orientated system of economic decision-making, is also a considerable complication. We shall return to this theme in a later chapter, but suffice it to say here that with influence of the *Boerenbond* (Flemish farmers' organisation) in Flanders and on the CVP; the strength of the 'Independents' and professional groups (doctors, pharmacists *et al*.) and the pluralistic structure of the unions (Catholic/Socialist) with their tendency to outbid each other, consensus, let alone tough decisions which can be made to stick, is extremely difficult to arrive at.

There are structural problems of considerable size — the obvious one is the over-capacity in the declining Walloon industries of the first industrial revolution — but there are also more subtle ones which have tended to exacerbate inter-regional difficulties as well as the complexity of economic decision-making in general. In Belgium the general level of investment as a percentage of GDP has lain below that of her main trading partners (see accompanying table).[35] Investment in new technological-based industries was 59 per cent in Flanders; 39.5 per cent in Wallonia and 0.02 per cent in Brussels. The

	Belgium %	France %	Germany %
1960	19	24	27
1977	22	24	22

cost of job creation has been considerably higher in Wallonia.[36] Each job created in Flanders cost only 0.111 billion BF in public investment and 1.435 billion in private investment, as against 0.234 billion (public) and 2.16 billion (private) in Wallonia.

One consequence of the openness of Belgium's economy is the high degree of penetration of multinational companies (MNCs).[37] These account for 40 per cent of value added in the economy and 49 per cent of sales (25 per cent in Germany, 25 in France, 19 in the Netherlands, 14 in Britain).[38] This is a mixed blessing. These firms have concentrated on the new science-based industries, and indeed 75 per cent turnover in these industries is accounted for by MNCs. Their productivity per worker is 0.8mBF against 0.53mBF for a national concern. They use 1.8 per cent of turnover in research and development as against 1.4 per cent for Belgian undertakings.[39] Their record in creating jobs has been considerable (+ 130,000 jobs 1968–75 and after the deduction of job losses caused by takeovers, + 80,000 jobs in the same period), showing a growth of 5.1 per cent as against a fall of 0.43 per cent in employment in purely domestic undertakings. This rate of growth could not be maintained in the recession, but it is not clear that MNCs have 'pruned' more jobs than the purely national concerns, though there is some evidence in that sense, (20 per cent of all lost jobs in 1960–75). In some respects they appear to be more robust; their employment rose by 0.41 per cent in 1975–8 as against a 3.97 per cent loss in national concerns.[40] The MNCs do however tend to obtain a higher market share, to specialise more and to produce more semi-finished products (38 as against 24 per cent for national concerns).

All those factors, quite independently of the power of the multinationals' foreign decision-making centres, tend to make the Belgian operations of MNCs vulnerable. The government does, however, face difficulties in defining a clear policy towards MNCs. Its 1978 'communication' on a new industrial policy[41] clearly seeks to ensure that its independence is not undermined in setting its economic priorities by decisions of the MNCs, which do not — even if they have created an *overall* increase in employment — take adequate account in their location decisions of the government's regional and employment policies. However, the government is forced to admit that in terms of the standards it seeks to set up for Belgian industry as

a whole — greater structural adaptability, investment, diversification, export promotion, research, penetration into science-based
sectors, improvement of competitive capacity to meet the occasion
and defend employment — the MNCs have a better record than
Belgian enterprises. This requires government to perform a delicate
balancing act in respect of multinationals, which means in effect that
their policy is extremely favourable to their activities, despite serious
and valid criticisms of their conduct, especially in Wallonia.

As we have seen, Belgian economic history is a perpetual see-saw
between the fortunes of the regions. Wallonia faces severe problems
arising from industrial decline, linked to her greater dependence on
'old' industries.' The new science-based industries are investing in
Flanders. The cost of job creation and maintenance is greater in
Wallonia. Unemployment is now higher in Wallonia. Taking the
country average as equal to 100, the gross value added per head (in
1978, at market prices) in Flanders was 124 and in Wallonia 103.
Whole sectors such as steel, glass, textiles and shipbuilding in
Wallonia are in frequent need of state support. The issue of support
for the Walloon steel industry was the central cause of the break-up
of the Eyskens I (1981) CVP/PSC-PS/SP coalition. Almost all
problems of economic policy degenerate into 'north-south' debates
about 'national solidarity', costs of regional policies, relative advantages and costs. There is an unending debate about the costs of
support for declining Walloon industries versus the cost of the new
Zeebrugge harbour or the true value of Walloon water which is
exported to Flanders and whose pressure in Wallonia is to be reduced
to permit works on the Schelde under the treaty with the
Netherlands. The fact that there are also political divergences
between Flanders, where the parties of the right have a comfortable
majority both in the Flemish Executive and in the Dutch-language
group in Parliament, and Wallonia where the PS is dominant and
where *'une Majorité de Progrès'* (PS, RW, MPW, PC, ecologists)
exists, which leads to quite different conceptions on state aids to
industry, public expenditure and other ideological touchstones, has
greatly complicated economic decision-making.

The Belgian political sub-culture: society

The nature of Belgian society has been constantly changing,
becoming more fragmented and pluralistic. At the start public
affairs and opinion formation were totally in the hands of the
French-speaking 'Unionist' (Liberal-moderate Catholic) élite, who
had provoked the 1830 Revolution and fashioned the new state
in their own image and interests. The nineteenth century was

dominated by the rise of new social groups, which came to play an important role in Belgian society and politics, though in some cases this role was then purely embryonic. These were the labour movement — originating in the industrial proletariat which the industrial revolution brought into being, above all in urban Wallonia — and, parallel to this development, a new class of industrial entrepreneurs and financiers, involved in trade and colonial development, which came to play an increasingly significant role in public affairs. Lastly, the Flemish cultural and political movement began to take shape and to find its voice, although this development was to become more significant in the twentieth century.

Within the framework of Belgium, there has been a generalised tendency towards fragmentation, with elements supportive of 'Belgian consciousness' or national unity tending to diminish over the course of time. Sub-cultures have developed, of which the Socialist working-class movement in Wallonia, with its many manifestations — trade unions, '*mutualités*' (non-governmental health insurance schemes, peculiar to Belgium and a few other smaller European countries), co-operatives, clubs — and its traditions making it self-contained and almost self-sufficient, was a prime example. The Christian trade unions, *mutualités* and socio-cultural organisations likewise constituted enclaves, self-contained and often isolated from or hostile to their Socialist counterparts.

The Flemish movement has matured and come of age, having surmounted the handicaps it suffered in the aftermath of two world wars. It is multi-faceted, having cultural, political and economic manifestations, each dimension enriching and reinforcing the other. The cultural foundations belonging to the Flemish movement — *Davidsfonds*, *Willemsfonds*, the *Ijzerkomitee* (see below, pp. 207-8) — and the Flemish universities and press contribute a permanent source of consciousness and pressure on the political parties other than the *Volksunie*, which already shares their ideals. This has produced a fragmented society or two societies, each of which has tended to turn in on itself, maintaining its own traditions and cultural development. Since the mid-1960s there has also been a defensive reaction in Wallonia to the Flemish movement: the tendency was for Walloon reaction, under the impulse of the *Mouvement Populaire Wallon*, the *Rassemblement Wallon* and the FDF, to shift radically first towards a defensive position and then — as the position of the PS in the 1981 election shows — towards a position not dissimilar from the Flemish attitude, in which each part of the country can and should be able to exercise considerable autonomy in a wide range of cultural and economic areas of policy. This had led to the two communities developing in separate directions — sometimes in confrontation — and often ignoring each other, which has made national unity ever more elusive and difficult.

The rise of a Belgian entrepreneurial class[42] (great captains of industry such as Baron Solvay, Coppée, Bunge, Anseele, Empain), based on rapid innovation, foreign trade and exploitation of the mineral wealth of the Congo, did much to stimulate the golden age of Belgian industry. This in turn created the basis for the high and continuing level of material prosperity in Belgium, the passing of which many are psychologically unable to accept, thus explaining the difficulty of the dialogue between the two sides of industry in the present crisis. At the same time, a structure of industry has been created based on interlocking trusts, often with the strong participation of banks, such as the Société Générale. This has tended to concentrate economic power in a very small number of hands or institutions, which can cause severe problems of control and accountability. It has created an economy in which there is probably less competitive behaviour than in most Western economies, which in turn leads to greater rigidities and poor adaptibility.

The decline of ideology in the 1950s and 1960s, which has been a feature of Western societies, has also been evident in Belgium. The accelerating social change, the changes in social and economic structures, have tended to undermine the 'collectivist' tendencies in Belgian associative life and reinforced inherent tendencies towards introverted individualistic materialism. These tendencies have always been in conflict. This later tendency has also no doubt done much to ensure that the broad movements which have influenced Europe and the world — the international fascist movement of the 1930s, the anti-war movement inspired by Vietnam, the student movement in the 1960s — only had a limited echo in Belgium, as if there were shock absorbers on the boundaries of the country. For example, there were only pale echoes of the French events of 1968 in Belgian universities in the following three years.

There has been little or no sign of a significant *Kulturkampf* between the generations in Belgium, but that is not to suggest that there has not been alienation and disaffection from traditional patterns and values. The sense of unease, the sense that society is in a state of crisis and of fragmentation, while certainly present, has tended to be incoherent and not clearly defined. Certainly, it is only in the recent past that it has found channels of expression of any significance. There are now signs that the recent reform of the education system, which created the '*Ecole renovée*', has begun to bear fruit in terms of creating a more questioning and independent generation. Belgium, with its strongly conformist and materialist tendencies and its high share of nuclear energy, seems an unlikely candidate for having the first ecologist national Deputies (since the 1981 elections). Perhaps the most immediately obvious explanation for this is to relate the phenomenon less to 'new leftism' or a latent 'green movement' than to the concept of alienation canalised into protest. Young voters — eighteen-year-olds now vote — and others reacted to the increasing inability of the Belgian political system to manage society and produce solutions to even the most pressing problems, by seeking refuge in protest parties and rejecting the traditional political parties and the consensus of post-war 'large is beautiful' growth-oriented policies fuelled by an ever larger and more bureaucratic public sector. Divergences between the three traditional parties have, after all, only concerned the *degree* and *extent* of these developments and not their reversal.

The arrival of large numbers of immigrant workers in Belgium in the 1960s and 1970s has also had a considerable impact on society. There has always been immigration to work in the mines, especially from Italy, France and Poland, but these immigrants came over a relatively long period and have become integrated into Belgian society without excessive difficulty. The situation has, however, been different with the arrival of large numbers of migrants from the Mediterranean — Yugoslavia, Morocco, Algeria, Turkey. These migrants have not been able to integrate into Belgian society and have often not wished to do so, preferring to maintain their own customs, religion and way of life in Belgium. Having been imported to undertake menial work, for which in 'the golden sixties' there were no Belgian volunteers, they are usually poor and confined to areas of poor housing in the inner city, especially in Brussels where in some communes (especially Schaarbeek and Anderlecht) they have come to represent nearly 30 per cent of the population, which has given rise to serious and even racist reactions, especially with the increase in unemployment in the recession. With well over 800,000 immigrants (up from 450,000 in 1961), the majority of whom came at first from Italy but subsequently from Spain, Turkey and North Africa, it is not impossible that serious problems will eventually arise.

The success of the anti-tax and anti-bureaucracy party, the UDRT, can be reviewed in the same light as the gains of the ecologists and the massive protests against the stationing of American Theatre Nuclear Forces (TNFs) in Belgium, as provided for in the December 1979 NATO agreement. The anti-missile movement, the ecological protest, the UDRT phenomenon, and the newly-assertive, self-confident and unapologetic regional consciousness are signs of the increasingly rapid rate of change of Belgian society, its fragmentation and renewal, behind the deceptive facade of relative stagnation and conformism. This suggests that the 1980s will see cumulatively radical changes in the old certainties.

NOTES

1. Figures on population are taken from *Basic Statistics of the European Community*, Eurostat 1981 (hereafter 'Eurostat'), table no. 1, and *Annuaire Statistique de la Belgique*, vol. 100, 1980 Institut National de Statistique (hereafter *Annuaire Statistique*).
2. Annuaire Statistique, table 6, p. 29.
3. Frans Van Kalken, *Histoire de la Belgique*, op. cit., 74–82, 99–114 and 120–64.
4. H. Haems *et al.*, *De Belgische Industrie: Een Profielbeeld*, De Nederlandse Boekhandel, Brussels, 1981, 14–16.
5. The development of Walloon industry is described in Haems op. cit., 17–22.
6. Haems, op. cit., 23–6, for the Flemish situation in the nineteenth and early twentieth century.
7. For discussion of the economic recovery, see Van Kalken op. cit., 707–12.
8. Haems, op. cit., 31–2.
9. Ibid., 38–43, and Van Kalken, 837–47.
10. Haems, op. cit., 39.
11. Ibid., 39–40.
12. Ibid., 42.
13. Ibid., 45–7 and table XXIV (pp. 210–11).
14. Eurostat, table 9.
15. Eurostat, table 110.
16. Data on agricultural production from Eurostat, tables 24–42.
17. Energy Data from Eurostat, tables 49–66.
18. Eurostat, table 64.
19. Eurostat, table 9.
20. Haems, op. cit., 55.
21. Ibid., table XXIV.
22. Eurostat, table 9.
23. Production data from Eurostat, tables 67, 69, 70, 73, 74, 75, 76, 77 and 78.
24. Haems, op. cit., 68.
25. Trade statistics from Eurostat, tables 95 (imports), 96 (exports), 97 (balance of trade); 102–111 (divertion of exports/imports and commodities traded).
26. Eurostat, table 111.
27. Data from Eurostat, tables 114 and 115.
28. Data composed from Eurostat, tables 119, 120 and 121.
29. Eurostat, tables 120 and 121.

30. Data from Eurostat, tables 133–137.
31. Health data: Eurostat, table 138.
32. Eurostat, table 132.
33. Eurostat, table 131.
34. Haems, op. cit., 63–5.
35. Ibid., table XXXVIII (pp. 230–1).
36. Following data from Haems, op. cit., 102–3.
37. Ibid., chapter IV ('Multinationalisering en Industrie Politiek') deals in detail with the role of MNCs in Belgium.
38. Van den Bralke, *Politiques d'Investissement, rédactions et cessation d'activitiés des multinationales en Europe*, PUF-CEEIM, Paris 1979, 32.
39. Haems, op. cit., 155–7.
40. Ibid., 150–5.
41. For the text see Chambres des Représentants 1977–8, Sitting of 22 Feb. 1978. Analysed in Haems, op. cit., 241–4.
42. For an analysis of the individual entrepreneurs — see F. Baudhuin, *Histoire économique de la Belgique*, Bruylant, Brussels, 1946, vol. 2., 205–58, and for financiers 259–86, where a colourful account is given of many leading personalities.

3

THE CENTRAL GOVERNMENT

The constitution of 1830 created a unitary state and a hereditary constitutional monarchy within a parliamentary system. The subsequent amendments in 1970 and 1980 have greatly reduced this unitary character, without however establishing a true federal system.

The Executive

The Crown

Executive power is vested in the Crown, but it is exercised by the Government. Under the constitution the King is 'irresponsible', that is to say his acts must be countersigned and covered by a responsible minister.[1] Indeed, although the King 'appoints and dismisses his ministers' (article 65), the outgoing premier must countersign his successor's appointment.[2] One would therefore suppose that the role of the Crown in Belgium is minimal, purely symbolic and beyond controversy. However, the reverse is true.[3] As we have seen, Leopold I sought to place a literal interpretation on his right to appoint ministers, Leopold II developed the Congo as a personal venture, Albert personally led his armies in the First World War and played a major part in imposing universal suffrage in 1919; Leopold III's controversial role in the Second World War almost ended the Belgian monarchy; and events have forced his successor Baudouin, after a predictably quiet start, to intervene more and more in political matters. All Belgian sovereigns have carried on extensive correspondence with their prime ministers and other ministers and have from time to time been prepared to go on public record on certain matters such as defence (Leopold II strongly supported a fairer conscription system) and foreign policy questions.

The key role of the King relates to the formation and resignation of governments.[4] The increasing ungovernability of Belgium over the last twenty years has made that role more frequently necessary and more difficult, in that the situation has often called for a greater royal discretion and freedom of choice, in the face of the immobilism of the politicians, than one would expect in a modern constitutional monarchy. It is essential to understand, though, that the King has not sought this role, but it has fallen upon him as the final arbiter in a system which is increasingly defective.[5]

In recent years the King has made increasingly frequent use of his right to refuse the resignation of the government. Since hardly any of the Belgian governments of recent years have fallen due to an adverse vote in Parliament or even because of the loss of their theoretical majorities, and resignation was usually the result of internal dissension as in the case of the Martens IV and recent Eyskens I governments, their ultimate fall was only delayed for a short period.[6]

When there is a crisis due to the resignation of the government or after an election, the King plays an important role in the rounds of consultations and the various customary procedures which have evolved in the matter. The procedure chosen by the King may well depend on how serious the difficulties in the way of finding a new government seem likely to be. He will first consult with the outgoing prime minister, the presidents of the two Houses of Parliament and possibly certain elder statesmen. In recent years, it has become more usual for the King also to see directly certain party leaders even at this early stage. This is not an obligation, let alone a custom, but precedents built up over time become difficult to break and thereby acquire a certain formalism.[7]

In earlier and perhaps simpler times, it was often possible for the King to proceed directly to the stage of naming a '*Formateur*' who would normally, but not always, become prime minister. Now it has usually been necessary to name an '*Informateur*' who will conduct negotiations and report on the situation to the King. The *Informateur* might be a candidate for the premiership but might, as with Mr Segers in 1968, Jos De Saeger in 1972, or Herman Vanderpoorten (PVV) in 1981, either simply have no wish for the task or, as in recent cases (Willy Claes [SP]), be disqualified for political reasons. The task of the *Informateur*, in theory to propose a *Formateur* to the King, has over time become progressively more complicated, since that choice would tend to presuppose a certain 'proto-agreement' between some parties on a coalition or programme, the more so in that during these discussions political life does not stand still. Party bureaux meet, and there are consultations and debates in the press and media, all of which — outside the formal consultations — may tend towards a *dénouement* of the crisis.

The gravity and length of recent crises — from December 1978 till March 1979 for the formation of the Martens I government — have complicated the King's task. He has been forced to have recourse to ever more imaginative and interventionist procedures. For example in 1979, he appointed Ferdinand Nothomb (PSC) and Willy Claes (SP) as *Co-médiateurs*[8] to try and bring the parties to agreement, and later in the same crisis Mr Vanden Boeynants negotiated and formed

the government in which it was clearly understood that he would not
be prime minister; in this process the King supported the *Formateur*
to the point of receiving in audience together, on 9 March 1979, the
six presidents of the parties of the outgoing coalition. He has thus on
occasions indicated a clear preference for a certain coalition. More
recently, at the time of the Eyskens I government (September 1981),
he clearly supported a coalition formula including the Socialists
which gained him some criticism from, ironically, the CVP.[9]

Once an agreement on the type of coalition to be formed has
emerged, the role of the King is over, except in the most formal
sense. The *Formateur* leads the negotiations, sometimes in day and
night 'conclaves' with the party presidents of his proposed coalition.
He will propose a programme, which forms the basis for discussions
and, when agreed upon, becomes the 'government agreement'. The
various parties then call congresses to approve the agreement. The
composition of the Cabinet, appointments of State Secretaries and
related issues (if an election has just taken place) such as the presidency of the Chamber and Senate are then agreed upon. The King
finally appoints the Cabinet. The prime minister then makes his
policy statement (*Déclaration gouvernemenᵼale*) to each House and
seeks a vote of confidence. At this point the process of forming a
government is complete.

The King must, with the countersignature of his ministers, sign all
bills and subordinate legislation of importance (*Arrêté royal* —
AR). This royal sanction may in modern times appear a formality;
however, several monarchs have objected to publicity being given
to AR agreed by the Cabinet, but not yet with the royal signature.
Well informed sources also consider that the King, via his Cabinet
(private staff), can and does keep a discreet watch on matters being
passed for signature when Parliament is dissolved or when a government, having resigned, is only responsible '*d'expédier les affaires
courantes* ('caretaker function').[10] Such matters as appointments are
held over to enable the new government to confirm or revoke earlier
proposals.

The Government

Formation. We have looked at the role of the King in forming
governments. What are the political constraints which play a role in
the formation of governments? These are indeed formidable and
have at times made for extremely protracted government crises. The
first essential point is that, apart from the 1950–4 period, no single
party has ever obtained an overall majority since proportional representation was introduced. A CVP-PSC majority has in any case

become impossible since 1968, because the PSC and CVP are two separate parties even if on many matters they remain very close. Governments must be coalitions or minority governments. Belgium, unlike Denmark, has no tradition of minority governments, which would, no doubt, be unable to meet other important criteria.

Since 1970 there has been a formal requirement for parity between Flemish and Francophone ministers — the prime minister excepted (article 86 *bis*) which means in effect that a coalition should have a majority in both Wallonia and Flanders, or come very close to it.[11] Since that time only the Tindemans I (1974–7) government has lacked a majority in the French-speaking linguistic group before its 'enlargement' to include the RW. In the provisional phases of the regionalisation, where the executives were committees of national ministers, it was likewise desirable for a government to have a majority in both Community Councils ('Cultural Councils' before 1980). Given the Brussels situation, this has not always been exactly the same as having a majority in Flanders and Wallonia.

Other majorities may be desirable if the government intends to proceed either with a revision of the constitution (two-thirds) or, since 1970, with the implementation of articles 59 *bis* and 107 *quater* of the constitution.[12] At other times such majorities may not be needed. When difficult economic questions have faced governments, there has been a tendency to seek broad-based governments representing left and right, and north and south.

Certainly coalition theory seems to have little relevance to Belgium. The most usual coalitions — PSC/CVP + PS/SP or the three traditional parties — are certainly not minimal winning coalitions, nor do they represent 'adjacent coalitions'.[13] For these theories to have applied, there should have been more Catholic/Liberal coalitions, but since 1945 there have only been four, as against eight PSC/CVP + PS/SP governments and more Socialist-Liberal governments before 1945 (there had only been one since 1945). Usually the election results permit the formation of at least three different types of coalition: a coalition of the three national parties; a Liberal/Christian Democratic coalition; a Socialist/Christian Democratic coalition. The elections may, by the losses of outgoing government parties (e.g. Socialists in 1974) or gains by certain opposition parties, have suggested a tendency in favour of one form or the other, but that tendency will, given the relative stability of the Belgian electorate, have been very small and may well be ignored by the politicians.

After the elections or the fall of a government, ideas will begin to crystallise in the larger parties, especially the CVP and the PS (Francophone Socialists). These, as the largest parties in their communities, have the basic responsibility for making the opening moves. The other parties can certainly block their moves, but if these major parties agree on the type of government to be formed, then it is likely that they can — in the long run — push that through. Where they disagree, the crisis will be long, each seeking to present the other as responsible for any breakdown.

A number of cases are worth looking at to illustrate this process in more detail. Usually — at least in recent years — certain basic issues will be on the table, dictating the type of government which is needed and the type of majority that it will need: predominance of 'community problems' (1973, 1974, 1977), predominance of economic and social questions (Eyskens I 1980) or 'mixed' (Martens II, III, IV). Even where there is clarity about the issues which predominate, some choice as to the coalition type may exist. The CVP/PSC will always face a basic choice as to its preferred powers in economic and social issues — Liberals or Socialists. Leo Tindemans and many others — but not all CVP leaders — have long had a basic preference for coalitions with or including the Liberals (Leburton, Tindemans I, Martens III and V), and indeed may have hoped to create such a coalition before the 1981 elections. The PSC is more evenly divided. It is in any case not so dominant in its own region as the CVP.

Attitudes both of and towards the Liberals themselves have often made such a strategy difficult. Since it is not just participation in a coalition which is important, but the balance of forces, a weak Liberal presence *together* with Socialists and Christians (PSC/CVP) may well be rejected by the Liberals, especially the Flemish PVV, which has always sought to avoid entering coalitions without the strengthened bargaining position which could derive from significant electoral success. The Walloon Liberals have often been less hesitant to enter government. PVV opposition prevented the formation of a coalition including Liberals both in 1977 and 1979.

The Socialists, especially in Wallonia, have been extremely reluctant to relinquish power.[14] In Belgium considerable patronage in terms of appointments, state finance for projects and job creation goes with office, and is exclusive to the parties of the majority. The Socialist trade unions have supported this concern. The SP is too weak in Flanders to adopt a genuine strategically independent line. It could hardly enter or leave government without the PS, although in recent years SP positions on defence policy and community issues have diverged notably from those of the PS. Both parties have tended to become more regional — witness the 1980 PS slogan *'Wallonie dominée, c'est fini'*,[15] which could have come from the RW or FDF, whereas the SP insists that if Wallonia wants to regionalise industrial policy, it will have to bear the cost alone. The fact that no reform of the state was possible without the PS, with its trade union links, made the SP indispensible, whatever preferences CVP leaders may have had for the Liberals, whom the Socialists have sought to keep out of government.

It is precisely the economic crisis and its attendant need for a social consensus, and the Reform of the State, — with its constitutional need for complex qualified majorities and the political need for support from a 'significant majority'[16] in each Region — which have dictated the presence of the Socialists in government since 1968, (with the sole exception of the 1974–7 period) up until 1981. The Reform of the State, with its special political and constitutional requirements, brought the community parties (RW, FDF, PU) into government after 1974, despite the fact that till then the traditional parties had refused to consider them as government parties. It became clear that the reforms would be a north-south compromise. Without 'compromising' the community parties, the 'traditional' parties — even though they had the necessary majority — could not take the political risks involved on their own. The tactic worked. The RW lost heavily after its experience of government in 1974, likewise the VU in 1978. The participation of these parties between 1974–9 compromised them sufficiently to make possible the final adoption of reforms by the classic tripartite Martens III government in 1980.

The length of a government crisis is not usually related to the choice of coalition patterns — tripartite PSC/CVP–PVV/PRL; PSC/CVP–PS/SP or classic tripartite; or inclusion of Community parties in a basic bipartite PSC/CVP-SP/PS coalition — since this option usually emerges fairly early. In 1974 it soon became clear that the Socialists would go into opposition and in 1977 that the Liberals were not serious candidates for office. In 1978–9 it was soon clear that the basic form was to be a PSC/CVP–SP/PS coalition with one or more 'Community parties' (in this event only the FDF). The real debate was about relative influence: Flemish/Walloon and ideological influence. This degree of influence expresses itself both in the government's programme and in the distribution and number of Cabinet posts accorded to each partner.

The entry into force of the next phase of the Reform of the State after the 1981 general election has at one and the same time complicated and simplified the political issues involved in the formation of governments. Three of the four Executives (the Flemish Executive, the Executive of the French-speaking community and the Walloon Executive) are now outside the central government, and may be composed of majorities which are different from those of the central government.[17] This factor no doubt made the formation of the Martens V government (December 1981) without the Socialists

(CVP/PSC–PRL–PVV) easier because there was no need for a 'Walloon majority'. On the other hand, a situation in which the PS is in power in Wallonia but not centrally can be the source of severe conflict, which may weaken the central government.

Government organisation. Each government is different in organisation and style, but certain characteristics may be observed. It is now almost inevitable that the prime minister will be Flemish, and furthermore from the CVP, while the main parties of the coalition will have a vice prime minister. There has also been a tendency in recent years for the size of governments to increase. There are two reasons for this. In the first place, the preparation for the Reform of the State created structures such as the Executives of Regions and Communities inside the national government. The second reason has been the need to balance the interests of larger coalitions — regionalised 'political families' (e.g. PS and SP), 'Community Parties', and the different wings of parties, especially the 'Christian Democratic' (left) wing of the PSC and CVP.

This expansion has however been continuous from five ministries in 1831 to seven in 1878, to nineteen in 1946. Most of the new ministries broke away from the old Interior Ministry. The expansion of the number of ministers has even been greater, but has varied considerably. The Eyskens government (1968) had twenty-nine ministers and the Leburton government (1972) twenty-two ministers and fourteen state secretaries (junior ministers); the Tindemans I government contained nineteen ministers and six state secretaries. The Tindemans II (1977) government — a coalition of eight parties — contained twenty-three ministers and seven state secretaries. The Martens II (1979) had twenty-seven ministers and nine state secretaries. The first government in 'regionalised' Belgium — Martens V (1981) — is much smaller, with sixteen ministers and eight state secretaries.[18]

Ministers need not be members of either House of Parliament, but most are. Political parties have followed varying practices in their choice of persons to be ministers. Some governments have seemed to be composed of second-level personalities, with the strong Party Presidents remaining outside the government. This was notably the case with the Tindemans II government (1977–8), whereas the Martens V government saw the entry into government of three Party Presidents (Tindemans, De Clerq, Gol). When a Party President becomes a minister, he ceases to hold his former position, and often leaves some more junior personality to keep the presidential seat warm for him.

The Party Presidents have often been required to mediate when difficulties have arisen in a coalition, to the point where the authority of the government as such has been reduced to almost nothing. Under the Tindemans II government, regular meetings of Party Presidents of the majority became almost institutionalised and in the minds of many, virtually usurped the government functions.[19] This tendency continued under the first Martens governments; it has now somewhat declined, but remains a problem.[20] The post of prime minister only gradually came into existence, and was not mentioned in the constitution till 1970. In the early years after 1831, it was the *Formateur* who was the head of government, in that he counter-signed the appointment and dismissal of ministers, but he was often at best a *primus inter pares*. The need for a leader and co-ordinator became more evident with the development of coalitions after 1918. Although in earlier times, the King did from time to time preside over the Cabinet, and the possibility still exists (last used in 1957),[21] the true head of the Cabinet is the prime minister. Until 1970, even the concept of a Cabinet was legally a grey area. The 1970 Constitu-tional Reform refers to the Cabinet (articles 86 *bis*, 91 and 91*a*), fixing the requirement that, with the exception of the prime minister, the Cabinet must be composed equally from both language groups. State secretaries are formally excluded from the Cabinet and are not subject to the language parity rule. The prime minister nominates and dismisses ministers in fact, since it is he who countersigns the necessary *Arrêtés Royaux*. He presides over the government and ensures co-ordination. He alone may also present the government's resignation, or propose the dissolution of Parliament. He also signs the Cabinet minutes. In a personality-conscious and media-conscious age, he represents the government to Belgian and foreign public opinion. One of his most important tasks in the inevitable coalition governments is to resolve inter-party disputes and maintain the government's coherence. The power of the Belgian prime minister is considerable and has grown, but it is less than that of his British counterpart. The fact that he leads a coalition government restricts his margin for manoeuvre, and he will often not be the leader of his own party, either in name or in fact.

Arrêtés royaux settle the respective competences of ministers and, under them, of state secretaries. In the early years, the Cabinet was not seen as a collegial body, as it has now developed. Indeed, apart from a certain number of particular cases where the law for example requires an AR on a given matter to be '*délibéré en Conseil des Ministres*' (discussed in Cabinet), there is no *legal* provision for collegiate decision-making. Ministers formally make and counter-sign proposals to the King, who exercises the executive power.

Political reality is of course quite different.[22] All important

decisions — the budget, bills, ARs, appointments in the public
services and state enterprises — are in fact debated and approved in
cabinet, and sometimes ministers of several parties countersign
measures or table bills. This is reinforced by the collective responsibility of the Cabinet to Parliament (to either House): this imposes
collective responsibility on ministers. However, since 1945, only one
government has been formally defeated on a motion of no-
confidence (the Spaak government of 1946). Defeat in votes on bills
or other matters does not automatically imply resignation and
usually does not have that consequence, but has sometimes done so.
Governments fail more because of internal dissensions than because
of parliamentary votes, to the point where many observers have
become critical of this tendency. Very often the collapse of a government will be followed by virtually the same team being reformed
after a two-week-long 'crisis'.

The Cabinet operates with a series of committees.[23] Some governments have set up a '*Kernkabinett*' (inner Cabinet) in which all coalition parties are represented. This tendency began to develop in the
early 1960s. The Lefèvre-Spaak (1961–5) government instituted a
Comité de Politique Générale. The Harmel-Spinoy (1961–8) government included six 'senior' ministers responsible for co-ordination of
policy areas, who formed a *Comité de Politique Générale*. The
Vanden Boeynants-De Clercq (1966–8) government was the first to
create a *Kernkabinett* and two committees: a *Comité de Politique
Générale* and a *Comité de Coördination Sociale et Economique*.
These committees survive. From time to time, other committees or
co-ordination functions have been created to deal with the Reform
of the State. The Cabinet does not take votes, but reaches its
decisions by consensus. This does not mean unanimity: ministers
may disagree with the 'sense of the meeting', but they must then
either defend the government's position in public or resign. This
practice corresponds closely to British Cabinet practice, but in a
coalition government more latitude for disagreement has to be
tolerated.[24]

The central administration

Each minister appoints a 'cabinet' of personal advisers who do not
form part of the Civil Service. These cabinets, which may include up
to twenty members, are important as a go-between in negotiations
between parties, ministers and 'social partners' (the two sides of
industry) and government, as well as being influential in policy
formulation within a ministry. These appointments are of course
political and personal to the minister concerned.

There has been a tendency for at least senior appointments in the civil service and what are called in Belgium *Organismes parastataux* (state enterprises or bodies) to become increasingly politicised, with coalition governments practising a *'Proportz'* (or share-out) system between themselves.[25] There has also been the problem of achieving linguistic equilibrium in appointments, at all levels, especially in some areas such as development co-operation, where for obvious reasons (Francophone Africa) French is a much more practically useful language than Dutch.

The power of appointment to posts in the central administration and diplomatic service is expressly given by the constitution to the King (article 66 [1]). The right to make other appointments may only be given to the King by express legal provision. This gives some safeguard to Regional, Provincial and local government autonomy in the appointment of their personnel. For example, articles 87 and 88 of the Special Law on the Reform of the State 1980[26] provide that the Executives shall appoint their own personnel but that the conditions of employment of each category shall be the same as those applying to the national administration. The basic statute of all national civil servants is laid down in a Royal Decree of 1937, although more recent laws of 1965 and 1972 have updated some of the earlier provisions.[27]

Contrary to popular belief, the number of civil servants has not increased dramatically, and indeed in some categories the numbers have actually fallen. In 1970 the central administration employed 67,074 staff in all categories (excluding 41,101 staff of the Post and Telephones), of whom rather more than half were Permanent Statutory Civil Servants. By 1978, this figure had only grown to 81,622. The largest ministries were Finance (25,623 in 1970 and 34,727 in 1978) and Public Works (9,205 in 1970 and 9,451 in 1978). There were also 132,044 other personnel in 1978 (61,448 teachers, 52,066 military personnel, 13,492 gendarmes) and 167,964 in 1978 (80,599 teachers and researchers; 63,350 military personnel and 15,770 gendarmes).[28]

Parliament

The constitution states that 'all power emanates from the nation' (article 25 [1]), and that power is exercised in accordance with the constitution (article 25 [2]). Article 26 provides that legislative power be shared between the Executive and the Legislature. This is the classic nineteenth-century liberal-democratic model. Power emanates from the people, but is constitutionally delegated to Parliament and other organs. Since in reality executive power is exercised by the Cabinet, which is responsible to Parliament, Parliament becomes in theory the central body in the state, representing the sovereignty of the people. However, Parliament itself is not sovereign in the sense that the British Parliament is; it is bound by the constitution, which it can only amend by a special procedure (two-thirds majority) after recourse to the electorate.

Belgium has not escaped from the tendency of modern Western democracies towards the erosion of this classic schema. Power is more and more concentrated and exercised outside Parliament — in the Cabinet, in the parties, through 'corporatist' arrangements between the state and the two sides of industry — making it little more than a '*Chambre d'enregistrement*' (a rubber-stamping body), giving its formal approval and therefore legal effect to decisions already taken elsewhere. Parliament, however, retains its function as an 'electoral college' from which the Executive emerges, though even here election results are often so ambiguous that the political parties can create coalitions which seem almost to defy the verdict of the electorate. One should not, however, overstate this case; Parliament is and will remain an important actor on the Belgian political stage.

As we have seen, bi-cameralism was originally introduced to provide a blocking mechanism against the (already limited) 'dangers of radicalism in the Lower Chamber'.[29] Gradually both Houses were democratised by changing the electoral qualifications, the electoral system and, for the Senate, the method of election. In more recent years, with the emergence of parties as the dominant feature of political life, the Senate's composition has become almost a carbon copy of the Chamber, with a slight advantage to the large 'national' parties. As such conflict between the two Houses is now virtually excluded, the Senate's role as a 'revising' body has never seemed important, since its political independence is non-existent. With the Reform of the State, however, it is to find a new vocation.[30] Its directly elected members now form the Assemblies of the Regions and Communities. The Agreement on the Reform of the State provides eventually for complete transformation of the Senate into a body with virtually no collective national role except in revising the constitution and in forming the elected Regional and Community Assemblies. This Reform has not yet been achieved, and as a result the Senate remains, as we shall see, a half-way house, with both a national and regional function.

Parliament is elected for four years, but the King may dissolve Parliament earlier. In recent years, few legislatures have come near their full term. Under the constitution (articles 7 and 56 *quater* [4]), the King — naturally only on the proposal of the Cabinet — may dissolve one or both Houses. When the Senate is dissolved, he may also dissolve the Provincial Councils which elect a proportion of the Senate. In fact, the dissolution of only one House is in modern terms very rare; this power is the *quid pro quo* of Cabinet responsibility to Parliament — an appeal to the electors where a government is censured. Since the mid-nineteenth century (cases occurred in 1833, 1851 and 1864), it has been almost impossible, although one might say that the 1977 election was caused by the fact that the Tindemans I government had lost its majority. Most dissolutions occur (as in 1981) because of internal dissensions in the ruling coalition.[31]

The Chamber of Representatives

The Chamber of Representatives has 212 members elected by universal suffrage for four years by proportional representation (PR). The original text of the constitution provided for a minimum of one Deputy (technically '*Représentant*', though '*Deputé*' is normal usage) per 40,000 inhabitants, which led to a growth of the House from 102 in 1831 to 212 in 1949. Since 1949, despite the increase in population, the various electoral laws have held the number of members static at the same level, and this norm was written into the constitution (article 49) in 1971. Each electoral district (*Arrondissement*) is accorded a number of seats proportional to its population revealed in each census (*not* its number of voters), which includes foreigners (260,000 in the Brussels *Arrondissement*). This gave, in the 1978 election, the distribution per Province shown in the adjoining table (1950 figures in brackets):[32]

	1978	1950
Brabant (incl. Brussels)	48	(44)
Antwerp	32	(33)
Hainaut	30	(32)
West Flanders	29	(30)
East Flanders	23	(24)
Liège	22	(24)
Limbourg	14	(11)
Namur	8	(9)
Luxembourg	5	(6)
Total	212	

Since 1965 in particular, there has been a tendency to increase the representation of the Flemish *Arrondissements*. Each Province is split up into a number of *Arrondissements*: Brabant has five, as has West Flanders, others have three or two. The *Arrondissements* of Brussels (34), Antwerp (20), Liège (14), Ghent (12) and Charleroi

(10) have the largest representation. Neufchâteau-Virton, in the Province of Luxembourg, only returns two members, as does Ypres in West Flanders.[33]

The electoral system

Since the European elections in June 1979, the right to vote has been given at eighteen years. This first applied to parliamentary elections in 1981.[34] However, candidates must be at least twenty-five years old. Since 1893[35] voting has been compulsory and fines, albeit derisory (1 to 25 francs), may be levied on those who do not comply. As a result, the number of non-voters is very small — 5.22 per cent for the whole country in 1978, with a high-point of 7.42 per cent in Brussels.[36] Voters must vote in their *Communes*, but can do so in certain cases by proxy.

Article 48 (2) lays down that elections to the Chamber of Representatives shall take place by 'a system of proportional representation, as laid down by law'. This does not of course tie Parliament to a particular form of proportional representation. However, since the introduction of PR in 1899, there has been little variation in the electoral system itself (although universal suffrage was introduced later).[37] The Belgian system is not completely proportional, since, according to article 48 of the constitution, the *Arrondissements* and Provinces are the basic units of electoral law. Article 48 would not permit, as in the Netherlands, complete proportionality. Obviously in some of the smaller Provinces, or where one party has a very strong position (Limbourg or Luxembourg), the application of proportionality within the Province would tend to be disadvantageous to smaller parties. To reduce this disadvantage, the law allows lists to form alliances within a given Province or Provinces, and permits a second distribution of seats for lists which have obtained for the Chamber, 66 per cent of the electoral quotient in the *Arrondissement* and 33 per cent of the quota for the Senate.

The Belgian system is a list system.[38] Parties or political movements may table lists. To do so they must be supported by between 200 and 500 electors (depending on the size of the *Arrondissement*) or three MP's. The list may contain candidates up to the maximum number of seats to be filled in the *Arrondissement* and an equal number of candidates as '*Suppléants*' (alternates who replace an elected candidate whose seat becomes vacant). The order of candidates is decided by the party in whatever manner it may determine (we shall look at this later). Voters may cast a valid vote in four ways. They may vote
— for the list as a whole;

— for a given candidate by preference;
— for a given candidate and alternate by preference; or
— for an alternate by preference.
A vote for the list implies acceptance of the order established by the party.

Each list then receives a number of seats allocated in accordance with the d'Hondt system, invented by a Belgian professor in the nineteenth century. The electoral law allows lists to conclude '*Apparentements*' (alliances) at the provincial level. Naturally lists of the same party do so. Sometimes 'cartel' lists are formed (as between the PS-RW in some provinces in 1974). These are not *Apparentements*, but 'mixed' joint lists. The distribution of seats and the election of candidates is arrived at by the following four basic steps:

1. In each *Arrondissement* of a province an electoral divisor is calculated:

$$\frac{\text{Total vote cast}}{\text{Seats to be filled}} = A$$

For each party an electoral quotient is calculated:

$$\frac{\text{Votes cast for that list}}{A} = B$$

The first distribution allocates a seat or seats to each list having an electoral quotient of one or more.

2. After this distribution, some seats will remain to be filled. Only those lists with an electoral quotient of 0.66 in one *Arrondissement* at least may participate in the second division. This reduces the value of *Apparentement* to small parties (e.g. to the Ecologists or Walloon list in Hainaut in 1981). For each qualified list, the number of votes cast in the whole province is divided successively by the number of seats already won plus one, then two, three, and so on. The quotients thus obtained are classified in descending order, until all the remaining seats are allocated.

3. It remains to allocate the second distribution of seats to an *Arrondissement*. Local quotients are calculated for each list as follows:

$$\frac{\text{Electoral quotient in the } Arrondissement}{\text{First-distribution seats} + 1, 2. \ldots}$$

The seats for each party are then allocated to an *Arrondissement* in accordance with the size of the local quotients of that party in descending order.

4. The final stage is the election of candidates to fill the seats allocated to each list. A 'list quotient' is calculated:

$$\frac{\text{Votes obtained}}{\text{Seats to be filled} + 1}$$

The votes given to the list as a whole are used as a 'pot' to top up the preference votes given to candidates, but the preference votes can upset the order of the list established by the party and do so, in the middle of the list, if not at the top, which is rarely affected. There has been a growing tendency to give preference votes.

EXAMPLE: List X obtains 100,000 votes and five seats. List quotient = 20,000. List votes = 50,000, preference votes = 50,000.

Candidates		Topping up of preference vote	Order of election
A	20,500	–	(1)
B	8,000	+ 12,000	(2)
C	3,000	+ 17,000	(3)
D	3,500	+ 16,500	(4)
E	2,000	+ 4,500	
		(remainder)	
F	3,500		
G	8,000		(5)
H	1,000		
I	400		
J	600		
	50,000	50,000	

Candidates E and F are thus not elected. It should be noted that a higher preference vote does not ensure election in better order, as for example D is elected after C. This example is typical in that a relatively modest preference vote for a 'middle order' candidate can reverse the order of the list, which is why certain popular figures accept a 'marginal' position on the list often called *'La Position de Combat'*.

The parties determine the order of candidates on their lists according to their statutes and internal procedures. There are various types of procedure, some being relatively centralised, others being more democratic. In the Socialist Party, especially in the Charleroi and Borinage Regions, there is a lively tradition of 'polls', i.e. votes by all party members, whereas in Brussels the PS Federation leadership has always avoided them. The CVP, in some *Arrondissements*, has the same tradition;[39] the party statute, as last amended in 1979, provides generally for such polls (para. 37), but it allows the National Executive to provide for exceptions where polls are not held: small *Arrondissements*, elections at short notice, and in any case amendments to the list by a three-quarters majority.[40] The FDF, on the other hand, for example, provides (article 23 of the statutes) for a '*Commission electorale élargie*', mostly chosen by the Executive, to fix the list after receiving candidatures from the sections, *additional* to the outgoing FDF Deputies and Senators.[41]

Election of the Senate

Originally, as we have seen, the Senate was intended to be and was a conservative abode.[42] At a later stage it was intended, via Provincial and co-opted Senators, to ensure representation of regional interests and to incorporate some new political personalities, who could contribute to public life much in the way that cross-bench Peers do in the British House of Lords. This has not worked. The Senate, which is, as we shall see, elected in three steps, has become as politicised as the Chamber, and has tended to be used as part of the pre-electoral carve-ups or as a possible refuge for those who have failed to gain election to the Chamber. The political composition of the Senate rarely varies much from that of the Chamber of Representatives, though in 1958 the CVP/PSC obtained an overall majority in the Senate and not in the CR. Smaller parties are at a slight disadvantage.

The most recent reform of the Senate — article 56 of the constitution, adopted in 1921 — attempted to ensure higher qualifications for Senators. Article 56 *bis* imposes a series of requirements, at least one of which must be met: a certain educational standard, higher civil service or business experience, an annual tax payment of BF 3,000, etc. Higher standards of education and inflation made these qualifications meaningless, and today no one would in reality be excluded. There is a lower age-limit of forty. None of these qualifications is imposed on provincial or co-opted Senators. The electorate for the directly-elected Senators is the same as for the Chamber. We shall now look at the three categories of Senators: those directly elected; Provincial Senators (introduced in 1893) and co-opted Senators (introduced in 1921).

— *Directly-elected Senators.* There are 106 Senators (fixed at half the number of Representatives)[43] allocated to the Provinces on the same basis (population) and using the same method of election as the House of Representatives.

— *Provincial Senators.*[44] Each Province is allocated at least three Provincial Senators. Provinces are allocated one Senator per 200,000 inhabitants and one for any 'remainder' above 125,000. These are elected by the Provincial Councils (which are elected by proportional representation on the same day as the Chamber of Representatives and the 106 elected Senators) and they meet to conduct the election a short time later. The figures for 1970, shown in the adjoining table, show that the number of Provincial Senators is not proportional to population. Luxembourg obtained one Senator per 74,000 inhabitants and Brabant one per 202,000.

	Directly elected	*Provincial*	*Co-opted Senators*
Antwerp	17	8	
Brabant	24	11	
Hainaut	15	6	
Liège	12	5	
Limbourg	7	3	
Luxembourg	2	3	
Namur	4	3	
West Flanders	11	5	
East Flanders	14	6	
Total	106	50	25

— *Co-opted Senators.* Twenty-five additional Senators are co-opted[45] — elected by PR by the two other groups of Senators. The number of co-opted Senators must always be half the number of Provincial Senators.

At present the Senate thus has 181 members, plus one *ex-officio* royal prince who takes no part in political life. The final composition of the Senate is only complete about ten to fifteen days after a general election. Intense bargaining both between and within parties occurs over the Provincial and co-opted Senators seats, both to 'rescue' defeated candidates and to create deals between small parties which are close together politically. Thus in 1981, the Socialists, RW and Ecologists co-operated in Wallonia to elect Provincial and co-opted Senators.

A politician whose star is waning may successively be a Deputy, a directly-elected Senator, a Provincial Senator and finally a co-opted Senator before sinking into oblivion. Given rules in some parties against '*le Cumul des Mandats*' (the holding of a series of European, national, regional and local offices), some politicians with varied aims may from time to time prefer merely to be elected as a *Suppléant* (alternate) to one or the other House, while serving as an

MEP (Glinne in 1981), a European Commissioner (Simonet in 1974) or a mayor.

The powers of the two Houses

With certain minor exceptions, the two chambers have equal powers and functions.[46] All legislation must be passed in the same form by both chambers. Financial appropriation acts must pass both Houses: however, financial measures must be introduced in the Chamber first. The latter alone may impeach ministers before the Supreme Court (*Cour de Cassation*). The Senate proposes candidates for appointment to the *Cour de Cassation*. The Senate may not meet when the House is not in session. De-composed into its two linguistic groups, the directly-elected Senators are intended to form the Regional Assemblies, which have important legislative powers in their own regions and communities under the provisions for the Reform of the State.

For matters relating to the succession to the throne, e.g. the declaration under article 82 (applied in 1945 to Leopold III) that the King 'is unable to reign' (*Impossibilité de régner*), the two Houses meet and vote in joint session.

In view of the fact that at least until 1893, if not 1921, the Senate had no real democratic basis, the tradition had developed to regard the Chamber of Representatives as the true representative of the people and the Senate as an Upper House, a revising or 'blocking' chamber. This tendency still survives. New governments first seek the confidence of the Chamber, which in fact virtually binds the Senate, although it in turn is called upon to approve a new government.

The organisation of Parliament

Each House is led by a President, whom it elects, but who is in fact usually chosen as part of the political bargaining surrounding the formation of the government. He is assisted by two Vice Presidents and a number of secretaries (eight in the Chamber), who are in fact merely members of the Bureau. The Bureau, responsible for the running of business and the administration, is made up of the President, Vice Presidents and Secretaries plus the Chairmen of recognised political groups.[47] In the Senate there is a 'college of quaestors' responsible for the administrative and financial matters of the Senate itself. Members may form political groups for which the minimum size is three in the Chamber.

The agenda is fixed by another body of similar composition called the Conference of Presidents, composed of the President, Vice Presidents, former Presidents, and the President and one member of each group. The opinions of committee chairmen may be heard. The prime minister or a substitute also attends. The proposed order of business is ratified by the Chamber. In the Chamber, twelve members or the government may propose an amendment, which is then voted upon.[48]

The two Houses set up a number of permanent committees each session. Until recently each House had one committee per government department,[49] plus some purely parliamentary committees (on rules, immunities, etc.). Then, during the 1960s, the members of committees multiplied to reach twenty-three in the Senate (1979–80 session) and twenty-two in the Chamber.[50] In the 1980/1 session both Houses reduced the number of committees significantly. This is linked to devolution and the impracticality of having too many committees. The most important committees are in the Chamber: Foreign Affairs, Defence, Economic Affairs, Finance, Legal Affairs, Social Affairs and Employment in all, thirteen committees. In the Senate there are now also thirteen of which one is only semi-permanent (Revision of the Constitution and Institutional Reform). The main committees are Social Affairs, Economic Affairs, Finance, Infrastructure, Internal Policy, Legal Affairs, External Relations and Defence.[51]

Both Houses also divide into *Sections* — six in the Chamber (External Relations, Internal Affairs, Economic, Social, Culture, Infrastructure) and four in the Senate (Social, External Affairs, Internal Affairs, Economic Affairs). These *Sections* are a sort of sub-parliament. They may consider bills up to the final vote stage and budgets, as well as *Interpellations* of the government. The final vote on bills must take place in plenary session. They are no longer very active, and are a relic of the early development of Belgian parliamentarianism. Between the 1976/7 and 1980/1 sessions, only one Senate *Section* met at all (Economic — six meetings). In 1979/80, Chamber *Sections* held five meetings and in 1980/1 there were none.[52]

Special committees may be set up to deal with particular bills. These are usually presided over by the president of the chamber in question.[53] Matters such as the Reform of the State or special powers bills (1982) are always handled in such committees. In the Senate there was one in 1980/1, on private militias (in fact an investigating committee) and five special committees of which only one (Reform of the State) was of any major importance. The others concerned parliamentary procedure (no meetings in 1980/1) or parliamentary immunity.

As well as working on bills, committees exercise control functions. They may hear statements from ministers. In the Chamber's 1980/1 session, there were twenty-one statements to various committees covering such matters as arms sales, the budget, African policy, social expenditure, the textile industry, and scientific policy. Some of these matters were discussed in several meetings. The committees may also hold hearings (none in 1980/1) and constitute sub-committees.[54]

Committee membership is proportional. However, in the small (Chamber twenty-three members, Senate twenty-two members) committees, some groups are not represented. The author of a bill or proposal may always participate as may one member per group not represented in the committee (the Chamber only). Staff of political groups may also attend and therefore report back to their groups. Any member of either House may make written observations to a committee even if he is not a member of that committee.

The two Houses usually hold an annual ordinary session from October to October.[55] Extraordinary sessions are held after elections. In an average session, the Senate holds about eighty sittings (morning and afternoon) — in 1977/8 there were eighty-three, in 1979/80 there were ninety-six and in 1980/1 there were seventy-seven sittings (333 hours). The Chamber met on seventy-one days in 1979/80 and sixty-six in 1980/1 (410 hours).[56] Normally the Chamber and the Senate sit neither on Saturday nor Monday, but in recent times, when dealing with measures such as special powers or the Reform of the State, have often sat on these days and Sunday as well. However, night sessions are rare (one in the Senate in 1980/1).[57]

The two Houses both provide for several methods of parliamentary control. Members may table written questions and these are to be answered within fifteen days. In the Chamber there were 4,990 in the 1979/80 session and 5,326 in the 1980/1 session. In the Senate there were 1,160 in 1976/7 and 2,351 in 1980/1. Opposition members ask the largest number of questions. There is also an hour-long questions time on Wednesday. In the Senate there were thirty-eight oral questions in 1976/7 and ninety-two in 1980/1. In the Chamber there were 299 oral questions in 1979/80 and 258 in 1980/1; no supplementary questions are allowed. Members may also table '*Interpellations*'. These are a longer form of question which permit a debate on the Minister's reply, and they may be followed by a motion which could be a motion of no-confidence. There were fifty-two Senate *Interpellations* in 1980/1 and 134 (139 tabled) in the Chamber on which forty-three motions were tabled.[58]

Motions (also no-confidence motions) may be tabled following debates on government statements. There was only one in the sessions of 1979/80 and 1980/1 which did not concern the formation of the government (economic policy on 17 October 1979, which also involved a censure motion).[59]

Speaking time is always limited except for ministers and rapporteurs (who may speak at their own request). The longest allocation is thirty minutes in the general debate on a bill; the author of an *interpellation* may speak for fifteen minutes.[60]

The legislative process

Naturally no two bills are totally alike and therefore each one has a different legislative history. However, some generalisations can be made concerning the legislative process. There are bills of different types:
— Routine, uncontroversial bills. These constitute the vast mass of legislative activity in terms of numbers of bills;
— Controversial, important legislation, under two headings:
(a) Reform of the State (special majorities required)
(b) other major 'political' bills, such as major taxation or social measures. These tend to be adopted government against opposition. Bills dealing with the structure of state bodies (*La Loi Communale*) are often called 'organic laws'.
Parliament has, as we shall see, had influence on bills in category *(a)*. Its influence is smaller on those in category *(b)*, and is often smaller than that of powerful pressure groups. There are other classifications of bills, as follows:

Special powers bills. These have been quite rare in recent years (1914, 1926, 1932, 1935, 1937, 1939, 1944–7, 1957, 1961, 1967, 1978, 1980 and 1982), but less so than one might expect. They are of two types: those conferring respectively special and extraordinary powers. None but the laws of 1939 and 1944 provided for extraordinary powers, which are usually only accorded in a war or major imminent crisis. Such laws permit the King (government) to take measures (decree-laws) with the force of law. These are not laws, but are not subject to the control of the Courts (under article 107 of the constitution) as are *Arrêtés royaux*. These decree-laws can themselves be carried out by *Arrêtés*. The laws usually refer to broad objectives which justify action, such as 'the need to ensure the security and independence of the national territory, public order and the protection of the country's financial and economic interests'. No powers could be broader. No special majority is required to adopt such laws.

Special powers laws are usually more limited in scope and time.

Arrêtés royaux adopted under them can amend laws if the basic special powers law provides for this.[61] After the expiry of the law, AR issued under the law can only be amended by law. Thus in 1982, the indexation of wages could be limited by AR.

Framework, programme and planning laws. All of these are modern innovations, which are made necessary by interventionism, but which reduce the power of Parliament to amend legislation. Framework laws (*Lois cadres*) are very general and allow the government wide powers to implement them; indeed, without the necessary AR the law would be too general to be operative.[62] The laws are, in effect, little more than directives. Programme laws are laws dealing with long-term infrastructure plans and the like. There have been six since 1973. They came close to mixing budgetary and legislative provisions in the same law, which is not permitted. An example of a planning law is that of 15 June 1970 which provides for five-year indicative plans with annual revision.[63]

These kinds of laws have all increased the power of the Executive well beyond the modest intentions of articles 29 and 67 of the constitution, which empower the government to implement the laws. It has been assumed that such wide delegations have a sound legal basis in article 78, which states that the King has (only) those powers granted by the constitution *or* by laws adopted under it.

Another classification of bills is according to their origin. Most important bills are now proposed by the government. These are called '*Projets de Loi*' and have priority in Parliament. Private members bills, often more propagandistic or kite-flying in intent, are called '*Propositions de Loi*', and are often refused even at first reading (*Prise en Considération*) and therefore never reach committee. In the Senate in 1979/80 there were 144 *Propositions de Loi*, of which only six were adopted in the Senate; some two *Propositions de Résolutions* on the Senate rules were accepted, but they were agreed texts. In 1980/1, seventeen out of 109 were adopted. This was above the average; in 1977 of 119 *Propositions*, three were adopted. In the Chamber, 223 *Propositions de Loi* were tabled in 1979/80 and only sixteen were approved; in 1980/1, 166 were tabled and only twenty-four were adopted, but many remained 'under consideration,' which does not assure passage. However, the success rate would seem higher than in Britain. However, on dissolution in 1981, 551 *Propositions* (mostly with no real chance) were in the pipeline and all were thus lost.[64]

Almost all government bills are passed, unless impeded by a governmental crisis. Government tables an average 120 bills (1979/80, sixty-five tabled in the Chamber plus fifty-six tabled in the

Senate = 121 bills; in 1980/1 sixty-two in the Chamber plus sixty-four in the Senate = 126). In 1980/1 Parliament examined in all 118 government bills and *in that* session passed 102 of them. The Senate passed 166 of those tabled in the Senate[65] or sent over by the Chamber (106).[66] These figures exclude budgetary measures, to which we shall return.

Tabling of a Bill. The law on the Council of State (*Conseil d'Etat*) provides that the government must refer many types of bills to its legislation section for an advisory opinion.[67] The government, the President of either House, or either House on a majority vote may thus refer any project or *Proposition de Loi*.[68] Such referrals in principle suspend the examination in Parliament. Amendments may also be referred. These opinions are only advisory, but in reality are extremely influential and often lead the government to undertake major modifications to its bills in response to objections of unconstitutionality or other legal problems. These opinions also influence parliamentary opinion. The *Conseil d'Etat* played a major role in the debate over the Reform of the State.

First reading (Prise en Consideration). Government bills bypass this step. Other bills need the support of at least five members and a favourable vote.[69]

Committee stage. The President refers bills to one committee, or one main committee with others being asked to give an opinion, or to several committees in joint session (as for the European Elections Bill) or to a special committee. Each committee nominates a rapporteur. It will call the minister, often on several occasions, and for major bills the prime minister. Government bills are frequently amended in committee, often in the light of external inter-party agreements (which has led to criticism) or because of the fall of the government. The committee reports to the House. This report contains the observations of the committee, its voting on the amendments and its revised text (if it adopts amendments).[70] Prior debates in *Sections* (rare) may be used to dispose of uncontroversial matters.[71]

Final vote. The Chamber then proceeds to a general debate and then to vote on each amendment (minimum of five signatories), on each article and then on the whole bill. Texts which affect the interests of one language group can be suspended and referred back to the government for fresh consideration, under article 38 *bis* of the constitution, if three-quarters of one language group so require (the so-called 'alarm bell' procedure — never used so far).[72] In the

Chamber, minor matters can be dealt with without report, where there are no amendments or observations. Each House follows the same procedure — and having equal powers must agree to the same text. No provision exists to break deadlocks nor even for conciliation by the Houses. However, in practice, it is the Senate which gives way.

Financial legislation

The constitution devotes several articles (110, 111, 113, 115, 116) to public finances. No taxation (or other levy) may be imposed except by an act of Parliament. Jurisprudence makes it clear that the title of the measure is not important but its real impact. The criterion is: is it really a tax? If yes, then it must be imposed by law. However, in complex modern times laws can provide for tax rates etc. to be fixed by *Arrêté royal* (article 100). Article 111 provides that taxes must be voted annually and at any rate for not more than one year at a time.

As to the State Budget (appropriations), these too must be voted annually by law and must include all expenditure and income. These principles have been given detailed application by a law of 1963.[73] The Draft Budget Law must be tabled in Parliament by 30 September each year and voted annually. However, modern budgetary techniques require long-term planning; hence the 1963 law permits the adoption of commitment (long-term) appropriations and payment appropriations for the year in question. In principle, transfers may not be operated between items, but there are permitted exceptions. In matters of great urgency, credits may be exceeded, but the Court of Auditors and Parliament must be informed and the higher appropriations must be approved in a subsequent law. Each year, no later than August, the government must present the accounts for the execution of the previous year's budget, together with the comments of the Court of Auditors, which itself must receive the accounts by 30 June. Parliament then must pass a discharge law. Failure to do so would represent a vote of no-confidence.

The Court of Auditors is an independent financial control body instituted by the constitution (article 116).[74] Its members are appointed by the Chamber of Representatives for a six-year term. There is a French and Flemish section, each with a president, four members and a clerk. In addition to reporting on the annual execution of the budget, the Court controls — during the year — the requisites and legality of the financial administration of the State, Communities, Regions, Provinces and *Communes*. The Court must give its approval ('*Visa*') for all expenditure. The government, deliberating in Cabinet, can on its responsibility override this refusal, which must be notified to Parliament. So-called fixed expenditure (rents, salaries etc.) can be paid without the '*Visa*'. The Court of Auditors also has a jurisdictional competence to discipline officials responsible for misuse of public funds. However, it can only impose financial penalties (repayment), and its rulings in all such cases may be appealed to the *Cour de Cassation*. The Court is the long arm of Parliament, its agent in this very complex and detailed area.

In Parliament, priority is given to budgetary bills between September and December.[75] The main budgetary bill, *Voies et Moyens* (ways and means), must be voted by 25 December and the other budgets by 30 March at the latest. The budgetary bills are examined both in the Budgets Committee (CR) or Finance Committee (Senate), and in 'specialised committees' for each ministry's budget. The committees work under a special rapid procedure. Reports are only approved by the Chairman. The budget debates in plenary session are the occasion for a general political debate; speaking time is limited, but votes do take place on individual items and on amendments. Budgets first examined in the Senate are not reported on or debated in detail in the Chamber and *vice versa*. Matters not pertinent to the budget may not be included either in the draft bill or in amendments. The Budgets Committee of the Chamber held thirty-nine meetings in 1980/1 and the Senate Finance Committee forty-six, only exceeded in each House by the Legal committee. There were fifty-five budgetary bills in 1980/1 of which twenty-seven were rectifying budgets for earlier years.[76]

Parliament and foreign policy

Through its powers in respect of treaty-making, appropriations and general oversight of the government, Parliament also exercises a role in the foreign policy field. As we shall see in chapter 7, the practical impact of parliament is quite modest.

Amendments to the constitution

Article 131 provides for amendment, but only by explicit amendment. The procedure may not be launched when Parliament is prevented from meeting freely in Belgium or in war time. Otherwise, the government prepares a *Déclaration de Révision* which must state which articles are to be revisable. This declaration is examined in a special committee in each House and then voted upon article by article. Amendments may be moved. Examples were those moved unsuccessfully in 1978 in favour of giving the vote in local government elections to foreigners resident in Belgium and the successful amendment to amend article 49 to ensure representation of the German Community in Parliament. It is not necessary to specify how to amend the article, though some declarations do so. For example, in 1978 it is simply stated that 'article 113 should be revised', but 'it is necessary to revise article 111 to provide for the annuality of the budgets of the regions.' The declaration is just that, and is published as such. It is not a law and is therefore not signed by the King.

Once a declaration is accepted, Parliament is automatically dissolved and elections are held. The new Parliament is *'Constituant'* and may modify the constitution by a two-thirds majority,[77] but only those articles mentioned in the 'declaration'.

The influence of Parliament

In the same way as in all Western democracies, the Belgian Parliament has undergone a crisis of confidence since the late 1950s. It has become clear that it has less and less real influence — less than it has ever had. Governments are made and unmade outside Parliament. The role of the majority is to support government policy. Often government Deputies may not table bills, amendments or interpellations without the approval of their groups. Only government Deputies who are close to powerful pressure groups may be able to exercise real influence. The opposition is weak because governments often have large majorities and because it is itself divided e.g. VU, FDF, PS/SP, PCB are now in opposition. They have no coherent alternative policy. There is no 'opposition', only 'oppositions'. As H. Van Impe has written, 'Parliament is marginal in legislation and only retains a subsidiary and residual legislative power.'[78] This is possibly exaggerated — especially on such issues as Reform of the State — but is in general an acceptable conclusion, especially in view of the recent (1982–3) year of 'full powers' delegated to the government.

The Judiciary

The judiciary in Belgium does not play a major political role as it does in those countries, such as the United States, Canada and Germany, where there is a tendency to refer to the courts difficult issues, which are in reality as much political as judicial. In this, Belgium more closely resembles Britain, in that a number of constitutional and legislative procedures and customs seem designed precisely to avoid the Judiciary taking decisions of a political character. The constitution provides in its articles 92–107 the classic guarantees of the independence of the Judiciary from the Executive and Legislative branches (especially articles 92 and 93); it provides that the deliberations of courts be in public, that judges are named for life but may be retired at a fixed age, that judges of the appeal courts are appointed by the Crown from lists proposed by the appeal courts themselves and by the Provincial Councils, and that the members of the *Cour de Cassation* (Supreme Court) are appointed by the Crown from lists proposed by the Senate and by the *Cour de Cassation* itself. Thus there is a democratic element in the appointment of senior judges. The constitution forbids special tribunals, but allows military, labour and commercial courts (articles 94 and 106) the competences of which are to be defined by law.

Organisation of the Judiciary[79]

The highest court in Belgium, the *Cour de Cassation*, only overturns decisions of lower courts on legal grounds, but does not reconsider the facts of a case. It is composed of judges, appointed by the Crown on a proposal from the Senate and the Court itself. Belgian courts, including the *Cour de Cassation*, do not have the same power to set precedents '*erga omnes*', as do British and American courts. Article 28 of the constitution gives to the legislator — national or regional — the sole right to give binding general interpretations of laws or decrees. The decisions of the *Cour de Cassation* thus only concern the particular case in which a judgement is sought. The decision to quash a judgement merely refers the issue back to the lower court, which — legally, at any rate, — is not even bound by the decision. Only after a second judgement of the lower court has been quashed does the ruling become binding.

The *Cour de Cassation* also has original jurisdiction over cases of impeachment of ministers (article 90 of the constitution) brought by the CR and over cases involving the removal of judges.

The constitutional revision of 1970 established five (as against three) appeal courts based on Brussels (for Brabant), Ghent (East and West Flanders), Antwerp (Antwerp and Limburg); Liège (Liège, Namur and Luxembourg) and Mons (Hainaut).[80] These courts hear appeals against rulings and judgements of lower courts in civil and criminal matters.

As the constitution permits, some technical courts have been instituted to hear cases arising in certain special matters — military courts (which include one civilian member) to hear cases against military law and those involving offences by military personnel, commercial courts and labour courts.

The basic judicial system has a close resemblance to the French system. Crimes are examined by the '*Parquet*' (a prosecuting authority consisting of the *Procureur du Roi* and his substitutes), which decides on the action required. It may refer the matter to a *Juge d'Instruction* for further investigation or referral to the *Tribunal correctionnel*, directly. The Justice Minister may only instruct the *Procureur* to proceed, but may not prevent proceedings.

Offences of a more serious nature are heard before Provincial assize courts, with a jury for criminal matters and political offences, although — and this was perhaps of dubious constitutionality — collaboration with the enemy during the two World Wars was afterwards treated as an ordinary offence and referred to military courts as an offence against the security of the state.

A very large proportion of criminal offences are referred to the *Tribunaux correctionnels* under a law of 1867 concerning mitigating circumstances. The *Tribunaux correctionnels* may impose lower sentences, but — and that is the advantage for the prosecution — they are less unpredictable than assize courts, where juries are often influenced by popular sentiment or effective advocacy.

In 1975, the *Parquets* received 884,558 criminal complaints, citations by police officers and denunciations. These were disposed of as follows:[81]

By agreement	32,053
Juge d'Instruction appointed	26,501
Tribunal correctionnel	59,779
Referred to another jurisdiction	121,828
Filed	609,812

Of the cases referred to a *Juge d'Instruction*, some 6,000 were dismissed without further proceedings. Assize courts received cases against 13,078 persons. In 1975 they pronounced judgements against seventy persons and acquitted eight. In 1976 22,681 persons were sentenced, five being sentenced to death. However, the death penalty is purely theoretical in Belgium, and is automatically commuted.

In civil matters the *Juges de Paix* (lowest level of jurisdiction) received 147,460 heard cases in 1975 and dealt with 141,885 of them. The *Tribunaux de Guerre* heard 56,506 cases and had a backlog of 46,544 cases.

The appeal courts heard 6,415 cases (3,790 accepted as a whole or in part — a high proportion) in criminal matters and dealt with

4,912 civil cases, while 7,650 new cases arrived. The *Cour de Cassation* heard 335 civil cases and 1,168 criminal cases, quashing 224.

Administrative justice

Administrative justice, i.e. the hearing of appeals against the acts of administrative bodies, is the province of the *Conseil d'Etat*, which we have already met earlier in this chapter in another guise, in relation to its advisory functions regarding legislation. It is the administrative section of the *Conseil d'Etat* which concerns us here.[82] When Parliament passed the law of 1946 which set it up, it carefully examined the constitutionality of such a step in relation to the jurisdiction of the normal courts, and concluded that the *Conseil d'Etat* operating *as part of the* executive branch, did not interfere with the competences of the courts. At the same time, since it does, in effect, exercise a judicial competence, the law seeks to ensure the independence of the members of the *Conseil d'Etat* by a series of measures. Its members are appointed for life by the Crown from two lists proposed by the *Conseil d'Etat* itself and by the two Houses of Parliament (article 70 of the law on the *Conseil d'Etat*). The 1978 declaration of constitutional amendment (repeated in 1981) proposed to devote a section of the constitution to administrative justice and the role of the *Conseil d'Etat*, but up to the time of writing no action has been taken in this matter. The *Cour de Cassation* is competent to decide disputes over the boundaries of competence between the courts and the *Conseil d'Etat*.

The function of the *Conseil d'Etat* is to consider the legality and validity of acts of the administration in relation to the law. This may lead it to pronounce on what would in British parlance be called delegated legislation — *Arrêtés royaux* and *Arrêtés ministériels*. This function, though based on other criteria of an administrative character, is more thoroughgoing than that accorded to the courts under article 107 of the constitution. A decision by the courts that a given *Arrêté* is not in conformity with the law implies only that it should not be applied in the case before the court. In other words, the judgement only applies *inter partes*. A judgement of the *Conseil d'Etat* may under article 14 of the law on the *Conseil d'Etat*, annul an *Arrêté erga omnes*. A request for an annulment must be made within sixteen days of the decision complained of. The right to ask courts not to apply an administrative act is unlimited in time and may be based on broader criteria such as the internal legality of the actions of the administration.

In 1973/4, the *Conseil d'Etat* rendered fifty-nine decisions on appeals from other administrative bodies, and 414 judgements in appeals against administrative rules of which 166 were annulled.[83]

The constitutionality of laws

As we have seen, article 28 of the constitution provides that only Parliament and the Regional or Community assemblies, as the case may be, can give an 'authentic' *erga omnes* interpretation of laws and decrees. This has not prevented debate on the difficult question of the right or otherwise of courts to control the constitutionality of laws. Here the constitution is mute although, as we have seen, it confers on the courts (article 107) the right to control the legality of secondary legislation.[84]

Legal doctrine and argument in cases have been divided on the issue. Neither the courts nor Parliament have shown any tendency to accept that the courts have or should have any such competence to control the constitutionality of laws.

The *Cour de Cassation* stated boldly in a judgement of 23 July 1849 that 'it is not the function of the courts to examine whether a law is in conformity with the Constitution.'[85] This jurisprudence remains unaltered and was — contrary to the opinion of the *Procureur-Général* — confirmed in a 1974 judgement. The *Conseil d'Etat* has likewise, on at least four occasions, taken the same line.

The position of decrees of the Community and Regional assemblies is somewhat different, in that article 107 of the constitution now provides for the setting up of an arbitration court to settle conflicts between laws and decrees, but not on their constitutionality on other grounds. Until this court is established, a complicated procedure involving the *Conseil d'Etat*, and giving Parliament the right to overrule the *Conseil d'Etat*, is provided for in the law of 9 August 1980 on the reform of the Institutions (Articles 24–28). It may be supposed that when the arbitration court is set up, it would be able to declare a decree — or, for that matter, a law — to be in violation of the provisions of articles 107 *quater* or 59 *bis* of the constitution in that it invades the 'Regional', 'Community', or 'national' sphere. This limited control of constitutionality is the most that is conceivable in the present Belgian context. We shall return to this in Chapter 4.

NOTES

1. Constitution, articles 63 and 64.
2. For a discussion of this procedure, see A. Mast, *Overzicht van het Belgisch Grondwettelijk Recht*, E. Story, Ghent, 1981, 355–6.

3. For a brief history of the Crown's role since 1831, see A. Molitor (formerly Secretary to the King), *La Fonction Royale en Belgique*, Centre de Recherche et d'Information Socio-politique (CRISP), Brussels, 1979, 13–25.

4. Mast, op. cit., 353–6, and Molitor, op. cit., 26–42.

5. Molitor, op. cit., 37–8.

6. Ibid., 28.

7. The procedures are described in Mast, op. cit., 353–5, and Molitor, op. cit., 31–4. There are also some useful articles, but they are not all very recent: A. Mast, 'La nomination et révocation des Ministres', *Journal des Tribunaux*, 1949, 649; and, on the 1977 crisis, L. Neels, 'Het leven van het Grondwet. De Kabinetskrisis', *Rechtskundig Weekblad*, 1977, 508–604.

8. Molitor, op. cit., 37.

9. See Erik Van Rompuy, 'Un Avertissement au Palais', *Le Soir*, Sept. 1981. Van Rompuy is Chairman of the CVP *Jongeren*.

10 Ibid., 78–80. The King signs an average of some 1,500 documents each month.

11. Mast, op. cit., 356–8.

12. Op. cit., 198–202, for the various types of 'special majority' as they arise in articles 131, 107*quater*, 59 *bis*, 62, 56 *bis*, art 1 (4), 3 *bis*, 38 *bis*. Some of the instances are of small practical importance.

13. See 'Belgium' in Henig (ed.), *Political Parties in the European Community*, PSI/Allen & Unwin, 1979, for a discussion of the preference for broad coalitions.

14. Xavier Mabille and Val Lorwin, 'The Belgian Socialist Party' in Patterson and Thomas (eds), *Social Democratic Parties in Western Europe*, Croom-Helm, London, 1977, 394, emphasises this point, even though the article was written during a rare period when the PS was in opposition and appeared to be moving to the left.

15. *Le Programme Complet du Parti Socialiste*, 1981.

16. This notion arose in particular after the 1977 elections, and led Mr Tindemans to form his second government with 'Community parties'. See X. Mabille, 'Le Système des Partis dans la Belgique post-unitaire' in *Courrier Hebdomadaire du CRISP* (hereafter 'CH') no. 864, 1979, esp. 22–4.

17. See 'Loi spéciale du 8 Août 1980 sur la réforme des institutions', *Moniteur Belge*, 15 Aug. 1981, articles 59 and 65 (1).

18. For details of size and structure of governments, see Mast, op. cit., 372. State secretaries are exempted from the parity rule, and are not members of the Cabinet. They may in some cases countersign *Arrêtés royaux*.

19. See J. Brassine, 'La Réforme de l'Etat: phase immédiate et phase transitaire', CH 857/8, 1979.

20. R. Urbain, *La Fonction et les Services du Premier Ministre en Belgique*, Edition de la Librairie encyclopedique, Brussels, 1958, and Mast, op. cit., 373–6.

21. Mast, op. cit., 374.

22. For a discussion of the legal and political issues, see ibid., 376–9, and in

more detail in L. de Lichtervelde, 'Le Conseil des Ministres dans le Droit Public Belge', *Bulletin de l'Academie Royale de Belgique*, XXXIII, 21, and B. Waleffe, *Some Constitutional Aspects of recent Cabinet Development in Great Britain and in Belgium*, Bruylant, Brussels 1966.

23. Details in Luykx, op. cit., 505 and 541.
24. Mast, op. cit., 378.
25. Patterson and Thomas, (eds), op. cit., 394–5.
26. *Moniteur Belge*, 15 Aug. 1980.
27. Mast, op. cit., 314.
28. Figures from *Annuaire Statistique de la Belgique*, vol. 99, 1979, 500–3.
29. Luykx, op. cit., 55: 'Un corps aristocratique. . . . et un pouvoir modérateur'.
30. Mast, op. cit., quotes the policy statement of the Martens II government to this effect, as from 1983 (p. 193).
31. See F. Velu *La dissolution du Parlement*, Bruylant, Brussels 1966.
32. *Annuaire Statistique* (1979), 112.
33. Ibid.
34. Constitutional amendment of 28 July 1981.
35. Mast, op. cit., 165.
36. *Annuaire Statistique*, 110.
37. Luykx, op. cit., 229–30.
38. The account of the election system is based on information supplied to the author by the Service des Elections of the Interior Ministry.
39. *Dossiers du CRISP* no. 10, 'Les partis politiques en Belgique' (1978), 20.
40. CVP, *Statuten en Reglementen* (last amended 1979), rules 36 and 37.
41. *Statutes du FDF* as amended by the Congress of 5 Nov. 1977 and 1981, paras 23 and 24.
42. For the historical development see summary in Mast, op. cit., 182–9.
43. Ibid., 185–6.
44. Ibid., 187–8.
45. Ibid., 188.
46. On powers see ibid., 189–93 and 286–7.
47. E.g. Chambre des Représentants. Rules (CRR), article 3.
48. E.g. CRR, article 22.
49. J.J.A. Salmon, 'Les Commissions des affaires étrangères du Parlement Belge', unpublished paper for the Colloquium on Parliamentary Foreign Affairs Committees held in Florence, April 1981, p. 6 (reference to article 48 of the 1850 Senate Rules).
50. Op. cit., p. 7.
51. Senate Session 1980/1, no. 1, *Commissions et Délégations*, and Chambre des Representants, *Revue Statistique de l'Activité Parlementaire 1980/1*, dated 27 Nov. 1981, p. 6. Hereafter '*Relevé*'.
52. *Relevé*, p. 3, and information supplied to the author by the Senate department of Committees, hereafter 'Senate information'.
53. CRR, article 13, and Senate Rules (SR), article 13.
54. CRR, article 21; Salmon, op. cit., 54–8 and *Relevé*, 10–13, for statistics.
55. *Relevé*.

56. *Relevé* and Senate information.
57. *Relevé* and Senate information.
58. *Relevé*, p. 5, and Senate information.
59. *Relevé*, p. 8.
60. E.g. CRR, article 31.
61. For a discussion of the constitutionality and use made of special and extraordinary powers, see Mast op. cit., 224–7.
62. Ibid., 222–3.
63. Ibid., 227–8.
64. *Relevé*, p. 4, and Senate information.
65. *Relevé*, p. 4.
66. Mast, op. cit., 254–5.
67. E.g. CRR, article 48. On amendments CRR 48 (5).
68. CRR article 50.
69. See CRR, articles 49–57, and Mast, op. cit., 195–206.
70. Mast, op. cit., 205–6.
71. Op. cit., 200–2.
72. CRR, article 57.
73. Provisions discussed in Mast, op. cit., 449–59.
74. Ibid., 460–4.
75. The following paragraph is based on CRR, articles 58–69.
76. *Relevé*, p. 4.
77. Mast, op. cit., 472–82.
78. H. Van Impe, *Le Régime Parlementaire en Belgique*, Bruylant Brussels, 1968.
79. See Mast, op. cit., 397–417.
80. See article 104.
81. *Annuaire Statistique*, 184–6, for statistics of cases.
82. Mast, *op. cit.*
83. *Annuaire Statistique*, 192.
84. Mast, *op. cit.*, 432–44.
85. Pas 1849 I 449.

4
REGIONAL AND LOCAL GOVERNMENT

In this chapter we shall deal both with the newly-created regional authorities resulting from almost twenty years of debate about what is usually called 'the Reform of the State' and with the traditional local and provincial authorities which have existed since the state was founded. Until the Reform of the State, Belgium was an extremely centralised state in that even the most minor acts and decisions of the *Communes* (local authorities) and provinces were almost all subject to annulment by the central government, usually in the person of the Minister of the Interior, under the system of '*Tutelle*' (administrative supervision). This *Tutelle* of local authorities has not been abolished, but it has now been given to the new Regional authorities.

It is perhaps at this point that we should define the exact meaning of the communities and regions which compose Belgium, and which will be the main actors in the narrative. Regions are a geographical concept, whereas the communities are linguistic and cultural entities. The Flemish *region* consists of the four Flemish provinces — Antwerp, Limburg, West Flanders, East Flanders. The Walloon *region* consists of the four traditional Walloon provinces — Hainaut, Liège, Luxembourg, Namur — plus part of the province of Brabant. The Brussels *region* consists of the nineteen *Communes* comprising Greater Brussels. The Flemish *community* is made up of all Dutch-speakers in both the four Flemish provinces and Brussels. It should be made clear that Dutch (*Nederlands*) is the language spoken in Flemish Belgium, although in everyday language — often Flemish dialects — there are considerable variations from the Dutch spoken in the Netherlands. The *Francophone community* is made up of all French-speakers in the Walloon and Brussels regions. (It is an anomaly that the 3–5 per cent of French-speakers living in the Flemish provinces do not belong legally to any community at all.) The German-speaking community consists of some 70,000 German-speakers who live close to the Belgo-German border.

The Reform of the State will be our main theme. As we saw in Chapter 2, under pressure from both the Flemish and the Walloon movements, it became inevitable in the late 1960s that some reform would have to be imposed. The history of the Reform process is of one long round of resistance and foot-dragging by the proponents of a strong central government and in particular the CVP, coupled with the difficulties caused by the contradictory demands of those who in principle strongly supported the Reform cause. As a result, after almost twenty years, the Reform is far from complete: the Senate has not yet been reformed; the Provinces still exist; the financial provisions for the Regions and Communities remain inadequate, their powers remain limited, and above all no solution has been found to the problem of the status of Brussels. Timid though it may be, it is a start.

The question is now sometimes raised as to the character of the new Belgian state, as it emerges from the Reform. Is it a federal state? After all, many such as the FDF who fought for reform called themselves federalists. The precise nature of the new system is hard to classify. It is clearly not a classic federal structure, because such a structure is based on the notion of equal geographical units with specific powers and structures below the level of the central government. Clearly, the establishment of non-contiguous Regions and Communities, with both geographical and non-geographical ('*Personalisable*') federalism, makes the Belgian system unique. (The special conditions prevailing in Belgium have necessitated the introduction of a novel kind of federation relating not only to the government of a given area, but to the provision of services to persons living outside the area although culturally linked to it. This is the meaning of the term '*personalisable.*') The Flemish structure, with one council for both cultural and regional matters, does come closer to classic federalism, however, but even here the participation in the Council of Brussels (geographically external) representatives breaches the classical schema, as does its exercise of 'cultural powers' in Brussels, which is *outside* its territory. A principle of federalism, namely that the existence and powers of the subordinate units should have a special legal and constitutional status, is however respected. Articles 107 *quater* and 59 *bis* establishing the Regions and Communities, are in the constitution itself. The special laws on their functioning can only be amended by the 'double' special majority, which of course was not the case in the proposed British devolution schemes for Scotland and Wales.[1]

Reform of the State

We shall look at the background to the move towards a Reform of the State as a solution to the 'Community Question', and then at the tortuous process whereby a first (but not final) major phase was achieved by the summer of 1980 and the institutions of a new Belgium were brought into existence.

The Community Question has become the dominant political issue in Belgium; by the 1960s it had become clear that the unitary structure of the state, created in 1831, was no longer viable and by the early 1970s it appeared increasingly — deceptively, as it happened — to have matured sufficiently to be ripe for a global and far-reaching solution. Simple 'geographical federalism' was clearly inadequate to meet the complicated reality of the Belgian situation. Such a solution would imply four 'states' (Flanders, Brussels, Wallonia and the German-speaking Cantons), all exercising the same devolved powers over both cultural and socio-economic matters. But Brussels is not a third linguistic Community — it is bilingual, and therefore can not exercise powers in the cultural domain. Furthermore, from a socio-economic and cultural (but not historical or political) point of view the French-speaking people in the 'commuter' suburbs should belong to Brussels, but this is politically impossible. No geographically tidy solution can therefore be found; to bring them into Brussels is politically unacceptable to the Flemish parties, and to ignore their specificity and leave them as part of Flanders is unacceptable to the French-speaking parties.

Secondly, the German-speaking Community in the five eastern *Communes* (about 70,000) is not a socio-economic unit, and its institutions could not usefully combine 'cultural' and 'socio-economic' powers. For these reasons a more complex and differentiated pattern of institutions had to be found; this was the aim of the Egmont Pact. The Egmont Pact (1977) is important, because it was the first politically realistic attempt at a coherent and intellectually consistent solution to the problem. Although it was never implemented as such, much of its inspiration, watered down and fudged, found its way into the less elegant solutions finally adopted. Under the Pact, Belgium would eventually have comprised the central state (government and bi-cameral Parliament) and three Communities (Flanders, Wallonia and the German-speakers), each with an elected assembly and Executive and three Regions (Flanders, Brussels, Wallonia), each with an elected assembly and Executive. There would be special guarantees of Flemish minority rights in Brussels and for French-speakers in the suburbs.

The roots of the problem go very deep. Indeed, they go right back to the origins of the Belgian state, but for a long time lay buried, only to re-emerge with increased virulence in the 1960s.[2] What is today Belgium already broke with the United Provinces over religious differences in the course of their common struggle against Spanish domination (Belgium is mainly Catholic). The French Revolution and the subsequent period of French rule in the period 1790–1810 saw the rise of a liberal, French-speaking middle class, not only in

Brussels and Wallonia but also in some of the larger Flemish towns, for whom the solution imposed by the great powers at the Congress of Vienna — incorporation into the Netherlands — was intolerable. The Revolution of 1830 against this imposition opened a long period of domination by the French-speakers. The very idea of a Belgian state was theirs; and it was they who had made the Revolution; the nature of the political institutions and the system of administration were determined by them. Since the late Middle Ages, economic power had passed from Flanders, and with the industrial revolution it moved decisively to the areas of Mons, Liège, Namur and Charleroi situated on the Sambre-Meuse coalfield in Wallonia.

In the twentieth century, as we have seen, Flemish nationalism began to emerge. At first it did so largely on a cultural level, and only after the First World War did it first find political expression.[2] Indeed, the war itself had proved a powerful catalyst to the movement. The two World Wars have on the one hand given the Flemish movement greater consciousness and even a certain impulsion, but on the other hand they greatly handicapped its wider political action. Rightly or wrongly, it became identified as anti-patriotic (which it may have been in the sense that it rejected the Belgian state) and pro-German and prepared to collaborate with the enemy. In many cases this was totally unjust, especially since in the Second World War many Flemish nationalists were anti-Nazi. Nonetheless, these sentiments provided the French-speaking establishment with a convenient alibi for refusing to respond to the Flemish movement's grievances.

The 1960s were a watershed in Belgian politics. It became clear that profound reforms were necessary. First, there was a reversal of the balance of power.[3] Not only was the Flemish community the national majority in numerical terms, but it was no longer on the defensive. The new economic dynamism of the country was in Flanders. The Walloon industrial base was in decline: coal, steel, ceramics, glass, chemicals. The Flemish movement became more self-confident and militant. There were the Flemish march on Brussels and the expulsion of the Francophone university from Louvain.

These changes led to something new: Walloon defensive movements. These on the whole tended to be ideologically left-wing, whereas Flemish nationalism is more right-wing. This of course responded to the Walloon working-class radical tradition, which was one of the Walloon particularisms which the new movements sought to defend. The movements were launched around the bitter strikes of the winter of 1960–1. They eventually fused first into the

Parti Wallon (1965) and then the *Rassemblement Wallon* (RW) in 1968.

Brussels was the cauldron of linguistic politics, and in the late 1960s was the front line. Many questions were raised: Was Brussels, as the Flemish movement proclaimed, 'Flemish soil'? Or was it a co-equal third region? What should be the rights of the Flemish minority in the city? On the other hand, what should be the rights of the French-speakers living in the Flemish *Communes* just outside the city? These issues were the battleground. With the rise of a more militant Flemish movement, the French-speakers of the capital felt increasingly vulnerable and feared that they would be the victims of any settlement between the two Communities. This led to the formation of the *Front Démocratique des Francophones de Bruxelles* (FDF) in 1964.

In the 1965 election the three regional parties obtained 8.7 per cent of the vote between them, and by 1968 their combined share of the vote had almost doubled to 15.7 per cent,[4] and it reached its peak in 1971 with 23.4 per cent of the vote. In the elections of 1974[5] (21.1 per cent) and 1977 (17.0 per cent) the vote for the Community parties (FDF + VU) fell back, but not by any dramatic degree, since their combined vote remained well above their level in the breakthrough year of 1968. In any case, the fall in 1977 was almost entirely due to the break-up of the RW. This global result also hides the fact that in Brussels the peak combined vote for the Community parties was not reached until 1974, but the fact that the FDF was no longer in a cartel with the small Brussels Liberal Party makes comparison difficult. Even if by 1977 the Community vote had ebbed slightly, it was clear that it was a permanent phenomenon in Belgian politics of which account would have to be taken. Furthermore, by 1977 the Community parties had achieved a major objective: to show that the Belgian unitary state was ungovernable and to participate themselves in the implementation of the necessary reforms.

It has been a long process. The constitutional revision of 1971 had done no more than establish general principles and procedures which subsequent legislation was to implement.[6] In the new article 59 *bis* it established the Cultural Councils for the three Communities. In article 107 *quater*, it established the principle of Regional councils with powers in the socio–economic field.

The implementation of these constitutional provisions was left to the legislator, but under conditions almost as onerous and complicated as constitutional amendment itself. Laws under article 59 *bis* and 107 *quater* have to be adopted by a two-thirds majority in each House of the legislature and a majority in each linguistic group in each House. These special majorities have dominated negotiations for the formation of a government and have often made one form of coalition preferable to another. This was the rationale behind the short-lived Leburton government of 1973–4. It was a 'classic' tripartite government (PSB/BSP-CVP/PSC-PLP/PVV); it had the necessary 'special majority', but suffered from internal tension on other issues (Socialists versus Liberals) and from the external pressure of the Community parties, which greatly reduced its freedom of manoeuvre. The first Tindemans government (1974–7) attempted to avoid these defects, narrowing its ideological dimension by excluding the PSB/BSP (which gave it only the barest parliamentary majority) while seeking a broad agreement among all parties on the Community issue through inter-party talks carried on outside the framework both of the government and Parliament (the Steennokerzeel meeting).[7] When this approach failed, Tindemans sought to enlarge his majority by taking in some of the Community parties, especially in Wallonia, where his government was weakest. He met with only partial success, and in the summer of 1974 he added the RW alone. This gave him greater strength in Wallonia and some protection against the threat of the Community parties, but no 'special majority'. Indeed, this mini-enlargement had other negative consequences: the RW was initially to the left of the government's centre of gravity and was to become more so. Participation in a centre-right government without the FDF imposed severe ideological and regionalist strains on the RW, leading ultimately to a rupture between the increasingly leftist party chairman, Paul Henry Gendebien, and the more moderate RW ministers. At the same time, the Tindemans government was open to attack by the PSB/BSP and the trade unions for its economic policies, which also strained RW loyalty. Furthermore, the CVP faced VU criticism on its Flemish flank. Even though the break-up of the RW was the ostensible reason for the collapse of the Tindemans I government, it seems to have collapsed more under the accumulated weight of these contradictions.[8]

Meanwhile the positive spirit of Steenokkerzeel had not been completely forgotten. In all the political parties, in inter-Community study groups, in various organisations and associations and on the part of individuals, an enormous amount of positive work[9] had been going on outside the formal framework of the government to increase mutual understanding, to narrow areas of disagreement, and to build up areas of agreement and a non-binding basis to test various solutions to the most serious problems. Since 1976 the Socialists of all three regions had agreed a common position. The CVP/PVV/VU had also attempted to reach a common approach

(October 1975). Two well-known figures, M. Claes (BSP) and M. Moreau (RW), published a plan.

A conference on the theme was held in Antwerp (10 January 1976). The Minister for Institutional Reforms, M. Perin (RW), published on a personal basis a political report on the institutions. None of these ideas gained universal approval, but they made a positive contribution to the debate and prepared the ground for the official inter-Community dialogue between all the parties represented in Parliament, with the government present as an observer.[10] This dialogue, under the joint chairmanship of Mr De Keersmaeker (CVP) and M. Hurez (PSB), lasted from 30 November 1976 to 3 March 1977 and was just entering a new phase of negotiations as distinct from 'dialogue' when the government fell. Its results[11] were available for the Egmont negotiators. Furthermore, as a result of these discussions, relations between the PSB and the FDF and the CVP had greatly improved.

The 1977 elections saw gains for the CVP, for the PSB, and the FDF. The RW were the main losers. Above all there was a real simplification. One party was clearly dominant in each region: the CVP in Flanders, the PSB in Wallonia, the FDF in Brussels.

When it came to starting negotiations for a new government, two points were clear. First, the PSB should be in, and secondly, the parties supporting the Community pact and those forming the majority should this time be the same. Tindemans' first preference was for a classic tripartite. Others still hoped to exclude the Socialists (the PSC/CVP and Liberals had a bare majority). The tripartite was rejected by the PSB, and even the Flemish PVV was not enthusiastic. Moreover, it would not outflank the Community parties. The exclusion of the PSB would weaken the government in Wallonia and mean that it would enjoy no special majority, furthermore, the socio-economic issue would not be resolved. Thus these coalitions were rejected in favour of the preference of André Cools (PSB) and Wilfried Martens (CVP) for a broad majority: CVP/PSC-PSB/BSP-FDF-VU.[12] This combination had the 'special majority': 172 seats out of the 212 in the Chamber and firm majorities in all regions. Politically too it contained the leading parties in each region and a socio-economic consensus. These parties then both entered the government and negotiated the Community pact (the Egmont Pact). These arrangements initially had a remarkably easy passage, obtained wide agreement in the Community parties and could even count on some support from the Liberal Opposition and the RW. Even in the VU defections were minimal.[13]

The Pact was to be implemented rapidly; indeed, speed was essential if the dynamism and impulsion of the original political will

— the spirit of Egmont — was to be maintained. Just how costly any delay could be was shown only too clearly when the objections of the CVP came to the surface in October 1978.

The Pact was annexed to the government declaration and approved by the Chamber of Representatives on 9 June 1978, by 165 votes to thirty-four with three abstentions. On 14 June the declaration was also approved by the Senate by a massive majority (139 votes to twenty-four with five abstentions).[14] As the Pact made clear, many of the final arrangements would require the revision of the constitution, which was not immediately possible since the 1977 Parliament was not *Constituant*. This defect, which had perhaps played a not unimportant role in the demise of the Egmont Pact, was rectified in later attempts at a solution since the 1978 Parliament *was Constituant*.

The government's immediate task was to prepare the first phase of the Pact, which required three bills: a bill to implement article 107 *quater*, a bill to extend the 'cultural matters' forming the powers of the Cultural Councils, and a third bill amending the laws on the administrative use of languages. Many details of the Pact were unclear, or problems had been exposed in the parliamentary debates or in the copious public discussions of the pact and its implications. Above all, the Pact had rapidly to be translated into legislative texts. The 'Committee of Fifteen' (the six party Presidents of the Majority, the prime minister, the two ministers for the Reform of the Institutions and some other advisers and party representatives) met at the Château de Stuyvenberg over the period from 24 September 1977 to 17 January 1978. Its deliberations led to an annexe to the government declaration being tabled in February 1978. It was then the task of the two responsible ministers — M. Hoyaux (French-speaking) and Mr De Bondt (Flemish-speaking) to put the finishing touches to the texts. This was not easy and required frequent interventions by the party Presidents. Even at this stage, CVP ministers were dragging their feet, especially Mr De Bondt. The texts were finally approved by the Cabinet and presented to Parliament on 11 July 1978.[15] This was Bill no. 461.

Looking beyond the difficulties of the moment, what were to be the main provisions of the institutional reform? What sort of institutions would Belgium have had in the 1980s if the Pact and the bill had been fully implemented, including the necessary constitutional amendments? Certainly it would no longer have been a unitary state. Powerful regional institutions were to be set up with wide powers which could not have been revoked; these institutions were in some cases to have power to impose taxation and to conclude international agreements. There were to be elected assemblies and Executives which were to have their own administrations, and not be subject to the tutelage of the central government. The political majorities in the regions and at the centre were likely from time to time to be different. At any rate, it was not to be a form of simple 'geographical federalism' with one central government and several co-equal regional governments. There would be two kinds of devolved authorities with either geographical or personalisable competence. It could be called a mixture of cultural and geographical federalism. It was perhaps just this realisation that provoked the eleventh-hour CVP opposition — on the ostensible grounds of constitutional problems. It was always clear, and indeed agreed, that the Egmont Pact,[16] even if politically it constituted an indissoluble whole, could only be implemented in stages.

First, some parts only required the 'special majority' in order to apply either article 59 *bis* or article 107 *quater* of the revised constitution of 1970. These provisions of the Pact were to be carried into force rapidly — before 1 January 1979. There would still be some transitional arrangements: the members of the Regional councils would not yet be specially elected, but would be existing members of the Chamber of Representatives.

And secondly, other parts required revision of the constitution (reform of the Senate, direct election of members of the Regional councils, financial provisions, etc.). For these matters, a *Déclaration de Révision de la Constitution* (article 131) would be required, followed by new elections and adoption of the amendments. The Pact provided for this, but only at a later stage. Hence this was a crucial watershed in Belgian politics. It was therefore inevitable that opposition would arise.

At first, however, the bill made reasonable progress in the special committee of the Chamber, chaired by the then CVP President, Wilfried Martens. It was approved, with amendments, after crisis interventions on specific points by the party Presidents, on schedule at the end of September. By then, however, CVP Senators and the CVP congress had begun to raise doubts about the constitutional validity of the first phase.

It is a commonplace of Belgian politics, which has been shown to be true time and again, that what is not gained now tends never to be attained at all. Bargains are rarely fully kept. Given the need to defer some aspects of the Pact until a revision of the constitution could be carried out, it was one of the most ingenious features of the Egmont-Stuyvenberg agreement that enough reciprocal guarantees and concessions were contained in the first part of the Pact to satisfy both the French and Flemish parties of the majority.

It was for these reasons that the constitutional objections raised late in the day by the CVP (in September 1978)[17] set off alarm-bells in the other parties — Flemish- and French-speaking — of the Majority, which saw in the attitude of the CVP a very thinly disguised effort to sabotage the Pact. Previous rumours of prime minister Tindemans' limited attachment to the Pact were only confirmed by his precipitate resignation. It is true that the advisory legal body, the *Conseil d'Etat*, had given an opinion which indicated that certain articles of the bill providing for 'various institutional reforms' which was to implement the provisional phase of the Pact, were in fact unconstitutional. But at the time, the government, through no less a person than Mr Tindemans himself, had rejected these criticisms.

It became clear that the objections were above all political. Indeed 'unitarist' sentiment had always remained strong in the CVP. Now the party also saw the chance of making even greater electoral gains by blocking the implementation of the Pact on three grounds: first, defence of the constitution; secondly, defence of the Belgian state; and thirdly, defence of Flemish rights in the periphery of Brussels. The other parties of the Majority, especially the French-speaking ones, thereupon insisted on the full and rapid implementation of the Pact.[18] Mr André Cools (PSB chairman) was particularly insistent on this. On the CVP demand for more discussions, he was totally dismissive: 'Everything that could be negotiated has already been negotiated.'[19] In this new climate a crisis was inevitable, and it was not long in coming. The other five parties of the Majority demanded an immediate vote on Bill no. 461 and insisted that the Prime Minister make the vote an issue of confidence to force the CVP into line. Mr Tindemans preferred his dramatic resignation on 11 October 1978.

He was succeeded by Mr. Vanden Boeynants (PSC), with the same coalition and the same team. The task of this 'interim' government was to agree a *Déclaration de révision de la Constitution*, which would be followed by elections within a few months. The new Parliament would be able to amend the constitution, which would presumably mean that the transitional phase could be dispensed with. Otherwise Mr. Vanden Boeynants considered that the Egmont framework remained valid.

At this point it is perhaps worth standing back before resuming the Byzantine narrative, and looking in more detail at the ingenious intellectual heritage of the Egmont Pact and Bill no. 461 which was based upon it, since this structure was very largely to form the basis of the solution adopted four years later. The Pact proposed to set up three Community Councils and three Regional Councils, to provide for their financial autonomy, to set up arbitration machinery to settle conflicts of competence, and to transform the Senate. We shall look at each of these aspects in turn.[20]

The Communities

The three existing Community councils — the Dutch Cultural Council established by the law of 21 July 1971 under article 59 *bis* of the constitution, the French Cultural Council set up by the same law, and the German Cultural Council set up by the law of 10 July 1973 — were to be changed into Community Councils with new powers over what are called 'personal' matters such as hospital services, local welfare services and vocational training — in addition, of course, to the existing powers over culture, the use of languages, local aspects of education and international cultural co-operation.

Each Community would have had a directly elected assembly in the sense that the assembly was to consist of Regional Councillors who were to be directly elected. The two larger Community Councils would have been composed of the Flemish or Walloon Regional Councillors plus, for the French-speaking Community, half of the French-speaking group of the Brussels Regional Council. The German Community Council was to continue to have twenty-five members directly elected for four years. Under existing apportionment, that would give 121 members for the Flemish Council (118 + 3) and ninety-one members for the French-speaking Council (70 + 21). The Egmont Pact and Bill 461 proposed that for a transitional period the Councils should continue to consist of Deputies and Senators as now, but that later they would be separately elected.

Bill 461 proposed a provisional executive composed of a minister and three state secretaries (article 75). These executives would be responsible for preparation of proposals for the Councils, execution of decrees voted by the Councils, execution of the budget, and general administration. They would be responsible before their Community Council, but also members of the national government. This rather difficult arrangement was perhaps made necessary by the fact that the constitution could not be modified. The German Council was to continue, as at present, without an executive.

In the definitive stage, after the constitutional revision, the Community Councils were to have (except in the case of the German Community) their own independent Executives (*Collèges*) with a President and three members, with one member from Brussels. The *Collège* was to be responsible to the Council, but the censure procedure was to be the 'constructive no–confidence' system found in clause 66 of the Basic Law of the German Federal Republic: a motion must replace the whole *Collège* or the individual member censured.

Members of the Regional Executives would have been able to take part in meetings of the Community Executives, but without the right to vote.

The Regions

There were to be three regions, as specified in article 107 *quater*: Flanders, Brussels (the nineteen *Communes only*) and Wallonia. Each region was to have a directly-elected Regional Council and an Executive elected by the Regional Council and responsible to it. The Flemish and Walloon Regional Councils would have a number of members equivalent to the number of Deputies elected in each Region (now 118 and seventy respectively). The Brussels Regional Council was to have forty-eight members, or double the number of Deputies elected in that Region. The Brussels members were to be elected on unilingual lists and form (as in Parliament) two linguistic groups (on present figures, six Flemish-speakers and forty-two French-speakers). The Councils were to be elected for four years, but if they failed to elect a new Executive within twenty-one days of rejecting a motion of confidence in the Executive, then they could be dissolved. There were special provisions for the Brussels Regional Council, in that censure motions and elections of the Bureau had to obtain a majority in each linguistic group.

In the transitional phase, Bill 461 proposed that the Regional Councils should be composed of Senators and Deputies from each Region until the revision of the constitution. Obviously, these transitional Councils could not be dissolved (and will be automatically renewed at each national election). The bill set out the procedures to be followed by the Councils, which closely parallelled normal parliamentary procedure.

Even in the transitional period, the Regions were to have an Executive of seven members, to be elected by the Regional Council in a separate election for each seat. The Executive was to elect its own President who would then be formally appointed by the King. The Executives were to act as a *Collège*, each member being obliged to bear collective responsibility. It would be responsible to the Council, which could adopt a 'constructive motion of no-confidence' against the whole *Collège* or against one member. Decisions were to be taken by consensus (neither by majority nor unanimously), and if a member could not agree with the consensus, he had to resign. The *Collège* would assign 'portfolios' to its members, as in government. The *Collège* would have the right to initiate *Ordonnances* (the regional equivalent of a bill) in the Council and to execute them, issue regulations (the regional equivalent of an AR), draw up and execute the budget; in short, it was to have all the normal powers of a government.

Brussels was as usual a special case. Its Executive had to include two Flemish-speakers elected separately by the Flemish linguistic group in the Council. Censure motions were to be adopted by both linguistic groups if they were against the whole *Collège*, but motions against individuals only needed to obtain a majority in the linguistic group of that member. The distribution of portfolios in the Brussels Executive was subject to special rules. If political agreement was not reached, there was an automatic procedure for assigning among its members six portfolios (Finance, Economic Policy and Employment, Housing, Public Services and undertakings for the French-speaking members and Urban Planning and Local Government for the two Flemish-speaking members).

The Regions and central state were each given exclusive competences. The state remained exclusively competent for foreign affairs, defence, justice, elections, macro-economic policy, taxation, credit policy, monetary policy, national health policy, social security, infrastructure, national transport undertakings. The Region was to be exclusively competent (by way of *Ordonnances*) for planning, housing, local transport, supervision of local government, licensing of mineral exploitation, regional economic development (state intervention, investment, etc.), water policy (vital in Wallonia) and agricultural land holding policy. The Brussels Region inherited the local government powers (fire service etc.) of the council for the 'Greater Brussels' area (*Agglomération Bruxelloise*), which was to be abolished.

Naturally neither the state nor the Regions could intervene in matters devolved to the Communities under article 59 *bis* of the constitution. The residual matters in the exclusive competence of neither, which are given to the Communities, are in the concurrent competence of state and Regions. As in Germany, the Regions could have intervened in these 'concurrent' matters but *only provided that* the state does not do so.

The Regions were to have several sources of finance. They were to be accorded a global grant by the state, to be apportioned between them according to a special formula. On condition that they acted in accordance with overall national policy, the Regions might seek loans. They could have been accorded a proportion of certain taxes, but this was not fixed in detail. Under the Egmont Pact, they were to have their own tax revenues, but only after the revision of the constitution. The Communities were to be authorised to take up loans, but were otherwise, as at that time, to continue to be financed from the state.

These new structures would have introduced a new and complicated '*Hiérarchie des Normes*'. Clashes between the law (the state), decrees (Communities) and *Ordonnances* (Regions), all of which had the same legal force *within* their respective spheres of competence, were inevitable. In the transitional phase all these norms were to be subject to the control of the ordinary courts and of the *Conseil d'Etat*. In the 'definitive phase' an arbitration court was to be set up, appointed by the King for a period of eight years.

Special provisions were to be made for Brussels and its periphery (where there were already facilities for the French-speaking minorities). As we have already seen, there were special provisions giving protection to the Flemish minority in Brussels. In addition, Cultural Committees (one for each Community) were to be set up in each of the nineteen *Communes* of Brussels and in the six *Communes à Facilités*. These were to be guarantors of minority rights in each case. Voters (this of course was for the French-speaking minority) in the six peripheral *Communes* and in some other peripheral quarters were to be able to exercise the right of a 'fictive' electoral and administrative domicile in one of the nineteen (bilingual) *Communes* of the capital. This provision was hotly contested, and the Flemish parties sought to minimise its fiscal and electoral impact (e.g. the taxes to be paid back to the *Commune* of effective residence), but it was imaginative in that it gave French-speakers rights without extending the boundaries of Brussels.

The Senate was to become a Regional chamber composed of the members of the Regional Councils. The government would no longer have been responsible before the Senate, and it would not have had co-equal legislative powers with the Chamber. It was to be able, within thirty days, to propose amendments to ordinary laws, which the Chamber could disregard. It would retain full rights (two-thirds majority vote required) in respect of constitutional amendment and over laws, requiring a special majority (e.g. those under articles 59 *bis* and 107 *quater*). It would also have the power to pronounce on motions from Community Councils on the protection of ideological minorities (in cultural/educational matters).

The provisions of the Egmont Pact seem at times excessively complicated, but such complexity was required to deal with the very real complexity of the situation. Indeed, the structure of the Pact corresponds in its main outlines to the structure proposed over the previous two years by almost all the different plans published by parties, organisations and individuals. The transitional period was necessary both because the 1977 Houses were not '*Constituantes*', and because it was thought useful to 'test' the whole edifice in a preliminary period; and so that a start could at least be made, exploiting the positive climate which reigned after the 1977 elections.

The breakthrough

The Pact was an imaginative synthesis or distillation of what was desirable and possible. It failed, not because of its own weaknesses, but through a failure of political will. Much of the detailed work was rescued from the debris and, with the exception of its Brussels provisions, formed the basis for the Reform of 1980, which telescoped into one phase the two phases of the Pact.

We return to the narrative after the shock elections of December 1978, which had taken place in an atmosphere of mutual recrimination and distrust. We are not concerned with the general political aspect of the elections, which are treated elsewhere, nor the acrobatics which marked the unprecedentedly long government crisis after the election.[21] The *Volksunie* suffered a severe setback; the CVP did not obtain its expected advance, but rather a marginal decline, as did the Socialists; the FDF made very slight progress. The PSC increased its vote. Among the opposition parties, the PVV advanced, but the Walloon Liberals declined and the RW made a slight recovery. No clear trend was evident except for the *Volksunie* which withdrew into its shell. At all events no lesson emerged for the future Reform of the State. It was the collapse of the Front of the French-speaking parties of the majority (PS-PSC-FDF) — which made it possible for the problem to be solved without Brussels, making the reform acceptable to the Flemish parties — which led to the breakthrough. This Front came into existence during the crisis to ensure that no new government, whatever it was, would do as some, especially in the CVP, wanted — namely put the Community question on a back burner.[22]

This, certainly, was not the case with the Martens I government whose declaration underlined the necessity of the Reform of the State. From its appointment in April 1979 it began work on a number of fronts.[23] First, there was an intermediate phase. This involved in effect what had earlier been called a preparatory stage. It required a law (of 5 July 1979) and forty-two *Arrêtés royaux*. Those matters which were to be within the competence of the Communities were increased, by the inclusion of some *Personalisable* matters (aid to the aged, public health, some research matters) and fixed regional competences in nine areas (employment, housing, refuse disposal, water policy, energy policy and so on). At the same time a very complex system of Executives *inside* the national government was created; these were in effect Cabinet committees under a minister but with their own regionalised administrations and with budgets, to be voted by the Community and Regional Councils and legislatures, again in the form of the various Councils. These Executives, being part of the national government, were of course not responsible to the Councils. For the first time an old CVP demand was taken into account: there was only one Executive for both Community and Regional matters on the Flemish side.[24]

Secondly, after a lengthy dialogue with the *Conseil d'Etat* over the constitutionality of the fusion of the two Flemish Executives and Councils, the responsibility of the Executives,[25] and the need for a constitutional revision to enable the Communities and Regions to raise their own financial resources — most of which the government accepted — drafts of revised articles 3 *ter* (Communities), 59 *bis* (Community competences), 100 and 113 (finance) were prepared, as well as a special law fixing the competences of the regions (the nine matters of the July Law and some new matters such as tourism, powers of *Tutelle*, borrowing powers and natural resources) and of the Communities (*Personalisable* matters), and the functioning of both. Finally, an ordinary law was prepared basically on finance and conflicts of competence. These bills were tabled on 1 October 1979 in the Senate.[26]

A special Senate committee began work on 24 October 1979 and held twelve meetings before Christmas. It soon become clear that many difficulties lay in the way of success.[27] The Flemish position — that nothing should be approved in this phase which would prejudice the final and definitive phase, especially in regard to Brussels, which the CVP sought to reduce to a lower status than the other regions, was an early warning of problems. These pressures grew as the CVP Congress of 16 December 1979 approached. In fact, the special committee became increasingly paralysed, which provoked a virulent reaction from the PS by J.M. Dehousse, who in a speech at Bossu on 2 December demanded in trenchant terms '*La Regionalisation à Trois*'.[28] The crisis was brewing. The CVP Congress adopted motions which made it difficult to see how the present debate could continue.[29] It refused to 'prejudice' future stages of the reform; it rejected the notion of Brussels as an equal third region; and it demanded that the regional *Ordonnances*, unlike the decrees of Community Councils, should not have the status of laws and thus (vital for Brussels) be subject to revision by law. Brussels was to be a 'City Region' only. More significant was the tone employed. Eric van Rompuy, Chairman of the CVP youth wing and often kite-flier for Mr Tindemans, said at the Congress: 'We intend to retain a free hand in the third phase and amend the second phase accordingly.'[30]

The crisis could not now be avoided. The French-speaking parties with their united Front reacted strongly. Mr Martens presented several series of proposals, and held meetings with all those concerned in an attempt to reach a compromise. His first proposals of 7 January 1980 sought to reduce the number of articles of the constitution to be revised, to 59 *bis* and those providing for financial autonomy for Regions and Communities. The vexed status of the *Ordonnances* would thus be solved as desired by the CVP. Brussels would not have the same competences. The measures would end at the latest on 31 December 1982, and if no solution had been found, the régime of 1979 would be reintroduced. The PS, which above all wanted assurance about a rapid and definitive (hence the issue about the 'life' of the proposal) regionalisation, did not reject these proposals; neither, at this stage, did the FDF.[31]

On 9 January, a mini-package, with almost no constitutional revision in the immediate short term, was put forward.[32] The PS accepted to obtain regionalisation at least now. After seeking Francophone solidarity, the FDF did not accept, and its ministers were forced out of the government. A new agreement on a bipartite PS/SP-CVP/PSC Cabinet was reached on 18 January on the basis of the 'mini-package'.[33] The FDF had broken (as the PSC-PS had) the Francophone Front. André Cools argued that the FDF had entered a trap sprung by the CVP in seeking too many guarantees which would be of little use. The political fact was there. The 'significant majority' basis for the government fell and with it not only its two-thirds majority, but also the need to include Brussels in any solution. With hindsight, it is possible to see that the way was now open for a solution.

The new bills were extremely modest. Regional authorities were not placed on the same level as the Communities. The *Personalisable* matters would not be included. The Regions and Communities would not have their own tax resources and Brussels would have a secondary status. It seemed a small advance. Even this provoked CVP opposition and on 2 April 1980 one article failed to obtain the two-thirds majority in the Senate due to CVP opposition (117 *ter*), which caused the fall of the Martens II government.[34]

Meanwhile, the Committee of twenty-eight, with representatives of all parties under the co-presidency of Mr Blankaert (CVP) and Mr Brouhon (PS), had been set up on 4 February 1980 to draft proposals for the definitive Reform of the State,[35] and was making progress. It therefore became possible to form a 'tripartite' government — Martens III — on 7 May 1980 with the CVP/PSC-

PS/SP-PVV/PRL. Ironically, while the CVP revolt had aimed at slowing down reform, all it had done was spectacularly to accelerate it. There was now movement, and the stage was set.

The new government returned to the more ambitious 1979 formula of Martens I, a solution not so far from the spirit of the Egmont Pact, except with regard to Brussels. This involved:[36]

(*a*) Revision of a series of articles of the constitution, 3 *ter* and 59 *bis* to add, *Personalisable* matters; 28, giving the decrees of the Communities and Regions equal status with laws; 107 *ter* setting up the arbitration court; 110, 111, 113 on finance and 108 on the *Tutelle* of Provinces and Communes which is given to the Communities and the Regions. The new 59 *bis* also authorised the fusion of the Flemish Community and Region into one body.

(*b*) A Special Law, setting out the organisation, functioning and competences of the Communities and Regions.

(*c*) An ordinary law on finance matters and the settlement of conflicts.

It was agreed that the constitutional revision was a precondition of phases (*b*) and (*c*) as the earlier opinion of the *Conseil d'Etat* had indicated. These amendments to the constitution passed rapidly and with relatively little difficulty, the only real opposition coming from the FDF, VU and some CVP and Brussels Socialists. On 21 May 1980 the proposals were tabled and all were passed by 28 July that year and some as early as July 4.

Parallel to these discussions the two bills were being examined. The government rejected the *Conseil d'Etat*'s opinion that the omission of Brussels made the law unconstitutional[37] as an incorrect application of article 107 *quater*; the government's view was that a progressive solution, as intended, was not opposed to the sense of the constitution. With some relatively minor amendments (the only important one relating to the creation of 'Title 4' in the Special Law on co-operation between the Communities) the bills passed Parliament as follows:[38]

	Senate		C.R.	
	vote	*date*	*vote*	*date*
Bill 434 (Special Law)	137:22:0	27 July	156:19:5	5 Aug.
Bill 435 (Ordinary Law)	132:23:2	7 Aug.	152:21:2	3 Aug.

Analysis of the new structure

The new structure of the Belgian state involved a central government, Communities (Flemish and French), Regions (Flemish and Walloon), Provinces and *Communes*. The Flemish Community and

Region have common institutions or, put another way, the Flemish Council and Executive exercise the powers of both the Flemish Community and the Region. The German-speaking Region has a Council, with smaller powers than the other Communities, but in 1983 a revision of article 59 *bis* is under way to equalise the position. Brussels has for the moment only those 'provisional' arrangements made under the earlier arrangements which anticipated regionalisation. The new institutions, resulting from the Reform of the State, are:[39]

THE COMMUNITIES

Powers

The Communities are competent to deal with:

Cultural matters, principally defined in article 59 *bis* of the constitution as amplified by article 4 of the Special Law:
— Language and use of languages;
— Culture, museums, scientific institutes, the library service;
— Radio and television;
— Youth policy, leisure, sport, tourism;
— Adult education, training in the arts, retraining of workers;
— Scientific research, applied scientific policy.

The so-called *Personalisable* matters (article 5 of the Special Law):
— *Health Policy*. Health care, outside hospitals and institutions, preventive medicine, but excluding matters of health insurance, general national norms and financing of such policies.
— *Welfare policy*. Family policy, protection of children, welfare and reception of immigrants, handicapped persons, protection of young persons, policy for the aged, probation service. All these matters exclude the fixing of basic national norms (e.g. pensions and family allowances).

International Co-operation. In the fields defined as Community competences (cultural and *Personalisable* matters), it is the Communities through their Executives and Councils which conclude treaties and agreements. Therefore such international agreements are ratified by the Community Councils and not by the national Parliament (article 16 of the Special Law).

Structure

The legislature in the Communities is the Community Council. The Community Councils are composed at present of the Deputies and elected Senators of, respectively, the Dutch- and French-language groups. Included, of course, are Deputies and Senators elected in Brussels. At present this means that the Flemish Council has 221 members and the French Council 172.

This gives quite different political compositions of the two Councils, as the adjoining table shows. In the Flemish Council, there is clearly a built-in right of centre CVP + PVV and perhaps VU) majority, even with the heavy CVP defeat in 1981. In the Council of the Francophone Community there is a '*Majorité de Progrès*' seventy-three seats out of 138 in 1981) made up of the PS, FDF-RW, *Ecolo* and Communists (the FDF-RW, *Ecolo* and Communist members have formed a twenty-strong group), just as there was in 1978. With the greater autonomy of the Councils and their independence of the national government, this 'progressive majority' gained in value and enabled a Socialist, Irène Petry, to be elected as President.

	Flemish Council		French Council	
	1978	*1981**	*1978*	*1981**
CVP/PSC	108	65	47	26
PS/SP	47	39	64	53
PRL/PVV	39	42	23†	37
VU	25	30	–	–
FDF	–	–	20	10‡
RW	–	–	10	2‡
PCB/BKP	1	–	5	3‡
UDRT	–	1	1	2
Ecolo	–	3	0	5‡
Vlaams blok	1	1	–	–

*1981 figures do not include Provincial or Co-opted Senators.
† Including one PVV.
‡ The FDF/RW-PCB-*Ecolo* formed a parliamentary group of twenty members.

As the Special Law provides, the Councils are organised much like the national Parliament, with their own rules of procedure, a *bureau* and a number of committees. The French Council has set up seven fifteen-member committees. The main ones are General Policy, Radio and TV, and Cultural Co-operation, both international and internal. The Flemish Council (which of course also covers regionalised matters) has set up fourteen committees with between fifteen and twenty-three members. Only some of these deal with 'Community matters', such as those on language policy and radio policy, whereas the Social Policy committee deals with both kinds of matters.

The Communities legislate by decree, which has the same status as a law. The right of initiative belongs both to Council members and to the Executives. The Executives promulgate the decrees, and there is *no* intervention by the national government. The Councils meet as of right in October each year for a session lasting at least fourteen days, but they may be called into special session by their Executive. They have the same right to conduct investigations, demand the presence of the Executive and put questions to it as does the national Parliament. The Executive may participate in the work of the Councils and is heard at its own request.

The present arrangement for the composition of the Councils is provisional in that once the Senate has been formed as provided for in the government declaration of Martens III of May 1980 (the articles of the constitution relating to the Senate may also be revised by the 1981 Parliament), the Councils should only consist of directly-elected Senators from each language group. The Senate would consist of 212 members, elected for a fixed term of four years and *not* subject to dissolution. The equal powers of the Senate in 'national' matters would be reviewed. This was supposed to be implemented by 1983, but has not been.

The executive power is vested in Community Executives. There is a French Community Executive with three members and a Flemish Executive (for both Community and Regional matters) with nine members. These Executives were initially 'inside' the national government, but left it at the first election after the entry into force of the Special Law. This occurred, more rapidly than expected, in November 1981. A second transitional arrangement, valid for one legislature only, was one important element in the Martens III compromise (important for the PRL and the SP), namely that the Executives are composed in proportion to council membership. Thereafter they will be composed by normal majority vote. They are elected by the Councils from among their members. The present system gives a Flemish Executive with four CVP, two PVV, two SP and one VU, with therefore a clear right-of-centre majority. On the French Executive there are two PS and one PSC with Mr Moureaux (PS) as President.

The Executives are organised on the Cabinet model. One member of each must come from Brussels. The Presidents of the Executives are elected by its members in a secret ballot if no consensus is agreed. Members are given portfolios and decisions are taken as a college, by consensus. Its role is to prepare proposals and the draft budget, to carry out the decrees of the Council and to represent the Community in relations with other authorities. They are associated with international negotiations covering their area of competence. On bills and ARs concerning them, the Executives must be consulted. The Executives can take decisions with direct legal effect to carry out decrees and policy generally. Each Executive will have its own administration.

Finance

Both Communities and Regions may be financed from their own tax revenues (charges, license fees etc.), from central grants and by borrowing. This financial system entered into force on 1 January 1982. The central government makes grants related to matters devolved to the Regions under article 107 *quater*, these therefore belong to the Walloon Region and the Flemish Community (which may use any revenue for either purpose). A proportion of central charges and taxes, such as television and radio licenses, also goes to the Communities and Regions.

The German Community, recognised in article 3 *ter* (new) of the constitution, has always had an inferior status. Under a law of 1973, a directly-elected Council of twenty-five members (elected at the same time as national elections) was set up with no Executive.[40] The Council can make regulations in relation to some of the cultural matters set out in article 59 *bis* of the constitution, which are carried out by national ministers, but it can not deal with *Personalisable* matters. It must be asked (with a time limit of sixty days) for its opinion on a number of matters — other matters in the field of education, culture and use of language. Ministers take part in the work of the Council. It is financed by a central grant. A revision of article 59 *bis* is in train to upgrade it to a full Community level with decree power and an Executive competent over the same matters as the other Communities. At the last two elections the PSC was over-taken as the largest party (with only eight seats against nine for the local *Partei der deutschsprächige Belgier* (PDB).

THE REGIONS

Powers

The powers of the Regions are potentially very wide, and much more important than those of the Communities, covering a large range of matters in the social and economic fields. These include:

— *Planning matters*: urban renewal, industrial location;
— *Environment policy*: protection of the environment, protection against dangerous materials, protection of the countryside, forestry policy, hunting and fishing licenses, polders, land-drainage;

— *Housing policy*: hygiene and safety of housing;
— *Water policy*: water provision, dams, cleaning of waste water;
— *Economic policy*: regional planning, exploitation of natural resources, search for investors, aid for industry, aid to tourism, aid to agriculture, except prices and incomes policy;
— *Energy policy*: provision of gas and electricity, improvement of coal mines, new energy sources (the Regions are not competent for nuclear energy or matters such as the rational use of energy, which require national norms);
— *Employment policy*: employment exchanges, work schemes, aid for retraining.
— *Supervision of the Provinces and Local Authorities*

The Executives must be consulted by the national government and consult with each other on a range of matters which involve both regions or are of national and regional interest, such as scientific research policy, national energy policy. The Regions can create the infrastructure and even enterprises with legal personality in order to carry out their functions.

Organisation

The Regional councils at present consist of the Deputies and Senators, as follows:
— *Flemish Region*: as for the Community Council (it is a single body). However, Deputies and Senators elected in Brussels may not vote on 'Regional' matters.
— *Walloon Region*: the Deputies and Senators elected in the Provinces of Hainaut, Liège, Luxembourg, Namur and those elected in Nivelles. In the case of Senators, the Councils will consist of Senators directly elected in each Region, who together compose the Senate, and are the same Senators as will form the Community Councils.

After the 1981 elections, the composition of the Councils was as follows (the Flemish Council is the same as the Community Council):

Walloon Regional Council (1981)

PS	48
RW	2
Ecolo	3
PCB	3
PSC	22
PRL	28
	106

As in the Walloon Community Council, there is a '*Majorité de Progrès*' (fifty-six seats), which enabled the election of a Socialist, André Cools, as President and ensured that the Socialists held three of the six seats in the Executive.

The Regional Councils function in the same way as the Community Councils; they also legislate by Decree.

The Walloon Executive is elected in the same way as the Community Executives. It has six members. At the time of writing the membership according to party is PS 3, PRL 2 and PSC 1. Because of the fact that the PSC and PRL, with three members between them, are in power at the national level, there was a month-long blockage in early 1982 over the presidency, It was provisionally exercised until the autumn of 1982 by M. Damseaux (PRL) and then by J.M. Dehousse (PS). The consensus rule will also limit the possibility for the Socialists, in opposition nationally since early 1982, to dynamise the Executive in both a progressive and an autonomist direction, at least until the next election. The Brussels member of the Flemish Executive is excluded from decisions on Regional matters.

Finance

The sources of Regional finance are the same as those for the Communities.

Conflicts

An arbitration court is to be set up to handle disputes, with article 107 *ter* of the constitution. In the original government bill (these provisions were later withdrawn), it was to be composed of one half judges and one half political appointees. A new bill is now before Parliament. The arbitration court is not a normal court and will only handle conflicts between decrees and laws. In order to avoid conflicts, a conciliation committee (consisting of the prime minister and Presidents of the Executives, three other national ministers and three other Executive members) has been set up. This committee is to seek solutions, by consensus, to conflicts arising from damage which draft bills, decrees, *Arrêtés royaux* or Executive decisions could do to the interests of the national government or the Communities and Regions. The *Conseil d'Etat* is also given certain advisory functions (which are in some cases obligatory), and where it finds that a draft goes beyond national, Regional or Community competence, the matter is referred to the conciliation committee.

The Walloon Region and French Community can fuse like the Flemish Council, if both Councils so decide by a two-thirds majority of the votes cast. The territory of the Flemish Region covers

Antwerp, Limburg, East and West Flanders, Louvain and Halle-Vilvoorde in Brabant. The Walloon Region covers the Provinces of Hainaut, Liège, Luxembourg, Namur and Nivelles in Brabant.

Brussels remains 'on ice'. The special and ordinary laws of 1980 do not apply.[41] In Brussels, French-speaking cultural, educational and health facilities are regulated by French Community or national legislation and Flemish institutions by Flemish Community or national legislation. For some regional matters there is, in accordance with 1974, 1977 and 1979 laws, a 'preparatory' regionalisation and various *Arrêtés royaux* (the latest of June 1980) which created an Executive *within* the national government — called the *Comité Ministeriel pour la Région Bruxelloise*, but there is no legislative body and at present, this Executive (CVP/PSC-PRL/PVV) is rather unrepresentative of the capital's electorate.

These reforms are in their infancy: time alone will tell whether they will operate well. Certainly views remain divided. At random two viewpoints taken from the same recent edition of *Le Soir* illustrate this. Jean Gol, Vice Premier and Liberal leader, stated: 'The Reform of 1980 may have given greater autonomy to the Regions, but it has also created greater complications and blockages. [. . . .] We have to ensure that the blockages and countervailing powers created by the Reform are avoided.' The reader is reminded that the PRL voted for these Reforms. On the other side, the *Bureau* of the RW stated: 'Wallonia still has no autonomous political existence, nor a proper Parliament or Government.'[42] 1983 has seen increased conflict over competences and finance with pressures from *both* sides for even more regionalisation.

PROVINCES AND LOCAL AUTHORITIES

The Provinces

The division of the Community into Provinces is set out in article 1 of the constitution, which authorises — by law — more Provinces to be created or may exclude certain areas from the division into Provinces and place them directly under the control of government. Such a law must be passed by a majority in *both* language groups and a two-thirds majority overall in both chambers. The constitutional division into Provinces is shown in the accompanying table.[43] There are thus four Flemish (F) and four Walloon (W) Provinces plus Brabant, which includes Brussels. The Provinces correspond to the historical structure of the Low Countries, but today have considerably less importance. The basic organisation and powers of the Provinces are laid down in the original Provincial Law (*Loi provinciale*) of 1836, which was considerably modified in 1975, and in various other laws. The Provinces have a provincial Council, its size depending on population. It is elected for four years, but may be dissolved with the Parliament, which in practice is now always done. The basic electoral unit is the *Canton*, a sub-division of the *Arrondissement*. The electoral system is as for the Chamber and Senate, with *Apparentement* being allowed between cantonal lists within the same *Arrondissement*.

PROVINCE (F = Flemish; W = Walloon)	POPULATION (1.1.1979)	Seats in Provincial Council
Brabant	2,216,938	90
Antwerp (F)	1,571,023	90
Hainaut (W)	1,313,204	90
East Flanders (F)	1,328,070	90
West Flanders (F)	1,076,326	90
Liège (W)	1,007,490	90
Limburg (F)	704,741	70
Namur (W)	402,488	60
Luxembourg (W)	221,374	50

The Executive of the Province is, as we shall see, relatively unimportant, since much of the executive power is in the hands of the Governor appointed by the Crown; it can also be reserved for the central government. This *Députation Permanente* (permanent committee) is elected by the Provincial Council for four years and may not be censured by the Provincial Council. Each *Députation* has six members. Each Province has a Governor, who presides over the *Députation* and can vote. In Brabant he is assisted by a Vice Governor, responsible for Brussels. The composition of the *Députations* is usually the result of inter-party negotiations in the days following the elections, which often means that no clear trend is visible as to the 'national majority'; this may lead to various combinations in different provinces. In some provinces one party traditionally has an absolute majority or has been very close to it: Luxembourg (PSC), though it fell well below in 1981; Liège (PS), (which came close to a majority with the Communists); Antwerp (CVP); Limburg (CVP), Hainaut (PS). These majorities are mostly very precarious (the CVP majorities were lost in 1981). Brabant and Namur are the most open, with no dominant party. In 1978 the CVP alone formed the *Députation* in West Flanders and Limburg; Brabant, Luxembourg and Hainaut saw alliances of the three national parties — Socialists, Christians and Liberals. Other Provinces saw PSC/CVP — PS/SP *Députations*. In 1981 even Socialist and Liberal *Députations* were found in some Provinces.[44]

The Provincial Council does not hold a very long annual session, meeting for a period, normally of fifteen days, which can be extended to a maximum of four weeks with the authorisation of the Governor, either from 1 July or 1 October each year. The Crown or the Governor may, for a specific agenda, call an extraordinary session. The main tasks of the Council are to elect the *Députation*, approve the Provincial budget, propose members of the provincial courts of appeal, vote expenditures for roads and hydraulic construction and for assistance to local authorities, and run provincial commercial activities and infrastructure projects. It must also give its opinion on local authority boundary changes within the Provinces and may deliberate on 'all matters of concern to the Provinces'.

The *Députation* prepares decisions when it is not in session. It authorises payment of expenditure, but must obtain the approval of the Audit Court, except for staff salaries and similar expenditure. The *Députation* presents an annual report and budget, as well as any other proposals it considers necessary for the Council's session. It may issue regulations (*Arrêtés provinciaux*) and fix penalties for their breach.

Provincial staff have increased from 16,415 in 1975 to 20,429 in 1979. Expenditure rose from 16,402 million FB in 1975 to 28,885 million FB in 1978, of which some 29 per cent was covered by Provincial taxation. The main items were further education (50 per cent), aid to commerce (10 per cent) and roads (9 per cent).

The independence of the Provinces is doubly limited. The Governor, a national appointment, presides over the *Députation* and prepares its work, and normally it is he, not the *Députation*, that carries out Provincial decisions and regulations. The *Députation* may appeal, but only to the central government. The Governor can also suspend a decision of the *Députation* by referring it to the King (i.e. the government), who has ten days to confirm the suspension. The Governor is also responsible for maintaining law and order in the Province. *Vis-à-vis* the Provincial Council too, the King and the Governor have far-reaching powers to disallow decisions which are *ultra vires* or affect the general interest. As well as this, decisions on the Budget, on the creation of provincial enterprises and on construction plans costing over 50,000 FB, can be referred to the King, who has forty days to decide whether to annul them or not by *Arrêté royal*. As a result, not only are the areas of its competence limited, but its actions are closely supervised by the central powers of *Tutelle* over the local authorities. It was intended under the Egmont-Stuyvenberg Pact that the Provincial level of government should be abolished, but no action has yet been taken on this. Thus there is a degree of over-government at the present time, which leads to excessive bureaucracy and frustration for the citizen.[45]

Local government (Communes)

The constitution (article 108) provides for local government on the
basis of *Communes*. It establishes as a principle the greatest possible
decentralisation; however, as with the Provinces, controls on the
activities of the *Communes* tend to reduce the real effect of this
provision. It otherwise simply provides for the direct election of
members of the Councils and for the fixing of their competences by
law. The constitution provides for the possibility of federations of
Communes being created, as well as *Agglomérations* in larger cities.
Little use has been made of these provisions, which were introduced
in 1970. *Agglomérations* have only been set up in Brussels, and five
Fédérations were created in the area near Brussels which were later
dissolved.[46] In general the need to provide for co-operation over a
wider area has been met — with mixed results, especially in rural
areas by amalgamation of smaller *Communes*. In 1920 there were
2,638 *Communes* in Belgium (Hainaut 444, Brabant 346, Liège 344,
Luxembourg 231). By 1958, at 2,359, the figure had barely changed.
But by 1975 a major reform had been introduced just before the
elections of 1976, leaving a mere 596 *Communes*. Luxembourg
Province was reduced from 329 very small *Communes* to forty-four
and Namur too fell to forty-four. Proportionally the smallest
changes were in the province of Antwerp from 144 to seventy-seven.
There is now only one *Commune* with less than 500 inhabitants and
only twenty-three with under 3,000 inhabitants. The largest number
are in the 5,000–15,000 range (306 *Communes*). There are sixty
Communes with between 25,000 and 50,000 inhabitants, twenty-one
with 50,000–100,000 inhabitants, and only eight with over 100,000
inhabitants. Brussels is, it should be remembered, composed of
nineteen *Communes*, one of which is also called Brussels (the city
centre).[47]

The organisation and powers of the *Communes* are laid down in
the *Loi Communale* as last modified in 1975.[48] The law is very
detailed, leaving the *Communes* little room for manoeuvre. The
minimum size of a Communal Council is seven members and the
maximum is fifty-five for *Communes* with over 300,000 inhabitants.
Most Communal Councils have between fifteen and twenty-five
members, except in the largest towns and in Brussels where the
average is about 35–40. In contrast to British local government,
Belgian *Communes* all have an executive, composed of the mayor
and the *Collège des Echevins* (lit. sheriffs). The mayor is appointed
by the King from among the Council members. With the approval
of the *Députation permanente* of the Province, the mayor may
be appointed from outside the Council. Originally these provisions
were intended to weaken the democratic element in local govern-

ment, making the mayor, in part at least, an agent of the central government under whose administrative supervision he is placed. But in modern times the appointment of mayors is a formality, ratifying politically negotiated arrangements. The problem of the appointment of M. Happart in the Fourons in 1983 — opposed by all Flemish parties — has shown that this is not always so. The *Echevins* are elected by the Council for a six-year term by absolute majority, *not* by proportional representation. The Council itself is elected for six years by proportional representation. The *Collège des Echevins* is thus, like the Cabinet at the national level, the emanation of the council majority only, unlike systems in countries with a *Magistrat* system, it is elected by proportional representation. This often requires pre- and post-electoral negotiations to create coalitions. These negotiations are necessary where no party has an absolute majority. At the 1976 elections, for *Communes* of over 50,000 inhabitants (twenty-nine in all) there were four CVP absolute majorities (Kortrijk, Hasselt, Genk, Roulers); three PS (Charleroi, La Louvière, Seraing); and two FDF (Schaerbeek and Etterbeek). Coalitions are often made on a purely local basis. There are, for example, many between opposition and government parties and there were PS-FDF or PS-PW coalitions well before these parties entered government together at the national level.[49]

The same general tendencies could be observed in the October 1982 Communal elections. Contrary to the wishes of the Socialist parties and the conventional wisdom of many observers, these elections retained a very considerable local content. In general one can say that the electorate returned to office those majorities — of whatever colour — that had been effective over the previous six years. Results varied widely over the whole country. Attempts by the PS/SP opposition to turn the elections into a plebiscite on the performance of the one-year-old CVP/PSC-PVV/PRL government were not successful. Certainly, in Flanders the CVP lost many absolute majorities, especially in Limburg, but both the CVP and the PSC recovered a good deal of the ground lost in the 1981 parliamentary elections. The Liberals could not hold all their 1981 gains. For their part, the PS only gained about 1.5 per cent on their 1981 result and lost by comparison with their 1976 Communal election results; in Brussels they suffered disastrous reverses. The only clear national lessons were the rough confirmation of the 1981 results and the confirmation of the breakthrough by the Ecologists, who entered the coalition in Liège. Almost everywhere, both in Flanders and Wallonia, where it was attempted, the concept of progressive alliances produced at best inconclusive results. Even in Liège, the Progressive Walloon list obtained a significantly smaller share of the vote than the PS and RW lists had done in 1976. It is clear that much of the RW electorate went over the PRL, in both the Provinces of Liège and Hainaut.

The Council is in a sense the 'legislature'. It must meet from time to time to study proposals from the *Collège*. It votes (in public) on the budget, loans, Communal taxes, by-laws which create penalties; urban sector plans (land use plans) and general rules relating to the Communal police (subject to general nationally fixed rules).

The *Collège des Echevins* usually divides up portfolios (e.g. Education and Culture; Social Affairs; Finance; Police matters; *'Etat Civil'* [registration of population, issue of identity cards, etc.]) among its members. The *Collège* is the administration. It prepares proposals for the Council and carries out the Council's decisions. It supervises the Communal administration, services and establishments. It administers the schools in the *Commune*. It has an important role in welfare administration; it issues permits for building (planning permission), entertainment licenses and the like; it is responsible for woods, forests and local roads in its area; and the mayor is also generally responsible for public order, being able, in the event of civil disturbance, to issue temporary Orders (forbidding assembly, etc.) and to requisition the gendarmerie or the army to assist him.

The *Commune* must have certain officials: a secretary, a *Receveur* (responsible for financial administration) and a police commissioner. The last of these is appointed by the King, but his deputy commissioners are appointed by the Council. Other officials and staff may be appointed by the Council.

Communal expenditure is financed from its share in the *Fonds des Communes*; direct state and Provincial aid, additional 'Communal' levies or other taxes (*centimes additionels*) and the product of certain charges and taxes (dog and vehicle licenses). Over the period 1974–8, Communal finances evolved as follows. Expenditure in 1974 was 96,500 million BF, of which almost 28 per cent was financed by borrowing, only 29 per cent by taxes, and 30 per cent by grants from the state or Province. Education and social services were (in that order) the largest items, alone taking almost 50 per cent of the budgets. In 1978 expenditure had risen to 177,068 million BF, of which 21.5 per cent was covered by taxes and 21.3 per cent by grants, whereas 34 per cent was covered by borrowing. The remainder in each case coming from charges and other income. Education and social services again led and took 50 per cent of total expenditure. Social expenditure had grown faster than the overall total, having more than doubled. Total Communal personnel rose from 117,027 in 1972 (police 14,085; CPAS [social services personnel] 32,202; *Inter-Communales* 13,824) to 149,148 in 1978 (police 14,878; CPAS 48,096; *Inter-Communales* 14,876).[50]

The *Communes* are, like the Provinces, subject to severe *Tutelle*. Many decisions require *prior* approval by the central authority now the Community or the Region or, for smaller matters, by the *Députation* of the Province (e.g. loans, by-laws, sector plans and even recruitment). Any matter — either decisions of the Council or the *Collège* — is suspended for up to forty days for annulment.

Local government in Belgium now faces something of a crisis. Not only are its already limited powers in the process of being further undermined by the collective inroads of central government and the new Communities and Regions, with which they co-exist uneasily; but they face very severe financial and even cash-flow problems, and increasing criticism, especially in the case of the Provinces and the *Agglomérations*, that they are a wasteful extra tier of government.

NOTES

1. See Mast, op. cit., 56–64.
2. See A.R. Zolberg, 'Les origines du clivage communautaire en Belgique', *Recherches Sociologiques*, VII, 2, 1976, 150–70, and M. Ruys, *De Vlamingen, een Volk in Beweging, en Natie in wording*, Tielt 1972. For the parties see also Rowies, *Les Partis politiques en Belgique*, CRISP 1977, no. 10.
3. See M.P. Heeremans, *Bref historique des tentatives de la Réforme de l'état en Belgique, Courrier Hebdomadaire du* CRISP (hereafter 'CH') 135, 12 Jan. 1962.
4. For analysis of these elections and results see N. Delruelle, R. Evalenko and W. Fraeys, *Le comportement des electeurs belges (1965 et 1968)*, Editions de l'Institut de Sociologie de l'ULB, 1970.
5. For later election results, see Dossiers du CRISP (no. 10) *Les Partis politiques en Belgique.*
6. For background, see J. Grootjans, *La Révision de la Constitution: l'évolution des idées et des textes jusqu'en juillet 1970*, CH, 518 and 519, 1971.
7. A. Alen and P. Van Speybroeck, 'La Réforme de l'état belge de 1974 jusqu'au Pacte d'Egmont', CEPESS 1977 (hereafter cited as 'CEPESS'), 7–9.
8. CEPESS, 23–28. Also *L'évolution du R.W. d'avril 1974 à mai 1977*, CH, 736, 1978, 12–18.
9. For the content of these schemes see CEPESS, 48–66.
10. For the position of the parties before the Dialogue Communautaire, see CEPESS, 68–110.
11. CEPESS, 111–24.
12. CH, 783/794, 1977, p. 3.
13. CEPESS, 12.
14. CEPESS, 144 and 154.

15. See CH, 857/8, 7 and 8.
16. See text of the Pact, preamble quoted in CEPESS, 289.
17. On the CVP objections see *Le Soir*, 7 Oct. 1978, 1 and 2.
18. Statements by André Cools and Mme Spaak in the RTB discussion programme 'Faire le Point' on 8 Oct. 1978.
19. Editorial by André Cools in *Le Peuple*, 7 Oct. 1978.
20. For full text of the Pact, see CEPESS, 289 and 299. For a description of the Egmont and Stuyvenberg Agreements and for an analysis of Bill 461, see *Les nouvelles Institutions de la Belgique*, CRISP 1978.
21. For full election results, see CH, 826–7, 'Les élection législatives du 17 décembre 1978', 4, 18 and 32.
22. Pact signed 14 Nov. 1978, see CH 874–5, 'La Réforme de l'Etat' (II)', 51, 52 and 53.
23. For an explanation in detail of these phases see CH 857–8, 'La Réforme de l'Etat: phase immédiate et phase transitoire', 9–11.
24. For the preparations and legislation on the 'immediate' phase, see CH 857–8, 12–24.
25. Ibid., 25–33.
26. Ibid., 34–7, for analysis of these texts.
27. CH 874–5, 'La Réforme de l'Etat' (II), 6–21.
28. Cited in ibid., 21.
29. Ibid., 22–5.
30. Cited in ibid., 874–5, 25.
31. For the crisis, see ibid., 26–41.
32. Ibid., 27
33. Ibid., 47–9 and annexe 6.
34. For parliamentary consideration and fall of Martens II, see CH 893–4, 'La Réforme de l'Etat' (III), 8–14 and 16–19.
35. Ibid., 14 and 15.
36. Ibid., 19–23.
37. Ibid., 24
38. Ibid., 26–42, for details of parliamentary discussions.
39. The analysis which follows is taken from Mast, op. cit., 236–51 (Councils — organisation and powers) and 380–4 (Executives); 'Loi Spéciale du 8 août 1980 relative à la réforme des Institutions', *Moniteur Belge*,
15 Aug. 1980; 'Loi ordinaire du 9 août 1980 relative à la réforme des Institutions', *Moniteur Belge*, 15 Aug. 1980 and CH 893–7, 21–3 and 36–9.
40. Mast, op. cit., 389–92, and *Unser Rat*, Rat der Deutschen Kulturgemeinschaft, 1978.
41. On Brussels see Mast, op. cit., 385–8.
42. *Le Soir*, 30 and 31 January 1981, 2.
43. *Annuaire statistique* (1979), 14–15, and 'Loi Provinciale' article 1 *bis*, published in *Codes*, Van In, Lier, 1977.
44. Le Soir, 9 Nov. 1981.
45. See Section of the Pact entitled 'Au niveau de la Sous-Region', but statement by Premier Martens in 1980, Senate Doc. 434 (1979–80), no. 2.

46. Dossiers du CRISP, 11, 7.
47. *Annuaire Statistique*, 5–7.
48. Published in *Codes*, Van In, Lier, 1977, 172–253.
49. Dossiers du CRISP, no. 10, 'La Décision politique en Belgique', 15.
50. Details of expenditure from *Annuaire Statistique*, 388–99.

5

THE POLITICAL PARTIES AND THE PARTY SYSTEM

The political parties are, as we have seen throughout this book, central actors in the political process. We shall here be concerned less with a dynamic analysis of their role, which this book continuously illustrates, than with an examination of the parties themselves — their history and origins, their structure and membership (which is very complex in all Belgian parties), their ideology and programmes. We shall then look at the interaction between the parties, which constitutes the party system. Finally, we shall look at the increasingly vocal criticisms of the political parties which have emerged over the last few years.

Any analytical structure of the Belgian parties inevitably suffers from the drawback that the reality of the Belgian situation today, as distinct from that before 1945, requires analysis in two dimensions simultaneously: the ideological and the regional. Indeed, one can talk about a national party system and three regional sub-systems (Flanders, Wallonia and Brussels), but at the same time one can talk about an ideological dimension of the classic left-right character. The method chosen here is but one of several possible analytical frameworks. The parties will be placed like pieces on a chess board and examined individually. Then their interaction in the national political system and the regional sub-systems will be examined. So we shall first look at the traditional 'political families' which dominated Belgian politics until the 1960s, with their respective regional components. Then we shall look at the *fédéraliste* Community parties and finally at the 'new' parties, such as the UDRT and the Ecologists.

The Christian Social 'family' *(CVP/PSC)*

The CVP/PSC family (the Catholic Party — CP), dominant in Flanders, is the largest *famille politique* in the country, but not the oldest. The Mechelen Catholic Congresses of 1863, 1864 and 1867 gave the philosophical impulses for the organisation of the Catholic Party.[1] Up until 1884, Catholic political forces were relatively disorganised and localised, obtaining support from such diverse organisations as the Antwerp Meeting Party, but essentially based in local *Unions Conservatrices et Constitutionelles*, the first of which was founded in Ghent in 1852, to be followed by Leuven (1854), Antwerp and Brussels (1858). Those were in fact little more than election committees. In 1864, they were federated into the *Fédération Nationale des Unions Constitutionelles et Conservatrices*. A parallel development was the establishment of *Cercles Catholiques* with a more spiritual and pastoral aim (Bruges, 1853). By 1868, there were some fifty *cercles*, which joined up in the *Union des Cercles Catholiques*, which increasingly concerned itself with political issues. These bodies represented the most conservative Catholic tendencies.[2]

On the other hand, bodies such as the Society of St Vincent de Paul (1845) and the *Fédération des Sociétés Ouvrières Catholiques* (1867), influenced later by the papal encyclical *Rerum Novarum*, formed the Christian Democratic tendency which also was important in the *Union Nationale du Redressement des Griefs*; this organised 'social congresses' in Liège in 1886, 1887 and 1890, which led to the foundation of the *Ligue Démocratique Belge* in 1891, precursor of the *Mouvement Ouvrier Chrétien* (MOC).

The Union des Cercles Catholiques and the *Fédération des Unions Constitutionelles et Conservatoires* merged in 1864 and were joined in 1888 by most of the Christian Democratic tendency, forming the Catholic Party under the leadership of Beernaert as chairman. Some of the Christian Democrats formed the *Parti Populaire Chrétien* under Daens, but this group never obtained more than two seats (Catholics averaged about ninety-six seats) and 3 per cent of the vote. From then until 1919, when universal suffrage was introduced (despite PR from 1899), the Catholic Party retained an absolute majority in both Chambers of the Legislature. In 1919, its share of the vote fell to 38.8 per cent and remained relatively constant down to the Second World War, with its high point of 41.3 per cent in 1921 and low point of 28.8 per cent in the unique election of 1936, recovering to 32.8 per cent in 1939. Apart from the years 1925–9 and 1936–9, it was the largest group in Parliament and always formed part of the varying coalitions: CP, Socialists and Liberals (1919–21; 1926–7; 1935–9), CP-Socialist (1925–6; 1939) and CP-Liberal (1921–5; 1927, 1935, 1939) and one Catholic minority government in 1925 which lasted one week.

The pressures of universal suffrage and the growth of the CSC forced a reform in the old Catholic Party. It had to recognise more clearly that it was a pluralistic party appealing to diverse social groups. Thus, in 1921, the old Catholic Party was reorganised as the *Union Catholique Belge*, a federation of four 'Standen' (lit. estates): the *Associations Constitutionelles* (the political 'Stand'), the *Boerenbond* (farmers); the *Ligue Nationale des Travailleurs*, and the Catholic middle-class organisation, the *Fédération des Classes*

Moyennes. In 1936, the Party was renamed the *Bloc Catholique* and two distinct wings, the Flemish *Katholiek Vlaamse Volkspartij* and the Walloon *Parti Catholique Social* (PCS), appeared. After the Second World War, the *Standen* system was abolished in favour of a 'classless' approach based on '*Personalisme chrétien*'. As before, the unitary structure was tempered by the recognition of two wings, which grew in autonomy after 1965. It was over the Leuven University affair (when the CVP wanted to transfer the university out of Flemish territory) in 1968 that the rupture (or so-called '*distancement*') came about. Since then two distinct parties, the *Parti Social Chrétien* (PSC) and *Christelijke Volkspartij* (CVP), have come into being, maintaining only minimum mutual co-ordination. With time, their positions on both 'Community' and economic and social issues have tended to diverge, especially with the greater and more radical trade union influence in the PSC.[2]

The Parti Social Chrétien (PSC)

The PSC only operates in Wallonia, the *Arrondissement* of Nivelles in Brabant and in Brussels, where it now competes with CVP lists. It had 38,327 members in 1966 and a peak of 45,998 in 1971, with 37,719 in 1973. By 1980, the Party had 53,000 members.[3] About 10 per cent of the membership is in Brussels. The basic level of party organisation, as for all the parties except the PCB, is the section based on the *Commune*.[4] It is at this level that members are recruited into the Party, which form associations for electoral purposes (districts for the provincial elections). At the *Arrondissement* level, at which parliamentary candidates are chosen, the Party has a structure parallel to that existing at the national level, with a Congress, a '*Conseil permanent*' (made up of representatives of the *Sections* and *ex-officio* members, such as Deputies) and a *Comité directeur* for day-to-day administration. At the national level, the Congress, which holds several preparatory seminars, is the supreme body. Apart from statutory Congresses every year, *ad hoc* Congresses may be held to decide on current political issues such as participation in the government, although this is rarer in the PSC than in the other parties. The *Conseil permanent* with 150 members (delegates of the *Arrondissements*, *ex-officio* members, members elected by the Congress) meets from time to time and usually decides on PSC participation in government. The *Comité directeur*, chaired by the Party President, meets frequently, often weekly, to deal with day-to-day matters. The leader of the Party — the President — is elected by all PSC members, voting by post. After the Party's defeat in 1981, Mr Vanden Boeynants resigned and was replaced by the

Christian Democrat leader (on the left wing of his Party), Gerard Deprez. The PSC and the CVP share the CEPESS (*Centre d'Etudes Politiques Economiques et Sociales*), a political research institute, linked to both Parties, which provides research back-up for the Party and its Deputies. The parliamentary groups in the Chamber, Senate and Community and Regional Councils elect their own Chairmen and leadership, which are in no way pre-eminent compared with the *Party* leadership and President, and are indeed subordinate to them.

The PSC structure is shot through with conflict between its two '*Tendances*' (wings). The right is generally organised by the *Centre Politique des Indépendants et Cadres Chrétiens* (CEPIC) and the left, the *Démocratie Chrétienne*, is closely linked to the CSC and the *Mouvement Ouvrier Chrétien* (MOC).[5] The 1976 Seraing Congress recognised these tendencies, but required them to support Party policy.

The MOC was founded in 1945, to link the various branches of the Christian Workers' Movement. It has not in more recent years exclusively identified with the PSC, but with a broader union and progressive movement. This led to the *Démocratie Chrétienne* under André Magnée as Chairman being set up in 1971. Its leading figures are Alfred Califice and Philippe Maystadt and the present PSC President, and its nerve-centre has been in the Charleroi area. Its main concern has been to maintain and develop the progressive strands in PSC policy and avoid the Party's isolation in Wallonia where it is a minority (now the third party). The MOC is, however, now in the process of setting up a new political movement which would be independent of the PSC.

The right wing, formerly active in the *Mouvement Chrétien des Indépendants et des Cadres* (MIC), set up in 1955, reacted to the establishment of the DC by setting up the CEPIC in 1972.[6] It established an extremely strong organisation: *Comité directeur, Conseil général* and congress, under Mr Vanden Boeynants as President. Its first major manifestation was a Brussels congress in 1974, and its first national congress was held in Brussels in 1977 with already over 600 members, several ministers and Deputies (Vanden Boeynants, Desmarets, Grafé, de Stexhe). Its main strength is in Brussels (50 per cent of PSC Councillors in 1976) and in Liège. It has a secretariat and a *Centre d'Etudes*.[7]

The CEPIC is the spokesman of a more radical pro-business doctrine: wage moderation, support for small business, and reaction to the leftward drift of the PSC, which since the early 1970s had ceased to be a 'party of the centre'.[8] The CEPIC's members are businessmen, managers and members of the *haute bourgeoisie*. Mr

Vanden Boeynants was a moderating force in the CEPIC, often at odds with the Party, especially during the periods of PSC/CVP-PS/SP government — over tax increases in 1977, *inter alia*.

There are also '*sans familles*' members of the PSC, associated with neither tendency. At present, the *Comité directeur* seems to be fairly balanced, but with fewer CEPIC members than DC members (nineteen DC to thirteen CEPIC and thirteen 'neutrals'),[9] there are perhaps, out of the total membership, 10,000 DC members and 8,000 CEPIC members. In 1978, only four CEPIC Deputies were elected as against twelve DC Deputies, but CEPIC dominates the *Arrondissements* of Brussels, Liège and, to a less extent, Tournai and Mons.

CEPIC has in more recent times become increasingly discredited. It is normal that its ideological reference-points should be those of the French *Rassemblement pour la Republique* (RPR) under Jacques Chirac or Valéry Giscard d'Estaing and that its main concern should be the defence of the commercial firm and its viability, reducing state intervention, and a strong position on defence. However, perhaps unjustly, its leaders have been associated with the far right: the Treasurer was suspected of links with the extreme right-wing *Front de la Jeunesse*. At the same time, the MOC decided in early 1982 to set up a new political movement (but not in alliance with the PS).

The PSC was thrown into a state of confusion. Under its new leader, Gerard Deprez, the CEPIC parliamentarians have agreed to leave CEPIC. No doubt a period of greater party unity is necessary. The PSC tends to choose its candidates by the method of '*Listes types*' — lists produced by the *Comité d'Arrondisement* and ratified by a delegate meeting by a two-thirds majority. The most severe problems, especially between DC and CEPIC tendencies, have arisen in Liège, where a postal poll of all members was even ordered in 1978.

The size of the PSC electorate traditionally depends to a large extent on the level of religious practice in an area.[10] It is strongest in the south of the Sambre-Meuse industrial valley. For the whole Walloon region, it was 19.8 per cent in 1981 and 26.7 per cent in 1978. Its post-war peak was 34.2 per cent in 1958, and its low point was 20.3 per cent in 1968. Its strongest positions in 1978 were in the Province of Luxembourg (44.6 per cent, with 48.5 per cent in the *Arrondissement* of Neufchateau-Virton). In the Province of Namur, it obtained an above-average 29.9 per cent, but only 11.1 per cent in Brabant (16 per cent in Nivelles) and 23.4 per cent in Hainaut, its worst score in a wholly Walloon Province. In 1981, it obtained only 33.1 per cent in the Province of Luxembourg and 18.0 per cent in Hainaut.

The PSC electorate[11] is about 57 per cent female and 43 per cent male and is therefore more predominantly female than the electorate as a whole. Only about 20 per cent of its electorate is under forty years old; 29 per cent are workers, 22 per cent white-collar workers (*'Employés'*), 19 per cent farmers, 13 per cent one-man or very small businessmen (*'Indépendants'*), and 8.6 per cent middle and senior managers. 83 per cent considered themselves to be practising Catholics. The PSC has an older and more 'bourgeois' electorate than its sister-party, the CVP. Of all workers, only 17 per cent voted PSC, whereas among farmers the proportion rose to 54.3 per cent among men and 62.9 per cent among women. Among male practising Catholics, 53.1 per cent voted PSC, which only 6.2 per cent of non-practising Catholic men did. The basic determinants of PSC voting are therefore in order: religious practice (although this is clearer among men than women, and less clear among working-class voters); the occupation of farming; age and sex (more women PSC voters).

The PSC, with its minority position, its divisions between strong CEPIC and DC wings, has always been a pragmatic party, a party with a governmental vocation. It has been in power uninterruptedly in various coalitions (CVP/PSC-PS/SP; CVP/PSC-PRL/PVV; CVP/PSC-PS/SP-PRL/PVV) and the broader coalitions including the RW (1974–7) and the FDF and VU (1977–80). Since the War, it has been in power for all but two short periods in 1945–7 and 1954–8). It has, however, progressively become the junior partner to the CVP, and has not provided a prime minister since 1968. Indeed, its subservience to the CVP led it to overcome its instinct to go into opposition after the November 1981 elections.[12] It has always sought to avoid both ideological and community isolation in Wallonia, hence its coalitions with the PS/SP and its participation in the *Front des Partis Francophones* in 1978.

The policy options of the PSC are the traditional concerns of Christian Democrats. A Christian 'personalist' ideology, based on 'reconciliation of class interests', has involved measures in favour of the less privileged without involving major structural changes in society. The key issues have been support for the Catholic education system and opposition to abortion and the permissive society, support for the family. In foreign policy, the PSC has been in favour of a strong defence posture and more rapid European integration. In more recent times, despite pressure from the *Démocratie Chrétienne* wing, the PSC has tended, in its economic policy, to move to the right on issues of the indexation of wages, state support for industry and public expenditure cuts.[13]

The Christelijke Volkspartij (CVP)

The CVP operates in the four Flemish Provinces and in Brussels and Brabant, where it competes with the PSC. It is the dominant Flemish party even after its defeat of 1981. In 1978, it obtained 43.5 per cent of the Flemish votes, and in 1981 36.9 per cent. This represented 26.1 per cent of the national vote in 1978 (PS: 13.1 per cent) and 19.3 per cent in 1981. Since the late 1960s, it has dominated its sister-party, the PSC, and as the main component of the largest political grouping in the country it has dominated both Flemish and national political life, giving rise to the criticism of the 'CVP-state'. It has (except for the 1973–4 Leburton government) invariably provided the prime minister since 1968 and now also dominates the Flemish Executive (four out of nine seats and the Presidency). It has, like the PSC, been in government in shifting coalitions continuously since 1958, and apart from 1945–7 and 1954–8 since the liberation. Its electoral high-point in Flanders was 60.4 per cent in 1950 and until 1981 its low-point was 39 per cent in 1968. Since the '*Distancement*' of the PSC and CVP in 1968, its high has been 43.9 per cent in 1977. In Brussels, where since 1968 there has been competition between the PSC and the CVP, the high for the CVP was 10.1 per cent in 1977 (PSC: 14.1 per cent) and its low was in 1981 with 5.5 per cent. The best areas for the CVP are Antwerp Province — 32.5 per cent in 1981 (45.6 per cent in 1978), but its results have been less good in the city of Antwerp itself — 28 per cent in 1981 (42 per cent in 1978), Limburg in 1978: 47 per cent. Its lowest results were in East Flanders with 45 per cent in 1978. Even in Ostende, its score was 28.3 per cent in 1978. Thus the CVP vote is fairly evenly spread throughout Flanders. Even after its heavy defeat in 1981, its lowest score remained 20.9 per cent in Ostende, and it still obtained over 60 per cent in a large number of *Cantons* (sub-divisions of the *Arrondissement*.)[14]

The profile of the CVP voter is similar, but not by any means identical, to that of the PSC voter.[15] The CVP electorate has a female majority (55 per cent to 45 per cent) but a slightly smaller one than the PSC. A larger proportion of the CVP electorate (34.7 per cent) are under forty; a larger proportion (35.6 as against 29.6 per cent in the PSC) are workers, and a smaller proportion farmers (15.3 per cent). Identification with the working class is felt by 57 per cent and with the middle class by 37 per cent, against 43.5 and 42.6 per cent respectively for the PSC. 92.7 per cent identify themselves as practising Catholics, but then Flanders is in general more Catholic. CVP voting is therefore determined by religious practice, coupled with working-class identification, and less with age and sex than for PSC voters. In Brussels both CVP and PSC voters are more likely to be

'*Indépendants*'. Women (52.2 per cent), over-sixties (54.2 per cent), farmers (75 per cent), middle-class identifiers and those who identify with no class (51.4 and 60 per cent, respectively) and practising Catholics (61.8 per cent) are the groups which predominantly vote CVP. Indeed, only 12.5 per cent of non-practising Catholics/non-Catholics voted CVP. More workers vote CVP than SP in Flanders. Figures for 1979 show that 53.4 per cent of the CVP vote is female and that 49 per cent of Flemish women vote CVP (only 40 per cent men). The Party's voters are mostly between thirty-five and forty-five (23.3 per cent), but it has more young voters (7.6 per cent) than any party except the VU; indeed of all voters under twenty-five, more vote CVP than for any other party (35.7 per cent). Of CVP voters 41.6 per cent are workers, 21.7 per cent *Employés*, 16.7 per cent *Indépendants*, 10.6 per cent managers and 9.4 per cent farmers. Of all workers, 41.4 per cent vote CVP and it remains the largest party in *every* social category. Of all practising Catholics 62 per cent vote CVP, and surprisingly 17.3 per cent declared non-believers voted CVP, a recent evolution. Of its electorate 73.3 per cent are practising, 22.5 per cent non-practising and 4.7 per cent non-believers. The CVP retains its broad appeal as a non-class party and has become less clearly confessional as religion has become less important, but still a by no means negligible factor in political choice.

The CVP appeals to three basic groups: Catholic workers, the 'middle classes' (small traders and businessmen) and the farmers. The Christian trade unions, the *Middenstand* organisations and the *Boerenbond* are closely articulated with the Party and co-exist more easily than the warring factions of the PSC. This has made for an even more pragmatic and 'classless' party than the PSC, with a strong element of hard-nosed defence of Flemish interests and a degree of cultural nationalism, coupled paradoxically with an attachment to Belgium, as conceived by the CVP, hence the expression the 'CVP-state'. At the beginning of the 1980s, under the pressure of figures such as its Party President, Leo Tindemans (1978–81), the CVP moved into a tougher and less centrist position on economic issues. Its chief slogans in the 1981 election were 'Take it or leave it: a strong new policy' and 'The truth is harsh, but only the CVP dares to say so'. This involved a harsh line on responsibility for the crisis both in class and 'Community' terms (no more concessions to the unions or to Wallonia). The five main elements of the seventy-page manifesto were:[16] 'Economic reconstruction; support for private initiative and the market; support for the family; an end to politicisation of economic policy, and the defence of Flemish interests.' The main themes were the need for a strong government, capable of acting; energetic action to compress costs of production (taxes, social security contributions, energy costs and, above all, wages); a resultant reduction in public expenditure, and a reduction in state interventionism. At the same time, measures for selective stimulation of certain sectors (agriculture, viable restructured sectors and new industrial sectors) are proposed.[16a] Taxation and social security policies should support the family and should be more selective. There is strong support for 'free' (Catholic) education. The CVP shows its colours as a Flemish party, in defence of Flemish economic, social and cultural specificity. The CVP accepts the Reform of the State, but insists on regional fiscal responsibility; in fact, it does not support greater devolution and above all is opposed to full regional status for Brussels, which it believes should have a special status. The CVP now believes in the regionalisation of five key industrial sectors, including steel for which Wallonia would then have to take financial responsibility.[17] In the international field, the CVP is a strong supporter of a federal Europe, seeking to 'give a new impulsion to the European Community' with greater political, monetary and industrial integration as urgent necessities. Europe needs to play a greater role in world affairs, especially in the North-South dialogue. NATO too needs strengthening, and the CVP supports the 1979 decision by NATO on Theatre Nuclear Forces or TNFs ('Pershing' and cruise missiles).

The organisation of the CVP is very logical, with parallel organs at every level:[18] the *Kongres* (Congress); the *Partij Bestuur* (Party Council), the *Bureau* (Executive) and the President. The basic level of organisation is the local *Section* based on the *Commune*, but it may be sub-divided into branches. Each section must be recognised by the *Bestuur* in the *Arrondissement* and a condition of recognition is a minimum membership equivalent to 7 per cent of CVP voters in the *Commune* or 3 per cent of the total electorate. The *Section* Congress, consisting of all members, meets at least once a year and elects the *Bestuur*, Congress delegations for the *Arrondissement* and national level, and the President. It also approves the statutes subject to national 'model' rules by a two-thirds majority. It adopts the manifesto for local elections. The *Bestuur* consists of a number of members elected by the Congress for three years, equal to the number of Councillors in the *Commune*, of which one-third must be under thirty-five and at least one-fifth women and one-fifth men, plus some *ex-officio* members. The *Bestuur* is responsible for policy decisions in the medium term, and it decides on alliances with other parties. The *Bestuur* elects the *Bureau* (President and members, each with a portfolio), including two women, for three years. The *Bureau* is responsible for the day-to-day administration of the Party. The CVP had 109,554 members in 1966, 114,843 in 1968, some 126,000 in 1976 and now about 130,000.

There is a similar structure at the *Arrondissement* level with a congress made up of section delegates and some *ex-officio* office holders. It elects the President and *Bestuur* (President, fifteen members plus one per 500 party members, plus national *Bestuur* members domiciled in that *Arrondissement* and up to one-third co-opted members). It elects the *Bureau*. The *Arrondissement* bodies are mainly concerned with parliamentary elections, campaigns and candidate selection.

The Provincial organisation is more sketchy, consisting of a *Bestuur* which has a number of members equal to twice the number of CVP Deputies and Provincial Councillors in the Province. It elects a *Bureau*. The *Bestuur* fixes alliances and chooses candidates for provincial senators. Alliance decisions (for the *Députation permanente*, for example) must be approved by the national *Bestuur*.

At the national level, there is a congress consisting of delegates of the sections, members of the *Bestuuren* of the *Arrondissements* and of the national *Bureau*. It meets at least once a year and may be called into session by at least five *Arrondissements*. It normally meets to approve any new government in which the CVP is to participate. It adopts the programme, controls the work of the *Bestuur* and by two-thirds majority may amend the statutes. It elects the President, whose term is a maximum of eight years. It elects a number of *Bestuur* members (fifteen plus one per 5,000 members, of whom one-fifth must be women). The *Bestuur* also includes CVP ministers and the *Bureaux* of the Senate and Chamber CVP groups and up to one-third co-opted members. Every *Arrondissement* and Province must have at least one member. It may sack office holders and exclude members by a two-thirds majority. It considers bills, decrees and policy statements from the CVP. Deputies must inform both their group and the *Bestuur* of all their initiatives. It considers current policy issues. It elects a *Bureau*, which meets weekly and is composed of the President, nine non-Deputies and some *ex-officio* members (Chairman of Chamber and Senate CVP groups, four deputies and four senators; CVP ministers, the Chairman of the CVP *Jongeren* [youth organisation]).

At the *Commune* level, polls are supposed to be held for candidate selection, but the *Bestuur* may, by a two-thirds majority, decide not to do so.[19] Except where Parliament is dissolved suddenly, there should be polls at the *Arrondissement* level for candidates to the Chamber and Senate, but again these are rare. Mostly the *Bestuur* of the *Arrondissement* draws up a 'model list' which is at best approved by an *Arrondissement* congress. In any event, by a three-quarters majority, the national *Bestuur* can modify the list, adding names or changing the order. Polls are now very rare. This is to maintain the delicate equilibrium between unions, 'middle class' and *Boerenbond* representatives. There is a theoretical age limit for Deputies and senators of sixty-five and an anti-cumulation rule, but these may be set aside by the national *Bestuur* by a two-third majority.[20]

There is also a '*Comité de concertation*' with the PSC to discuss common problems; this is composed of both *Bureaux*, and it is supposed to elect a joint national PSC/CVP President. However, this post has remained vacant and the two Parties have tended to drift apart.[21]

The Socialists

As we saw in Chapter 1, the first Socialist party, the *Parti Ouvrier Belge*, was founded in 1885, avoiding the term 'Socialist', which was even then considered a threat to the Party's essentially pragmatic outlook. Its basic doctrinal charter, the *Charte de Quaregnon* (1894), remained in force long after its quasi-revolutionary rhetoric had in the pre-1914 period been superseded by more specific pragmatic demands, to the point where the reformist current in the Party forced through an anti-clerical cartel with the Liberals in 1912. The Party first entered the Chamber in 1894 with twenty-eight seats and first entered the government in 1916. Apart from a short Catholic Socialist government in 1925–6, the Party only participated in '*Union Sacrée*' governments in the early post-war period, and in the crisis years in the 1930s. However, it soon surpassed the Liberals as the second party, and even became the largest party in 1925–9 and 1936–9. After the end of the *Union Sacrée* period in 1921, it moved to the left, but in the 1930s espoused the non-Marxist and nationalist theses of Hendrick De Man in his quasi-Keynesian '*Plan du Travail*'. De Man became President in 1939, succeeding the 'grand old man' of Belgian Socialism, Emile Vandervelde on his death. De Man dissolved the Party in 1940, and entered into open collaboration. A new party, the PSB (without collective union affiliations) was born clandestinely and from the activity of P.-H. Spaak in exile in London; it was less clearly a 'workers' party'. Since 1946, it has always been the second largest 'family', with a high of 36.7 per cent in 1961 and a low of 25.1 per cent in 1981. Before the ravages of the 'Community parties', its low was 29.7 per cent in 1949. It has often been in government since 1945; in the period 1944–7 in 'national' or 'left' coalitions, in 1954–8 with the Liberals, in 1961–5, 1968–73, and 1981 in coalitions with the CVP/PSC, and in 1973/4 and 1977–81 in broader 'tripartite' or 'Community coalitions'. It has only twice provided the prime minister since the late 1940s (Mr Van Acker 1954–8 and Mr Leburton 1973–4).[22]

The PSB/BSP long resisted the inevitable in the matter of region-alisation. The holding of separate and simultaneous congresses of the Walloon and Flemish organisations in 1967 did not wreck national party unity. A number of expedients, such as linguistic parity in all governing bodies and a system of co-presidents (since 1971), were tried until the collapse of the Egmont Pact and the result-ing radicalisation of positions made separation inevitable. The Party split in 1978 into the SP in Flanders, more pragmatic and open to Christians (its manifesto entitled *Doorbraak* [breakthrough] of 1979), and the Walloon PS with diametrically opposed view on 'Community questions'. Initially PS and SP doctrine on other issues was very close, but over time the two have moved apart in cultural, economic and, above all, defence policy issues.[23]

The Parti Socialiste (PS)

The basic unit of organisation[24] is a local section in each *Commune* which holds periodic general meetings and elects a committee to run its affairs. Organisations may affiliate to the PS, but they have no voting rights. These bodies may set up joint committees with the Party at various levels for common action. The section has a model statute laid down by the *Bureau*.

In each *Arrondissement*, there is a *Fédération d'Arrondissement* (FA) with a model statute. It holds periodic Congresses which elect a committee and national Congress delegates. The secretaries of the FA form a college, which the *Bureau* may consult on administrative matters. In each *Canton* (provincial electoral unit), there is a Cantonal Committee for campaign work. In the four Walloon Provinces there is a Provincial committee composed of not less than two delegates per FA, which holds a Provincial Congress at least once a year; this nominates the Socialist candidates for the *Députa-tion permanente* and as Provincial Senators. The *Fédérations* of Brussels and Brabant also co-ordinate their activities. At the request of the *Bureau* of one FA, the Provincial Committee must call a meeting of the FA (Congresses or Committees). The *Bureau* attends these Congresses.

The *Fédération de Bruxelles* and the four Walloon Provinces have a Regional Committee and Congress, which is responsible for taking decisions on regionalised (107 *quater*) matters. The Walloon Congress meets no less often than once a year or when it is called by the Regional Committee or by at least three Walloon FA. Repre-sentation (in addition to the Bureau and the Regional Committees which attend as of right) is on the basis of delegates from the appropriate FA.

At the national level, there is the Party Congress, which meets at least annually and always before the opening of the parliamentary session. Congresses may be called by the *Bureau* or by a minimum of three FA representing at least one-fifth of all members; they are also held to endorse PS participation in governments. The Congress defines party policy, elects the President, receives a report from the *Bureau*, which it may censure, and elects the *Bureau* for two years. If an FA so demands, voting takes place by *Fédération* block vote. Each *Fédération* has one delegate per 250 members. *Bureau* members, Deputies and *Deputés permanents* may attend and speak, but may not vote. The Congress is run by a *Bureau* and a *Commission des Resolutions* (Compositing Committee).[25]

Between Congresses, the supreme body is the *Conseil Général* (CG) which appoints Party officials, editors of Party papers, candidates as co-opted Senators and discusses urgent policy issues which the *Bureau* may submit to it. Three FA can demand a meeting of the *Conseil Général*. The voting members are delegates of the FA (one per 750 members) elected by their Congress for three years, Deputies and the *Bureau*. Representatives of various Socialist organisations may attend. In the *Bureau*, there are twenty-five voting members: the President, the two Vice Presidents (the President of the Walloon Regional Committee and the President of the Brussels *Fédération*), the General Secretary, and twenty-one members elected by the Congress. The parliamentary group Chairman and representatives of various Socialist organisations, ministers, representatives of the *Action Commune* (which includes the FGTB) are non-voting members.

The *Bureau* appoints the Deputy General Secretary, and takes day-to-day political decisions, consulting if necessary the *Conseil Général*. The Executive, consisting of the President, Vice Presidents, Secretary General and the latter's Deputy, are responsible for day-to-day administration and finance.

A wide range of bodies surround the Party: its youth, women's, educational and cultural organisations, as well as the unions (FGTB), co-operatives and *Mutualités*, which form the *Action Commune*. These make up the '*Monde socialiste*'. The Party shares the *Institut Emile Vandervelde* with the SP as a Party research institute.

The statutes of the Party provide for the statutes of the Parliamentary groups to be submitted to the *Conseil Général* for approval, and lay down that all parliamentary initiatives must be concerted within the group, and for matters not in the Party programme must obtain a favourable opinion from the Party *Bureau*. The PS is one party which still holds polls to designate parliamentary candidates, especially in Wallonia (not in Brussels), although this practice is declining since the Congresses of the *Arrondissements* usually decide against a poll. However, in 1978 polls were organised in the *Arrondissements* of Charleroi (9,800 voters), Mons (8,170) and the Walloon part of Brabant (2,500). No other *Arrondissements* held any polls.[26]

In 1972 the PS had 112,140 members in Wallonia and 28,433 in Brussels; in 1975 118,502 in Wallonia and 24,636 in Brussels; in 1979 it had 135,000.[27] Looking at the profile of the PS voter,[28] 51.9 per cent are women; 26.3 per cent are under forty and 35.2 per cent are over sixty. Workers account for 64.4 per cent; 16.8 per cent are *Employés* (white-collar workers) and only 1.8 per cent are farmers; 43.5 per cent identify with the working class and only 17.9 per cent are practising Catholics. The major characteristics of the PS electorate then are that they are older, almost equally male and female, working-class and non-practising Catholic. Of Walloon workers, 60.6 per cent voted PS and of those over sixty, 44 per cent voted PS (17.7 per cent only in Brussels). Of practising Catholics, only 16.5 per cent voted PS (this figure has no doubt increased) and 56.1 per cent of the non-practising voted PS. Of workers over sixty, over 65 per cent voted PS, whereas of workers under forty only 49.6 per cent did so.

Of the national vote in 1981 the PS obtained 12.7 per cent (13.0 in 1978) and 37.1 per cent in Wallonia (37.5 in 1978). In Brussels, the PS obtained 12.8 per cent in 1981, continuing its long-term decline (18.5 per cent in 1974). Its best results were in the Provinces of Hainaut (41.4 per cent) and Liège (37.4 per cent). Its worst results were in Luxembourg (24.7 per cent — however, this was up on the 1974 figure of 24.2 per cent). Its best *Arrondissements* were Huy-Waremme (Liège) with 47.9 per cent (45.7 in 1978); Soignies and Charleroi both with 41.1 per cent. Its poorest result — 23.3 per cent — was in Neufchâteau-Virton (Province of Luxembourg). In Liège, the PS was allied to some ex-RW members who figured on its lists and this led to the gains, and perhaps elsewhere partly compensated losses. In some *Cantons* in the Province of Luxembourg, the PS obtained less than 20 per cent and even less than 10 per cent in Bastogne. In some *Cantons* in the *Arrondissements* of Mons, Soignies, Liège, the PS passed 50 per cent of the vote.[29]

The election of Guy Spitaels as President, which was quite close-run (Spitaels gained 53 per cent, as against 47 for the left-winger Ernest Glinne), has led to a number of changes in the PS. He seeks to turn it into a more modern party with a clearer doctrine. This was the aim of the 1981 Congress, which had been planned since 1979, but only the energy of Spitaels enabled the doctrinal and administrative

Congresses entitled *'Renover et Agir'* to be held in March and October 1982. There has also been the opening to federalists and Catholics such as Yves de Wasseige, Jean Mottard and Marie Caprasse, who have been elected on PS lists. This was strongly contested in Charleroi and by more traditional Party members, but on the whole the more autonomist démarche of the Party has been easily accepted. There has also been a clear 'presidentialisation' of the PS, with the considerable use of the personality of Guy Spitaels in the election campaign in 1981, which was a new and effective phenomenon.[30]

The PS programme for the 1981 elections was, like the other party programmes, a closely argued and detailed text.[31] Its mainspring was the need to find a coherent response to the economic crisis, without accepting the logic of the market economy as inevitable. The basis of the PS response was to give absolute priority to employment and measures to create and conserve employment, especially for the most disadvantaged groups, using an interventionist approach to industrial and taxation policy. The PS accepts the need to control production costs, but refuses to see salaries as the sole element involved. The Party accepts the need to limit public spending, but to do so only in a moderate way covering all areas (including defence) and safeguarding acquired social rights, with a greater effort of national solidarity being required from those with higher incomes, in the framework of a more equitable tax system. Above all the state — both in the form of intervention and of public enterprise — is seen as having a positive role in reviving the Walloon industrial infrastructure in a socially acceptable manner.[32] The PS has moved to a rigorously autonomist position, espousing a federalist viewpoint for the first time. Not only does the PS fully assume the Reforms of 1980 and urge their completion, but it proposes to regionalise five key industrial sectors: steel, textiles, energy production, glass and shipbuilding. The powers of the regions should be extended to other areas such as applied research, agricultural policy, major public works and nuclear materials policy under public (Regional) control.

The PS is not influenced by the economic crisis to abandon its ambitious objectives in the social field, for youth, for equal opportunities for women, in environmental protection which should be increased by better planning and land use legislation, in health care, housing (a major effort needed) and consumer protection. Measures are favoured to improve the situation of immigrants, including the right of EEC nationals to vote in local elections. The Party remains fully committed to the NATO alliance, but wishes to see reductions in military expenditure and measures to reduce tension. It is opposed

to the Neutron bomb and favours the so-called 'zero option' on TNF
— dismantling of Soviet SS-20s in exchange for non-deployment of
'Pershing' and cruise. The Party remains strongly in favour of the
EEC, but seeks a more dynamic community with genuine social and
regional policies. It seeks to maintain public development aid at the
present 0.55 per cent of GDP at least, and to extend the North-South
dialogue.

The programme was pragmatic rather than ideological, although
it proposed some important structural reforms. The '*Renover et
Agir*' Congress sought to give the Party a clearer ideological basis,
anchored in a coherent analysis of the crisis, a resolutely federalist
démarche, and support for the new phenomenon of an active '*Vie
associative*' (lit. 'associational life'), involved in environmental,
consumer and labour battles at the grassroots, which has hitherto
by-passed traditional party structures.[33]

The 1982 *Communal* elections saw some practical attempts to put
these concepts of '*Ouverture*' into practice in the form of progressive
alliances before or after the elections, of which the most spectacular
example was the RPW/PS/*Ecolo* alliance in Liège under which two
Ecolo members become *Echevins*. The results of these experiments
were rather inconclusive.

The Socialistische Partij (SP)

As a permanent minority in Catholic and nationalist Flanders, the
SP has lived in a completely different environment from the PS. It
has been forced much earlier than the PS to become a strongly
Flemish party, and its style, rhetoric and policy have had to be more
pragmatic and more nationalist in order to survive in an essentially
hostile or indifferent environment, which it could do little to control
or shape. Since it has almost as large a share of the *national* vote as
the PS, the SP's weakness should not be overstated, but given the
greater size of Flanders, this has left it in a minority position as the
only left-of-centre party (except the very small Flemish wing of
PCB/KPB), with only two seats in the nine-member Flemish Executive. The SP obtained 12.4 per cent of the national vote (1981 and
1978), which represented 20.9 per cent of the Flemish vote in 1978
and 21.1 per cent in 1981. This is its lowest result; its highest was in
1961 (29.7 per cent of the Flemish vote — CVP 56.6 per cent). It has
traditionally been the second largest party, but with only about half
the CVP vote. In 1981, it fell into third place behind the PVV. After
1977, the long-term decline stabilised and even halted. Despite a
small overall gain in 1981, results were variable, with gains and
losses. The worst loss was in Antwerp *Arrondissement* (– 2.3 per

cent) and its best gains were in Hasselt (+ 2.6), St. Niklaas (+ 2.3). For the four Flemish provinces, its 1981 results were Antwerp 20.5 per cent (– 1.1), Limburg 23.9 per cent (+ 1.5), West Flanders 21.4 per cent (– 0.7), and East Flanders 19.8 per cent (+ 0.2). The best *Arrondissement* was Hasselt with 28.3 per cent (+ 2.0) and Ostende 26 per cent (+ 1.5). These results show the very even spread of the SP vote and the tendency towards greater evenness. In Brussels, the SP (competing with the PS) obtained 3.0 per cent (– 2.4) and yet for the Senate obtained 6.3 per cent (+ 0.7) and in the *Arrondissement* of Leuven 21.3 per cent (– 1.6).[34]

The profile of the SP voter[35] is somewhat different though not totally dissimilar to that of the PS voter. In 1968, 55.6 per cent were male (against 48.1 per cent in Wallonia and 45 in Brussels for the PS). This had become accentuated by 1979 with 60 per cent of SP voters being male. The Party had marginally more voters under forty (29.8 per cent against 26.3 for the PS). In 1979, 5.3 per cent of SP voters were under twenty-five; 37.8 per cent were 25–35 and 20.5 per cent were 35–45, which means that 52 per cent were under forty-five, representing a considerable change in the age structure of the Party's voters. The occupational structure was 58 per cent workers (64.4 for PS) in 1968 and 60.3 per cent in 1979. It had 27 per cent of *Employés* (16.8 for PS) in 1968 and 22.5 per cent in 1979; more (9.4 per cent) *Indépendants* than the PS (5.6) in 1968 and 11.3 per cent in 1979. It had 5.3 per cent middle and upper grade management in 1979 and 0.7 per cent farmers, fewer than in 1968 (1.5). Its Catholic electorate is much larger (34.5 per cent) than that of the PS, but well below all other Flemish parties except the PCB/KPB and the extreme left. If non-practising Catholics are included (1979), it has an electorate which is 78.2 per cent Catholic, not far behind the PVV (79.3). In 1979, 28.7 per cent of its voters were declared non-believers, and 1.6 per cent were of 'other religions', probably Jews. In 1968, of all men in Flanders 24.6 per cent voted SP; only 19.4 of the women did so. By 1979, 21 per cent of men and 16 per cent of women voted SP. In terms of age it was (1968) in the 40–60 age group where the largest proportion voted SP (24.1 per cent); in 1979 it was in the 25–35 age group (18.7 per cent). Among workers 32.2 per cent voted SP in 1968 and 22.3 per cent in 1979 (41.4 for the CVP). Even among the lowest income groups (under 28,000 BF income per month), only 20 per cent voted SP and 45 per cent CVP. Whereas among managers and tradesmen its support had risen to 18 per cent, it had fallen to 2 per cent of farmers (3.3 in 1968). Only 31.5 per cent of those (1968) with a clear working-class identification voted SP, but 84 per cent of its voters were such identifiers. The Party has become younger and more middle-class, more open to Catholics, but more male.

The organisation of the SP is very similar to that of the PS:[36] *Sections* at the *Communal* level, with a General Assembly and Committee. The general meeting must meet to prepare for *Arrondissement* and national Congresses and to appoint delegates. The Committee must include at least 25 per cent women and 25 per cent members under thirty-five.[37].

Arrondissement (fédération) organisations (AF). The AF holds a Congress which elects its Executive. This must include 25 per cent women and 25 per cent of members under thirty-five; up to half its membership may be elected officials (Deputies *et al.*) *Sections* within an electoral *Canton* co-operate in an *ad hoc* structure, as do the AFs within the same Province, particularly for the nomination of candidates for the *Bestendige Deputatie/Députation permanente* and as Provincial Senators.[38]

National organisations. The Congress is the highest body, meeting at least once a year; it gives its approval to the political report of the *Bureau*. It elects, every two years, the Party President (now Karel Van Miert), the *Bureau* and the administrative commission. The Congress delegates are appointed by their *Fédérations* on the proposal of the *Sections*, on the basis of one delegate per 300 members. Members of the *Algemene Raad* (General Council), *Bureau* and Administrative Commission, Deputies, Provincial Councillors may also participate, but not vote. The Party also has an *Algemene Raad* which meets to appoint the General Secretary and co-opted senators, and to discuss major political issues. Voting members are Deputies, MEPs, members of the *Bestendige Deputaties* and delegates of the AFs (1 per 500 members elected for two years). More day-to-day work is split between an administrative commission (responsible for administration, finance and audit, and information) and the *Bureau*, which deals with political questions. However, since the administrative commission (twenty members) includes the President and four representatives of the *Bureau*, there is a close overlap and co-ordination. The *Bureau* deals with political matters, but must present a report and a political resolution on future policy to the Congress. The *Bureau* has nineteen members (sixteen of them elected by the Congress on proposals from the AFs, and the President, the Secretary General and the latter's deputy).[39] The Party has a retirement age of sixty-five for elected office-holders and rules against '*Cumul*', which became stricter with effect from 1983.[40] The Party now rarely organises polls to select parliamentary candidates. Indeed, in 1978 there were none, and in the *Arrondissement* of Antwerp the Federal Congress specifically voted down a proposal for a poll[41]. The Party had 107,553 members in 1972, 107,155 in 1975 (representing about 13 per cent of its electorate, the highest of any party[42]) and 130,000 in 1979. There is a '*Concertation* committee' with the PS, composed of the two *Bureaux*, which rarely meets; indeed the Parties have moved further apart since the split in 1978.

SP policy has always been more pragmatic and less ideological than that of the PS. Its statutes speak of the 'establishment of a classless society, permitting the full self-realisation of every individual', and states that 'the action of the Party is in the humanist tradition. . . .'[43] Under Karel Van Miert, the Party has been modernised and become more open to new ideas, to Catholics, and to the new activist environmental and other grassroots groups. At the same time, it has lost the national Belgian viewpoint which characterised it as a junior partner of the PSB in the old unitary PSB/BSP, and has fully adopted Flemish positions on the Reform of the State and cultural matters. It has begun to review its policy with a series of conferences devoted to the development of specifically Flemish Socialist policies in various fields (housing in June 1978, education in March 1981).[44] It has also distanced itself from the PS on foreign policy matters, strongly opposing — even when in government — the use of Belgian territory for 'Pershing' and cruise TNFs, considering these weapons unnecessary and provocative; emphasising instead the need for negotiations. The SP however, is *not* anti-NATO, nor is it unilateralist or neutralist.

The Liberals

The Liberals were the first group to organise a political party in Belgium, and since they did so, the history of the Liberal family is one of splits and reunifications. Brussels has always been a strong Liberal centre, which has made the 'Community tensions' more difficult to handle. It was precisely the *Alliance Libérale* in Brussels, founded in 1841, which took the initiative in organising the first Liberal Congress (1846), which led to the formation of the *Parti Libéral*. The Party was later to be split between a conservative wing on one side, differing from the Catholic right-wing only in its anti-clericalism, and the 'Radicals' led by Paul Janson on the other, who favoured universal suffrage and social reform imposed by the state. The two sides splintered in 1887 and only reunited in 1900. The Party played an important part in political life down to 1884, forming many governments between 1848 and that year, when the Catholic Party obtained an absolute majority which they were to retain until 1919. By that time the Liberals had been surplanted by the *Parti*

Ouvrier Belge (POB) as the country's second largest political force. During the period of Catholic rule between 1884 and 1919, the Party often acted in close concert with POB; both were 'out' parties excluded from power, both were anti-clerical, and both supported universal suffrage, which would break the Catholic monopoly. After the First World War, and indeed until the *Pacte Scolaire* of 1958 finally ended the battle over education, the Party had been torn. In economic doctrine, it was more attracted to alliances with the CVP/PSC, but anti-clericalism remained enough of a live issue to make an anti-Catholic Liberal-Socialist alliance a real possibility. As a result, the Liberals served (apart from tripartite coalitions in the aftermath of both World Wars and in periods of severe economic crisis) in both kinds of coalition — Liberal/CVP/PSC in 1921-5, 1931-2 and 1932-5, and in Socialist-Liberal governments in 1946-7 and 1954-8. The last Liberal prime minister was Frère-Orban in 1878-84.[45]

In the 1960s, the Liberals evolved rapidly in several directions. The Party gradually and with success dropped its anti-Catholic bias and began to attract Catholic voters (by 1979, 10 per cent of all practising Catholics and 22 per cent of non-practising Catholics voted PVV) in Flanders.[46] With the creation of the more left-leaning PSC/CVP-PSB/BSP coalition after the strikes of 1960-1 and the 1961 elections, the old *Parti Libéral* was reformed as a more overtly neo-Liberal party, which obtained the support of some ex-PSC figures and personalities from smaller right and centre parties, under the name *Parti de la Liberté et du Progrès* (PLP/PVV) under Omer van Audenhove. The new party accepted the *Pacte Scolaire*, and sought to become a *Rassemblement* for believers and non-believers, in defence of the free market and Belgian national unity. The dominance of the French-speaking Brussels group in the Party was also reduced.

The Party was unable to remain untouched by the Community problem which swept through the country in the 1965 and 1968 elections, despite its record performance in doubling its vote between 1961 and 1965, reaching a high-point of 21.6 per cent in the latter year which was almost held in 1968 (20.9), thereafter to decline between 1971 and 1978. There was a shift in Brussels in 1970, which shattered Liberalism in the capital and created considerable confusion. The first group to break away from the 'official' Brussels PLP/PVV was the Flemish group, which left in December 1969 in protest against the refusal of the 'unitarist' and 'Francophone' PLP/PVV to grant parity in the Party organs in Brussels. This group entitled itself the *Blauwe Leeuwen* (Blue Lions). Then the French wing split into a rump 'official' group and a group which sought cooperation with the FDF in the coming elections for the Brussels

Agglomération. First of all, the PLP as a whole and other Franco-phone parties in Brussels joined in the *Comité du Salut Public* organised by the FDF, which led an aggressive anti-Flemish campaign in the 1970 *Communal* elections. After these elections, a group under Mundeleer split off in protest against co-operation with the bilingual list of Mr Vanden Boeynants in the Brussels *Commune*. Out of this was born the *PLP de la Région Bruxelloise*, which formed an electoral cartel with the FDF, but in which Mr Mundeleer did not participate, tabling, along with the rump PLP, his own list. The cartel, under the name *Rassemblement Bruxellois*, won an absolute majority in the Council and 49.8 per cent of the vote, leaving the PLP (official) and the Mundeleer Liberals with 4.1 and 1.9 per cent respectively. In some of the Brussels suburbs, the PLP and the *Blauwe Leeuwen* were also in competition. As the two wings of the Party were separating in 1972, the two Brussels groups also held separate Congresses. At the 1974 election, the pro-FDF group renamed the *Parti Libéral Démocratique et Progressiste* (PLDP), formed a cartel with the FDF-RW which, when the results were compared with the 1971 election (FDF and the PLP and Mundeleer lists together), shows a very serious loss for the Liberals. The PLDP became the *Parti Libéral*, and this in 1975 re-absorbed most of the old unitary PLP. What remained of it was shown in the 1976 *Communal* elections to be marginal.[47]

Meanwhile, at the national level, the PVV and PLP became auto-nomous, each holding a separate Congress while at the same time maintaining some national structure (national Congress and President). When the RW split in 1976, its centrist wing under Perin, Gol and Knoops joined the PLP in the formation of a new party, the *Parti des Réformes et de la Liberté Wallone* (PRLW) under André Damseaux (November 1976). It held its first Congress in January 1977, and declared itself to be 'pluralist, reformist and federalist'. While liberalism in Brussels continued to decline (only one Deputy in 1978), the PRLW prospered. The fusion of the PL and PRLW was thus proposed and carried out in Congresses of May and June 1979, creating the *Parti Réformateur Libéral* (PRL), which declared itself to be 'pluralist, popular and favourable to a federalism of union'. It elected the ex-RW Jean Gol as President. The Liberals retain a national Chairman, Pierre Deschamps (PRL), ensuring co-operation between the PRL and the PVV.[48]

The Parti Réformateur Libéral (PRL)

The structure of the PRL is relatively classic:[49] local *Sections* with an *Assemblée Générale* of all members electing a committee;

Arrondissement Fédérations, with a Congress, a *Bureau* and an Executive; provincial organisations, and a national organisation with a Congress, *Bureau*, Executive and President. There is also a '*Régionale*' (until 1983) for Brussels, presided over by Mr Van Halteren, Mayor of Brussels, who is also first Vice-President of the PRL. Jean Gol took control of the new Party (he had only entered the Liberal fold in 1976 when the PRLW was formed) with the help of a mere 300 ex-RW militants. André Damseaux retired from the leadership, and Jean Gol obtained 80 per cent of the Congress vote against Michel Toussaint. Gol has created a presidential style, surrounded by a strong team of ex-RWs and 'new men' such as Robert Henrion. The pieces have been put back together again in Brussels, and the old liberalism and the new tendencies have been integrated by a judicious association of the 'old barons' of the Party with decisions. Candidates are chosen by Congresses or polls. There were several polls in the Province of Hainaut in 1978.[50]

Traditionally, the Liberals have been the third party in Wallonia (second in 1965, 1968 and 1981, third to the Communists in 1946 and fourth in 1971 behind the RW and the PSC), with a peak in 1968 of 26.5 per cent and a low of 9.3 per cent in 1946 and otherwise of 10.5 per cent in 1958. Indeed, before 1965, the Party never attained more than 12 per cent of the Walloon vote. The Brussels comparisons became difficult after 1971. Its low point was 13.4 per cent in 1946 (otherwise 13.5 in 1971) and its high point 33.4 per cent in 1965. With the FDF-PLDP cartel in 1974, obtaining 39.6 per cent and the PLP/PVV only 5.9, it would appear that the decline continued. In 1977, the PL obtained 9.4 per cent and in 1978 a mere 6.4. The 1981 elections saw a considerable recovery to 16.1 per cent. The main bastions of the Liberal Party in Wallonia are Nivelles with 27.7 per cent (1978, 17.7), Luxembourg with 27.1 per cent (20.7) and its poorest results are in Hainaut with 18.8 per cent (14.7), Liège with 21.6 per cent (16.5) and Namur with 22.7 per cent (20.4), where it registered its smallest gains (+ 2.3). Its best *Arrondissement* was Arlon-Marche-Bastogne with 29.3 per cent and its worst was Charleroi with 15.7 (11.6).[51]

The profile of the Liberal voter in Wallonia and Brussels is as follows:[52] The (1968) electorate of the Liberals was 51 per cent female in Wallonia and 51.9 per cent female in Brussels. The age profile shows the Walloon Liberals with 42.4 per cent of their electorate under forty and 22.7 per cent over sixty (in Brussels only 28.6 under forty and 24.9 over sixty). The socio-economic structure was as follows: 15.8 per cent of workers (the lowest share for any Walloon party); 23 per cent *Employés*; 20.9 per cent *Indépendants*; 23 per cent managers, and 11.2 per cent farmers. This gives them the highest proportion of *Indépendants* and '*Cadres*' (middle/upper management); 59 per cent identified with the middle class and 11.7 per cent with the 'bourgeoisie'. The proportion of middle-class and 'bourgeois' identifiers was even higher in Brussels (59.3 and 17.8 per cent). Practising Catholics accounted for 43.9 per cent (only 28.4 in Brussels). Of all voters under forty, 32.1 per cent (twice the PSC figure) voted liberal. Of all Walloon workers, only 8.6 per cent voted Liberal, whereas 38.7 per cent of *Indépendants* did so (26.4 for the PSC). Of practising Catholics 24 per cent and of non-practising Catholics/non-believers 22.4 per cent voted Liberal; but in Brussels 30.6 per cent of the latter voted Liberal. It is therefore in Brussels, at least until 1968, that the traditional anticlerical, bourgeois liberalism had most clearly survived. The PRL had 28,000 members in 1972, 34,700 in 1975 and 40,000 in 1980.

Gradually, as the 'school war' lost relevance, the Liberals have moved to the right of the PSC, becoming a pluralist conservative party, but retaining in Wallonia especially, both among traditional supporters and among the ex-RW contingent, some of the radical liberalism of the past, updated as federalism and radical individualism. The economic crisis and the related pressure from new parties like the UDRT have led the Liberals to espouse a more radical neo-liberalism, inspired by the Chicago School and even by Mrs Thatcher. Jean Gol has repeatedly taken up the themes of the need to attack bureaucratic statism, to reward effort and to re-establish order in government, in the firm and in the family. At the same time, the PRL opposes greater Walloon federalism as likely to add to these dangers despite the earlier federalism of the PRLW. The strategy of the Liberals after the formation of the PRL was to maintain their position in Wallonia and to advance in Brussels (they did better than this) by taking votes from the PSC and the FDF.[53] This was so that they should constitute *the* strong conservative force in Wallonia and Brussels as a counterweight to the PS, and force the PSC to change alliances — as it reluctantly did in 1981. In line with this image, the PRL has attracted well-known military figures previously outside politics such as General Close, who have taken up the issue of the Soviet danger and linked the need for a strong defence with the need for a strong conservative policy internally.[54]

The Partij voor Vrijheid en Vooruitgang (PVV)

The PVV began to obtain autonomy in the late 1960s and was organised as an autonomous party at a Congress held in Blankenberge in May 1972 with Mr De Clercq as President and Mr Grootjans and Mr Vanderpoorten as Vice Presidents. It declared itself open to 'all who supported Liberal ideals irrespective of religion or philosophical beliefs'. The Congress also dealt with such delicate issues as abortion, which the PVV wants to see liberalised.

Throughout the post-war period (until the 1981 election), the PVV has been the third party in Flanders, behind the CVP and SP, and from time to time it has been the fourth party, dropping behind the *Volksunie* as well (1968, 1971, 1977). Its low point was 7.7 per cent of the Flemish vote in 1946, and otherwise 9.4 per cent in 1950. Its high point was 17.3 per cent in 1977 and then 20.6 per cent in 1981.

The PVV's fluctuations have not followed those of the PLP (or PRL). The PVV lost in 1977 while the PRLW gained, and it gained in 1978 while the PRLW lost. Both gained massively in 1981. The best PVV result in 1981 was in the Province of East Flanders with 24.1 per cent (21.7 in 1978). In 1978, its best result had also been in East Flanders, but it had made its biggest gain in West Flanders (+ 4.1 per cent). Its lowest results were in Limburg (17.9) and Antwerp (17.7) Province. Its best *Arrondissement* was Oudenaarde (35) and its worst, oddly enough in the same Province, were Sint-Niklaas and Antwerp (both 17.7). In Brussels, the PVV obtained 4.9 per cent (– 2.1) and in the Leuven area rose from 20.8 to 25.0 per cent.[55]

In 1968, 51.7 per cent of the PVV electorate was female, but by 1979 there had been a radical change in that 56.3 per cent of its electorate was male. In 1968, 30.5 per cent of PVV voters were under forty; in 1979 5.5 per cent were under twenty-five; 23.9 per cent were 25–35; 22.9 per cent 35–45; 21.2 per cent 45–55; 21.2 per cent 55–65 and 11.0 per cent over sixty-five (the lowest figure apart from the VU). Thus, 52.3 per cent of its voters were under forty-five (50.2 for the CVP and 53.5 for the SP). In 1968, 25.7 per cent of its electorate were workers (31.8 in 1979), the lowest percentage of workers for any party. 24.3 per cent were *Employés* in 1968 (22.5 in 1979); 19.3 per cent were *Indépendants* (22.7 in 1979); 19.3 per cent were managers (21.8 in 1979), and 9.3 per cent were farmers in 1968 (5.5 in 1979). Only 38 per cent identified with the working class while 49.8 per cent identified with the middle class or 'bourgeoisie'. In 1968, 65.3 per cent were Catholics. In 1979, 33.5 per cent were practising Catholics, 46.0 non-practising, 3.2 of other religions (Jewish) and 17.5 non-believers. Of all workers, only 8.5 per cent voted PVV (1979) and of all *Indépendants* 15 per cent voted PVV (less than for the CVP).[56]

The PVV structure is fairly classic. It had 43,794 members in 1975 and 50,000 in 1979, organised in local *Sections* based in *Communes*. Each *Arrondissement* has a *Fédération*, with its own Congress and *Bureau*. At the national level, there is a President, a *Politiek Komittee* which takes major decisions between Congresses, and the

Uitvoerende Bureau (Executive), which runs the Party's day-to-day affairs, with naturally periodic ordinary and extraordinary Congresses. The PVV shares, with the PRL, the Centre Paul Hymans, (1956), a Liberal research institute, and it has set up an institute to train party cadres, the *Instituut voor Volksopleiding en Kaders Omer Van Audenhove*.[57]

The PVV is, as we have seen, pluralistic, i.e. open to Catholics, but it also favours freer abortion. On economic and social policy, defence and international relations, it has become markedly more right-wing. Its basic programme *Handvest* [manifesto] *van het Moderne Liberalisme* — the Kortrijk Manifesto (1979) — is, according to Mr Grootjans, 'influenced by the theses of Milton Friedman, who has provided the intellectual basis for modern Liberalism'.[58] The Manifesto makes it clear that the PVV is calling for a new start, a new liberalism attuned to 'economic realities' and to the 'doubts and alienation' created by 'ambiguous and meaningless political compromise.' It states that the whole programme 'is based around one central theme: the restoration of a belief in the freedom of the individual in a free society as the first pillar of our society, made sick by bureaucratisation and 'state intervention'. The Manifesto itself advocates the need for a new liberalism, which it calls 'radical Liberalism', to provide a more coherent liberal ideological perspective in government. It identifies the individual and his free choice in a market economy as its central value. It supports measures to 'free the market', reduce costs by controlling bureaucracy, the welfare state and trade union pressure; it supports the small independent enterprise, profit is to be rehabilitated and structural change accepted. In social policy, it seeks more self-help and selectivity. It takes a strong stand on defence issues as a necessary guarantee of freedom, and supports greater integration in the European Community.[59]

The Communists

The Communists are not normally considered as one of the major national political families, and indeed their small influence does not justify such an approach, but as a long-standing national and still unitary (not Community) party, the PCB/KPB falls more into this category than do the two other groups we shall consider (Community parties and new movements).

The Belgian Communist Party (PCB/KPB) was born in 1921 of a forced marriage imposed by the Communist International on two antagonistic groups: the '*Ancien Parti*' — the *Parti Communiste de Belgique* led by Van Overstraeten, which was anti-parliamentary and favoured workers' councils — and the *Parti Communiste* of Jacquemotte which grew out of the group called *L'Ami des Exploités*, whose ideology was more moderate. They wanted to return the POB to a more left-wing class line. At its birth the PCB had only about 500 members. In 1925 the Comintern imposed the cell structure for the then 700 members and the expulsion in 1928 of the 'leftist' Trotskyite fraction. In the 1930s the Party moved into the trade unions and obtained some success, especially in the Borinage coal mines, and membership grew to above 8,500 at its high point. The Party espoused the notion of '*Front uni à la base*' (united front at the grassroots) until 1935 when at its VII Congress it adopted the *Front populaire* line. In 1937 a specifically Flemish wing, the KPB, was formed. There is some evidence that, even before the German invasion of the Soviet Union in June 1941, the PCB or rather groups within it were organising strikes and working-class resistance to the Germans in the Walloon industrial areas, but the Party as such followed the Comintern line that the war was 'imperialist'. After June 1941 the PCB entered active resistance and played a major role in the underground in the *Front de l'Indépendance*, a pluralist co-ordination body.[60]

The Party's parliamentary representation began in 1925, when it won 1.64 per cent of the vote and two seats. Until 1936 it never held more than three seats, but it did obtain votes as high as 6 per cent in some areas. With the radicalisation of the late 1930s its support increased to 6.06 per cent and nine seats in 1936 and 5.36 per cent and nine seats in 1939, but it played no part in parliamentary politics. In the early post-war period it saw considerable success. In 1946 it obtained 12.7 per cent and twenty-three seats. As in many European countries, it participated in several coalition Cabinets between 1944 and 1947 when the Cold War began in earnest. Throughout the 1950s and 1960s its support fell and then remained stable, but the Party was isolated in a political ghetto. The manner of the post-war reorganisation of the Socialist unions (FGTB) had also ensured that Communist influence would be small. The Party can scarcely be said to have climbed out of this isolation, but since the early 1970s, with the Socialists proposing a *Union des Progressistes* and the PCB itself evolving in response to the Euro-Communist movement, though remaining relatively traditional, the Party has — in a regionalised Wallonia, where it is strongest — more potential now than at any time since 1950. However, that is still not saying much.

Organisation is based on factory or local cells grouped into *Sections* under *Fédérations* (which do not always correspond to *Arrondissements*). Each *Fédération* holds a Congress and elects a Committee. The national Congress meets every three years and takes decisions by a 'double majority' (in the whole Congress and in each language group). The Congress elects the Central Committee on the basis of Community representation, and the *Bureau politique* (for one year). The President and Vice President are also elected by the double majority. Since 1980, measures have been taken to create more open debate and to establish Regional conferences (Wallonia and Flanders). Candidates are nominated by the Central Committee.[61] In 1976 the Party (PCB/KPB) had 14,847 members (11,000 in Wallonia).

The Party's greatest voting strength lies, as noted above, in Wallonia, with a peak of 21.7 per cent in 1946 (otherwise 12.7 in 1949 and 9.8 in 1968). Its low point was 4.5 per cent in 1958. In 1981 it obtained 4.9 per cent. Its best province was Hainaut with 6.3 per cent (8.6 in 1978) and its worst Namur with 2.4. It presented no list in Luxembourg. Its best *Arrondissement* was Mons with 12.5 per cent. In Flanders its support is small, with a 'high' of 5.5 per cent in 1946 and a low of 0.1 per cent in 1958, with a normal level of about 1.5. In 1981 it obtained 1.4. Its best result was in Antwerp Province (2.3) and Antwerp *Arrondissement* (2.7).[62] Its Walloon voters (1968) were 70.8 per cent male, 41.7 per cent under forty and 50 per cent under forty in Brussels. 66.7 per cent of the PCB electorate was working-class and 81.8 per cent were 'working-class identifiers'. Only 9.1 per cent were Catholics. Of all workers only 3.9 per cent and of all non-Catholics only 4.2 per cent voted PCB. In Flanders (1979), only 2.3 per cent of voters under twenty-five voted KPB; for all other age groups the figure was less than 1 per cent except for the 45–55 age-group (1.4). Of all workers only 0.5 per cent voted KPB and of *Employés* only 2.0.[63]

The PCB/KPB is a unitary party. It has made some organisational concessions to federalism, but it supports federalism '*à trois*' (Flanders, Brussels, Wallonia as equal regions). It is a '*Laïc*' party, but, since adopting the policy of the *Rassemblement des Progressistes* at its 1973 Congress, has emphasised its socio-economic programme, favouring considerable nationalisation. This strategy led it to experiment with a cartel in 1977 with the *Union Démocratique et Progressiste*, which was not renewed in 1978 or 1981. The main emphasis is placed (resolution of the XXXII Congress [1979]) on the need for an 'anti-monopolies alliance', prepared to resist the 'inevitability of the crisis' by greater intervention and control of investment decisions and financial institutions. The Party does not state explicitly that Belgium should leave NATO or the EEC, but it criticises their effects and argues against their policies. Against this background it elaborated an 'emergency plan' on employment (working week of thirty-six hours, etc.), defence of the social welfare system, enlargement of democracy and federalism, and a policy of peace and détente by the dissolution of NATO and the Warsaw Pact.[64] The Congress of March 1982 confirmed – despite strong internal turmoil — the PCB's 'Euro-Communist' identification and its federalist orientation.[65]

The Community parties

The denomination 'Community parties' only came into current use in the 1960s, applying to the *Volksunie* (VU), in Flanders; the *Front démocratique des Francophones* (FDF) in Brussels and the *Rassemblement Walloon* (RW) in Wallonia. As we have seen, the Flemish movement was much older, having been represented in Parliament by the *Front Partij* (1920s) and the *Vlaams National Verbond* (VNV) in the 1930s. The *Volksunie* was not formed until 1954, and grew slowly until 1961 and especially 1965. The increasing Flemish consciousness and the strikes of 1960–1 provoked a response in both Brussels and Wallonia, with Walloon lists and then the RW and the FDF, both from 1965. The three parties are pluralist, but the VU leans to the right, the FDF is of the centre, sometimes with serious disputes between its ex-Socialist and ex-Liberal tendencies, and the RW, especially since 1976, leans to the left.

The Rassemblement Wallon (RW)

Before the dramatic strikes of 1960–1, which saw the creation of the left-wing *Mouvement Populaire Wallon*, Walloon federalism had developed here and there — in the Liberal and Socialist parties, in the Walloon *Résistance* (and the *Congrès National Wallon* of 1945) — without finding any clear organisation and focus. It remained a defensive reaction to the rise of the Flemish movement. After 1961 various other Catholic and Liberal Walloon movements also came into being: the *Wallonie Catholique*; *Rénovation Wallonne* and *Wallonie Libérale*.[66]

In 1964 the *Front Wallon pour l'Unité et la Liberté de la Wallonie* was created out of the MPW and another small party, and 1965 saw the creation of the more left-wing *Parti Wallon du Travail* (PWT) under M. Perin. The PWT and the *Front Wallon* each obtained one seat and, together with the FDF, 2.3 per cent of the national vote in 1965. In Wallonia, the two lists obtained 2.4 per cent. After the election, the PWT, the *Front Wallon* and some independents formed the *Parti Wallon*, later (1968) the *Rassemblement Wallon*. The RW made significant electoral progress, in alliance with the FDF in 1968 (10.8 per cent in Wallonia); in 1971 (21.2 per cent and fourteen seats), the RW became the second Walloon party; but the 1974 election saw it decline to 18.8 per cent. The 1977 elections, after the RW had been in power, were disastrous for the Party, which had also meanwhile split; it obtained only 9.1 per cent. In 1978 the Party's results stabilised at 9.4 per cent, but in 1981 once again the Party was beset by a split which reduced it to two seats and 5.5 per cent of the Walloon vote, with many votes going to the dissident lists led by the former Party Chairman P.-H. Gendebien, and others going to the Socialists who put some ex-RW members on their lists. In 1978, a more representative year, the best RW vote was in the Province of Namur (10.9 per cent) and its worst was in the Province of Luxembourg (5.5 per cent). In 1981 its best result was in Namur again with 8.5 per cent and its worst in Luxembourg (2.5). Its best *Arrondissement* in 1978 was Thuin with 20.5 per cent (5.0 in 1981 due to the dissident candidacy of Paul-Henri Gendebien) and its worst 2.5 in Arlon-Bastogne. The best 1981 result was in Namur with 12.6 per cent (+ 0.2) and Nivelles 9.8.[67]

The typical RW voter is male (50.4 per cent in 1968), under forty (47.8), working-class (42.0) or middle-class (44.9); 31.5 per cent are *Employés*, 17.1 per cent *Indépendants*, 20 per cent *Cadres* and only 1.4 per cent farmers. It is more working-class than the PSC, and 43.9 per cent are practising Catholics. Of all workers 5.8 per cent and of all non-believers 8.2 per cent vote RW.[68]

The Party is based on local *Sections*, and *Sections d'entreprises* in some large factories. Its main organs are the Congress, its *Bureau fédéral* (seventy members) and the *Bureau* (President, Vice President and General Secretary). In 1979, it had 9,500 members.[69]

The RW went into the 1974 elections as a candidate for office. At last the inter-Community dialogue seemed to be producing results, and a government involving the Community parties was a possibility. The Steenokkerzeel conclave had not produced enough results for an 'opening' to the FDF-RW and the VU. However, the Lambermont talks of May 1974 made possible a 'small opening' to include the RW only in the PSC/CVP — PRL/PVV Tindemans I government in June. The RW's *Bureau fédéral* had authorised, not without some doubts even at this stage, a small opening without the FDF. The Party Congress at Tournai in October 1974 saw P.-H. Gendebien elected President in place of M. Perin who had become a minister. Gendebien defined the Party as 'federalist, progressive and pluralist' and its rôle as 'the left wing and motor of the majority especially on regionalisation and social issues.' On a number of issues — the slowness of the preparatory regionalisation (necessary because the new government, despite later attempts, was never enlarged to have the necessary special majority for a full regionalisation) on budgets, the rules for the state holding company, trade union elections — the RW's *Bureau* and Deputies chafed at the bit and requested the government to act.[70]

Almost from the start two strategies were being pursued: that of the ministers, led by Perin, of maintaining the government in office in spite of and even against Party interests (indeed Perin cared little for the fate of RW as such) in order to advance the inter-Community dialogue and provoke later, as the Socialist initiatives in June 1976 were to do, the conditions for a definitive regionalisation, as in the Egmont Pact. The other strategy pursued by Gendebien and the Party as such was favourable to the Party staying in the government in order to ensure a continuation of the 'dialogue', but was also concerned about a distinct future for the RW and the ideas it represented.[71] These tensions built up continually from mid-1975, and were actually exacerbated by the F-16 versus 'Mirage' affair in which the RW *Bureau* and Deputies initially opposed support for the 'non-European' F-16 and finally agreed only with bad grace after receiving concessions, in order to keep the government in being. At the same time it redoubled its pressure on the government to implement the Law on Provisional Regionalisation (August 1974). From October 1975 there arose a serious cleavage between the ministerial group and the Party itself, which reached a rapprochement with the FDF. The 'Perin report' on institutional reform was badly received by the *Bureau fédéral*, and the strange affair of the Flemish counters* in the Schaerbeeck town hall led to tensions between the 'base' of the RW and the ministerial group. As it later transpired, the Perin-Gol-Knoops group were already looking for an alternative option, in negotiating their collective membership of either the PSC or PLP, and to that end Perin created a political base in the *Club Réformes Europe-Régions*, a factional organisation inside the RW, in July 1976. On the other side Gendebien presented (26 October 1976) on behalf of the *Bureau restreint*, without consulting the *Bureau fédéral*, a doctrinal manifesto, and proposed a Congress on 4 December. The atmosphere had not been improved by the poor RW results in the *Communal* elections. In most party *Sections* there was no debate between the factions, but a split pure and simple. The Perin group took the offensive and left the RW to join the PLP — later to become the PRWL on 29 October. This eventually required a government reshuffle to give posts to 'loyal' RW men. In the interests of the Community dialogue, the RW remained loyal to the government, until it became clear that the dialogue was making no progress; it then voted against the budget in March 1977, and this precipitated an election which proved disastrous for the RW.

*This was a linguistic quarrel in a Brussels borough, where the FDF mayor established separate counters in the town hall to serve Flemish speakers. This action was ruled illegal, and when he still refused to accept bilingual counters, they were symbolically destroyed in a Gilbertian night commando raid by the *Gendarmerie*.

The Doctrinal Congress of 4 December 1976 oriented the RW to the left, but the Party was still open to Christian Democrats, for whom, together with Progressives, it was able to act as a centre-left pole, forming a component of a progressive majority in Wallonia with the PS after regionalisation. It was to be a progressive, libertarian, new-left party with an important ecological and '*auto-gestionnaire*' strand. After Gendebien left the Presidency in 1978 to run for the European Parliament, the new leadership under Henri Mordant moved closer to the FDF; this, in 1981, caused the second split in which the former MPW elements and Gendebien left the RW because of their opposition to tying the RW and Wallonia to Brussels. Some ran on Walloon lists (Gendebien obtained 15 per cent in Thuin) and others were given places on the Socialist lists. The RW subsequently found itself in deep trouble, and reduced to two Deputies. The Walloon movement is split, over both tactics and policies. A new grouping is probably needed.

The Front Démocratique des Francophones (FDF)

The FDF was formed in 1965 by federalists and non-federalists in Brussels to defend the French language and immediately obtained 10.0 per cent of the Brussels vote and three seats in the Chamber. Its rise thereafter was spectacular, with 18.6 per cent in 1968 and 34.5 per cent in 1971 when, with allies, it also captured an absolute majority in the Brussels *Agglomération*. In 1974 the FDF obtained 39.6 per cent of the Brussels vote, 34.9 in 1977, 35.1 in 1978, and a dramatic collapse to 20.3 in 1981.

As a result of the theory of the 'significant majority in each region', the FDF entered the 'Egmont Pact government', which would have created a separate Brussels Region if it had survived. The FDF remained in power in the Vanden Boeynants interim government and in the Martens I government until early 1980, when CVP pressure made its position impossible: it was in power, but was obtaining no results. It left the government — or was forced out of it — especially as the Francophone Front (PS-PSC-FDF) collapsed at the same time. After this experience, the FDF sought to strengthen its links with the RW in a Brussels–Wallonia alliance of solidarity. This produced the split in the RW and the electoral disaster in 1981, with an electorate which, in the face of the economic crisis, is less and less concerned with Community issues as such.

The FDF is a 'pluralist' party with Liberal, Christian and Socialist components. The Liberal wing has frequently in more recent years felt itself to be marginalised, hence the resignation of the FDF Deputy Havelange in 1981. The Party has also overcome clerical/

anti-clerical divisions, supporting abortion in 1973. The FDF is however more centrist than the RW, whose federalist theses it espoused
in 1970.[72]

The FDF had also proclaimed some left-of-centre positions on
workers' co-management and energy policy, but it remains to a great
extent the defender of the Brussels *Indépendants*. Its statutes declare
it to be 'a pluralist and federalist party committed to political action
for the defence of the rights of the French Community in Belgium
and of the Brussels region'.[73] The statutes also refer to the Party's
support for the Walloon cause (a recent amendment). The Party (in
its 1981 election manifesto) has argued that the key crisis in Belgium
is an institutional one, and demands full regionalisation to give
Brussels equal status with the other Regions and (a new demand in
line with its alliance with the RW) improvement of the 1980 arrangements for Wallonia. It also demands an extension of the boundaries
of the Brussels Region beyond the nineteen *Communes*.[74]

On economic and social issues, it regards the maximum autonomy
for Brussels as the best guarantee that its absolute priority — the
fight against unemployment — will be met. It proposes 'another
kind of economic growth in public and social services', maximum
support for SMUs, and an end to pro-Flemish employment policies
in Brussels. In its view, public spending is controlled by Flemish
interests which take 15 per cent of taxation from Brussels and return
6 per cent of public spending. For it, the unitary state is powerless
and paralysed. It places a new emphasis on an energy policy based on
energy saving and new energy sources (it is reticent on nuclear
energy), with state intervention.[75] The FDF proclaims itself to be
an 'Ecological party', especially in terms of the improvement of
the quality of urban life in Brussels — public transport, green
belts, parks — better planning and conservation of buildings and
districts.[76] On welfare policy, equal pensions for all (especially
Indépendants) is an absolute priority. The FDF (with a woman
leader, Mme Spaak till 1983) is committed to women's rights and to
measures against racism and political violence. On education, the
FDF argues for co-operation between the public and Catholic school
systems.

The FDF is pro-EEC and federalist, supporting the idea of a
'Social Europe of the Regions', open to the Third World. On
defence, it opposes unilateral disarmament, but favours mutual
reductions by negotiation and a more autonomous European
defence. The FDF-RW alliance is stated to concern only 'the Community platform of Wallonia-Brussels solidarity' and not economic
and social issues, on which the FDF is probably more centrist than
the RW.

The FDF has (1975) 10,990 members.[77] Its membership has been fairly constant since the late 1960s. The profile of the FDF voter is 64.1 per cent female; 20.8 per cent under forty and 25.0 per cent over sixty; 15.3 per cent workers, 39.0 per cent *Employés* and 12.7 per cent *Indépendants*. Of FDF voters 59.3 per cent identify with the middle class and 17.8 per cent with the upper middle class; 25 per cent are practising Catholics, the lowest figure except for the PS.[78]

Given its limited territorial coverage, the FDF's organisation is somewhat simpler than that of the other parties, but not very much so. The basic unit is the *Section* which has a General Assembly, a Committee and a President. *Sections* are grouped into '*Commissions de district*' which cover electoral districts; these *Commissions* draw up their lists for Provincial elections in Brabant and propose for ratification by the *Comité directeur* candidates as Provincial Senators. The Presidents of *Sections* also meet in a committee to co-ordinate activities. At the central level, the supreme authority is the bi-annual Congress (the *Conseil général* may call other Congresses), in which *all* members may participate and vote. It elects the Party President and General Secretary for two years, and votes on party policy. Between Congresses, the *Conseil général* is the supreme body — it may even amend the statutes by a two-thirds majority. It is composed of delegates of the *Sections* (one, plus up to seven extra for membership up to 1,000 and then one per 300 supplementary members); delegates (10 per cent of the total) of FDF *Communal* Councillors; all Provincial Councillors, *Agglomération* Councillors, mayors, *Echevins*, FDF administrators of the RTBF and other state bodies, representatives of the women's and youth organisations, of which there are ten and twenty respectively, all Deputies, Senators and Members of the European Parliament. It meets at least four times a year, and in any case whenever there is a government crisis. The smaller *Comité directeur* (meeting monthly at least), based on the same principles of representation and chosen from within the *Conseil général*, is an executive arm of the *Conseil général*. The *Bureau permanent* is the day-to-day decision-making body; it is even smaller, but still includes the President and General Secretary, all Deputies and number of members elected by the *Comité directeur* for two years, among its own members and representatives of the FDF-*Femmes et Jeunes*-FDF. The *Bureau permanent* can therefore have at times up to forty or fifty members, but it may delegate certain decisions to a smaller group (e.g. President, Vice President and General Secretary). The party also has a *Commission électoral* which makes up the lists for national elections on the basis of proposals from the sections, but these lists must be approved by the *Comité directeur*. The party has its own research institute.[79]

The Volksunie (VU)

As we have seen, the Flemish movement first entered Parliament in 1919, under the banner of the *Front Partij*, with five seats. After its defeat in 1932, this Party gave way to the more radical and right-wing *Vlaams Nationaal Verbond* of Staf De Clercq, which won sixteen seats in 1936 and seventeen in 1939. However, the collaboration of some Flemish nationalists with the Nazis caused the movement to be discredited after 1945. Only in 1949 did a dissident group from the CVP contest the elections under the name *Vlaamse Concentratie*. In 1954 this group was enlarged and became the *Volksunie* (VU),[80] entering Parliament with 3.9 per cent of the Flemish vote and one seat in the Chamber. Its low point was 3.4 per cent (one seat) in 1958, and its high was 18.8 per cent of the Flemish vote and twenty-one seats in 1971. Despite a fall in its vote in 1974, it reached its high point in terms of seats, with twenty-two. Its participation in government and hence its approval of the Egmont Pact cost it dear. Its vote fell back to 11.5 per cent in 1978, and the dissident (anti-Egmont) *Vlaams Blok* was formed, receiving 2.1 per cent of the vote and one seat (1981, one seat). Its high point in Brussels was 6.2 per cent in 1976 — in 1981 it obtained 5.94 per cent.

The Party's best vote (1981) was in Limburg (17.3 per cent) and its worst was in Antwerp (14.9). Its best *Arrondissement* was Tongres Maaseik (Limburg) with 20.7 per cent. The VU vote is very evenly spread.[81]

The VU (1968) vote was 51.5 per cent female; 49.5 per cent under forty and only 14.3 per cent over sixty. Workers accounted for 28 per cent; white-collar workers too for 28 per cent; *Indépendants* for 19 per cent; managers 18 per cent; and farmers 6.4 per cent. 42 per cent identified subjectively with the working class and 50.6 per cent with the (lower) middle class. 74.2 per cent (second only to the CVP) were practising Catholics. In 1979, 50.5 per cent of the VU's electorate were women, 11.3 per cent were under twenty-five, 23.9 per cent were in the 25–35 bracket, and 22.9 per cent were 35–45; so 58.2 per cent were under forty-five and only 13.2 per cent were over sixty. 37.1 per cent of VU voters were workers, 35.1 per cent *Employés*, 20.6 per cent *Indépendants*, 6.2 per cent managers and 1.0 per cent farmers. 55.7 per cent were workers or *Employés*, 54 were practising Catholics and 36.4 were non-practising Catholics and only 9.1 non-believers. The main determinants of VU voting were (young) age and middle-class identification among workers.[82]

The organisation of the VU is fairly typical of all Belgian parties, but is relatively complicated. In each *Commune* there may be more than one *Section*; indeed, there may be several. Each *Section* elects its executive for two years, which itself elects (with the approval of the *Arrondissement* executive) its Chairman and Secretary and its representatives in the *Arrondissement Raad*. Elected officials may attend such meetings, but they must not be in a majority. Where there are several *Sections* in a *Commune*, their representatives (five votes plus one extra vote per fifty members above twenty-five members), two representatives of the *Arrondissement* executive and elected members (Deputies and councillors) make up the *Politieke Raad* (Political Council), which elects its own executive (a quarter of its members must be women and people under thirty-five). It runs *Communal* election campaigns and chooses *Communal* candidates. All decisions on cartels and alliances must be approved by the *Arrondissement* executive. Each *Arrondissement* has a council made up of representatives of the *Sections*, co-opted members (up to 15 per cent), Chairmen of political Councils, VU leaders on Councils and Provincial Chairmen. The *Arrondissement* Council elects its executive of seven members plus a Chairman and Secretary, who must be elected by a two-thirds majority. The national *Partij Raad* (PR) names a Provincial President and may set up other Provincial co-ordination bodies. At the national level the Party is led by a *Partij Raad* which is composed of *Arrondissement* Chairmen, ministers, Deputies, Senators, MEPs, representatives of *Arrondissements* (one per 1,000 members) and some other *ex-officio* members. The *Partij Raad* can co-opt up to ten extra members by a two-thirds majority; it elects a *Partij Bestuur* and five committees for organisational matters. The Party Chairman is elected by a two-thirds majority of the *Partij Raad*. The *Partij Bestuur* elects a smaller political committee (Chairman, Vice Chairman, General Secretary and parliamentary group Chairmen) and an administrative committee. Candidates are chosen by the *Partij Bestuur* based on the proposals of the *Arrondissements* and then approved by the *Partij Raad*.[83] The Party now has 60,000 members, of which about 9,000 are in Brussels.[84]

The VU claims to be a social and federal party. It espouses radical Flemish nationalism, which it identifies with the concept of a Flemish state, rather than with the '*Grootnederland*' (Greater Netherlands) idea.[85] It bases its analysis on the failure of the present political system and of the national parties. It sees the link with Wallonia as a permanent financial liability. In response, it argues for 'political autonomy for a Flemish state in a federal system'. The federal concept is needed in order to safeguard links with Brussels, which it regards as a Flemish city. It favours an 'integral federalism' with all tasks being performed at the objectively most appropriate level. It has therefore proposed a 'confederal model' for Belgium, in which the Flemish state would enjoy the greatest possible autonomy, and with Brussels (limited to the nineteen *Communes*) as a confederal capital where both Communities would enjoy equal rights.[86]

In more recent times the message has become radicalised. The Party argued in its 1981 manifesto 'No half measures: Flemish money in Flemish hands and a Flemish state', thus condemning the 1980 regionalisation as totally inadequate. Its nationalism is based on progressive social and national radicalism, favouring more equality but rejecting both doctrinaire Marxism and Liberal egoism. It favours a 'social Flanders' with special policies for the family and weaker social groups. It favours more local democracy and more democratic decision-making in the trade unions. On education and culture, it is nationalist and pluralist. In economic policy, it gives priority to a Flemish employment policy, and has proposed a five-year plan to create 50,000 jobs by a new industrial policy based on a 'new co-operation between classes'. Profits must be rehabilitated as the mainspring of investment, public expenditure controlled, tax and social contribution charges on businesses and wage costs stabilised. The Party has, for some vital 'national sectors' such as energy, favoured a more radical approach with partial nationalisation and greater state control. Peace and disarmament are an important component of Party policy: the VU seeks the nationalisation of the arms industry, resolutely opposes the installation of NATO cruise missiles on Belgian territory and seeks an increase in development aid.[87] Its policies make it difficult to classify the Party on a right-left spectrum, but its 'gut-level' centre of gravity is probably to the right of centre, though on some issues it is closer to the SP than to either the CVP or the PVV.

Other parties

There are several smaller groups, unrepresented in Parliament, on both the extreme left and the extreme right.

Extreme left. There have been many groups, of which the most important is the *Ligue Revolutionnaire des Travailleurs* (LRT/RAL), affiliated to the Fourth International (Trotskyite). Its main competitor, since 1973, has been the AMADA/TPO (*Alle Macht aan de Arbeiders*), which exerted its most significant influence in the Antwerp dock strike of 1973. It has been renamed (1979) the

Parti du Travail. These groups were in competition in both 1978 and 1981, but did not contest all seats. The best results gained by AMADA/PVDA (*Partij van de Arbeid*) were in Antwerp with 3.5 per cent in the city (an increase of 0.1 since 1978). For the LRT/RAL, its best results were also in Flanders, but usually well below 1 per cent. Walloon results in both 1978 and 1981 were usually under 0.5 per cent for these lists.

Extreme right. The extreme right has no electoral influence. The *Forces Nouvelles* list, which stood in one or two *Arrondissements* in 1978 and 1981, obtained virtually no votes. However, movements on the extreme right, often of a para-military character, have been very active, linked by the extreme right-wing weekly, *Nouvelle Europe Magazine*. Here the Flemish *Vlaamse Militanten Orde* (VMO), which has existed since 1949, and the *Front de la Jeunesse* can be cited.

New parties

New parties are not an unknown or new phenomenon in Belgian political life. The left-wing Christian Democratic group under Daens, dissident lists, the *Front Partij*, *Vlaams Nationaal Verbond*, emanations of the Flemish movement, the Rexist Party under Léon Degrelle, all passed briefly across the stage of Belgian political life and then, especially those of the extreme right, disappeared after 1945. The new centre-left UDB (*Union Démocratique Belge*), which hoped to start a new progressive movement, obtained only one seat in 1946 and never dented the traditional parties. Of course, the Communists and the Community parties were once 'new' parties which threatened the stability of the established political system, and indeed the Community parties have become both a durable and a significant part of the political scene in Belgium. More recently, two new 'tendencies' have erupted on to the political scene and may carve out a position in the political spectrum as genuine representatives of a new political sensibility, to which the traditional parties or Community parties do not cater. This concerns the *Union Démocrate pour le Respect du Travail* (UDRT/RAD), a radical anti-taxation and anti-bureaucracy movement similar to Møgens Glistrup's Progress Party in Denmark, and the various ecologist movements of which the most representative and successful has been *Ecolo* and in Flanders AGALEV (*Anders Gaan Leven*, 'alternative life-style').

The UDRT-RAD

The UDRT originated in an initiative of a small group of readers of '*Défense Sociale*', the organ of the *Fédération Générale des Travailleurs Indépendants* (FGTI) and in particular Mr Robert Hendrick. In late 1977 they formed the *Centre d'Action Démocratique* which, with the energetic support of Mr Pauwels of the FGTI and '*Défense Sociale*', became the UDRT in April 1978, adopting a seventeen-point charter. Between then and the 1978 elections, the UDRT concentrated on Brussels and on forging links with potential competitors, the basically Flemish *Parti Radical* of Mr Delahaye, the *Union Radicale Belge*, the *Verenigde Onafhankelijke Partij* (VOP) and, most important, the *Centre Démocratie et Solidarité* (CDS) led by Mr Delforge, being the last remnants of the old PLP in Brussels. These groups formed a cartel for the 1978 elections, and in 1979 the UDRT-RAD enlarged itself to include the *Parti Radical* and some VOP and CDS members, and became a party with about 5,000 members mostly in Brussels. It established local *Sections*, for each *Arrondissement*, Provincial *Bureaux*, a national Congress open to all members, and between Congresses a more restricted *Assemblée générale*; an eighteen-member *Conseil national* of which fifteen members are elected by the *Assemblée générale* and three co-opted, and a *Bureau exécutif* composed of the Co-Presidents — Mr Hendrick (Francophone) and Mr Delahaye (Flemish) — and two other members and a Treasurer. The Party has also set up campaign and information cells. The structure is unitary.[88]

Its voters are mostly young, in the 26–35 age group; 30 per cent are *Cadres*, 28 per cent *Indépendants* and 11 per cent *Employés*.[89] At the 1978 election it took 0.88 per cent of the national vote, with 0.7 per cent in Flanders, 0.8 per cent in Wallonia and 2.3 per cent in Brussels; with 5.84 per cent in Arlon as its best score. It obtained one Deputy in Brussels. In 1981 it obtained 2.71 per cent of the national vote and 0.9 per cent in Flanders, 2.72 per cent in Wallonia and 6.97 per cent in Brussels, with 10.84 per cent in Uccle as its best result. It obtained three Deputies (two Francophone and one Dutch-speaker), *all* in Brussels, enabling it to form a group in the Chamber. The Party was disappointed with these limited gains.[90]

The UDRT rejects labels such as 'Poujadist', and declines to be considered right- or left-wing. It is a 'different' party or an anti-system party. Its main targets are the established political parties, which it regards as incapable of reform, being too encrusted in a system from which they profit, as parasites on the business community. It attacks this 'political class' and its appurtenances in the

Partenaires sociaux. It rejects the 'dictatorship of the unions and employers', but is much more against the unions than against the employers' body, the FEB. It does, however, dislike large multinational capital, favouring the small businessman. But this has been a problem in the Party, since its leadership wants to broaden its base from being a defence body for *Indépendants*. Thus, with difficulty, the candidates list for 1981 was purged of obvious representatives of the *Indépendants*. It opposes state interventionism, seeks radically to reform the tax system (maximum rate 35 per cent), to reduce bureaucratic regulations and unproductive public expenditure on bureaucracy, and 'excessive' social welfare. It proclaims attachment to the rights of entrepreneurs and to the free market. It seeks equal pensions for all and 'privatisation' of much of the welfare system. It argues for a stop on immigration from non-EEC countries and controls on welfare abuses by immigrants. On many issues such as defence and foreign policy it has no position, and on the Reform of the State it developed no policy until the debates of 1980. It favours decentralisation to the provinces rather than the present type of regionalisation, which it regards as a rather costly bureaucratic exercise. It may best be compared, as already mentioned, to the Danish Progress Party suspected likewise of extreme right-wing tendencies, while in reality it is probably better classified with the paradoxical label 'right-wing anarchist'.[91]

Ecologists

There were several Ecological lists in both Flanders and Wallonia in 1978, with various political characteristics — socialist, pluralist and purely environmental protection lists. None of the Ecologist lists made much impact in Flanders, but AGALEV was the most significant. In Wallonia, '*Ecolo*' was the most successful list, obtaining 1.26 per cent in Wallonia (Charleroi, Neufchâteau, Virton, Nivelles, Namur). Its best result was in the *Arrondissement* of Namur (2.78 per cent), Nivelles (2.78) and Liège (2.04). Its best *Cantonal* result was in Namur (5.21). The Ecologists found it easier to penetrate rural than urban areas in Wallonia and the reverse in Flanders. The 1981 elections saw an important advance for *Ecolo*, despite the divergences between the various tendencies which had threatened the movement, especially in Brussels: it obtained 4.8 per cent of the national vote, as against 0.8 in 1978, returning four Deputies and four Senators. *Ecolo* (Walloon) obtained two seats and AGALEV (Flanders) two seats. In Wallonia it obtained 6.3 per cent of the vote, while in Flanders AGALEV only obtained 3.5 per cent of the vote; In Brussels *Ecolo* obtained 7.5 per cent of the vote, which was

above the national average. In Hainaut it obtained 7.5 per cent.[92]
The Ecologists were more united in Flanders, but, their division in
Brussels has not been detrimental to its advance. The movement has
suffered from internal disputes and discussions about its structure
and ideological orientation, especially in Brussels, where in the 1981
election two other lists (*Ecologie Bruxelles* and *Ecolo-J*) were tabled
as well as *Ecolo*, though these other lists, largely particularist
Brussels lists, obtained little success. In Wallonia *Ecolo* was
dominant, as was AGALEV in Flanders. Such divergences are of
course only to be expected in a movement brought together from
such diverse origins and sensibilities (rural, urban, ideological and
so on).

The main components of the movement were bodies like *Les Amis
de la Terre* (Friends of the Earth), *Inter-environnement* and ARAU
(*Atelier de Recherche et Action Urbaine*), a body committed to
grassroots urban action. *Ecolo* and AGALEV are also quite
separate, though they agree on the approach to the 'Community
problem' based on a 'real federalism' working up from small 'basic
communities' which would be self-governing. AGALEV has done
more programmatic work than *Ecolo*, but is less structured. The
latter has problems over its health and education policies, in that
they lack detail on the kind of decentralisation and financing that the
Party proposes. It proposes a new model of economic activity, and is
not primarily a party interested in the environment, but as Mr.
Dubrulle (AGALEV) stated 'offers a real political alternative.'[93] The
Ecolo/AGALEV lists also have some quite concrete policies, for
example the thirty-four-hour week and the use of popular
referenda.[94] For them the need now is to become more structured in
order that they can benefit from their advance, and to use the parliamentary platform to increase their audience and credibility. The
Ecologists also refuse to be classified; they are 'elsewhere', and
although their basic sympathy is in a socialist direction, the PS/SP
cannot depend on any automatic support from them. Measures will
be voted on in accordance with a pragmatic evaluation in relation to
the Ecologists' aims.[95] It seems mainly but not exclusively to have
benefited from a certain rejection of traditional politics and the
youth vote (850,000 18–21-year-olds voted for the first time). Thus
Belgian Ecologists became the first Ecologists to enter a national
parliament, with two AGALEV Deputies and Senators and two
Ecolo Senators and Deputies.

Voting behaviour and the party system

We have already examined the basic factors determining voting behaviour in the course of looking at the profile of each party's electorate. Here we shall look at two issues related to the evolution of the party system. These are, first, the degree of the volatility of the electorate and the proportion of the vote going to the traditional parties and, secondly, the 'distance theory' approach — an examination of how the parties relate to each other in a continuum. Such an analysis is a basic element in a discussion of party interaction.

A significant and useful measure of electoral volatility is 'external mobility' (EM) expressed as a percentage, a notion close to the concept of 'swing' developed in Britain. The peaks of EM were 16.86 per cent in 1936 and 21.60 per cent in 1946, both these years being times of stress and realignment. EM became more stable in the 1946–65 period, falling to 4.55 per cent in 1958 and 4.61 per cent in 1961. The irruption of the 'Community parties' in 1965, maintained in 1968, gave an EM level of 16.9 per cent in 1965 and 6.46 per cent in 1968. The new equilibrium established in 1965–8 was maintained in the 1968–77 period, with an EM level of 6.77 per cent in 1977. In 1978 the level was 6.50 per cent in Flanders, 8.45 per cent in Brussels and 4.90 per cent in Wallonia, all roughly average. In 1981, the levels were considerably higher and approached the 1965 levels, due to the PRL/PVV and *Ecolo*/AGALEV gains.[96]

The level of support for the 'traditional parties' (PSC/CVP, PS/SP, PRL/PVV) has been above 90 per cent, except in 1936, 1939 and 1946, until 1965 when it fell to 84.3 per cent and 80.61 per cent in 1968. In 1978 it was 79.7 per cent (83 if the PCB/KBP is counted as a 'traditional party'). In 1981 it fell to 73.0 per cent (75.3 including the PCB/KPB). For the three groups of parties the situation was as shown in the table. This shows a new trend — will it be maintained? — towards three sizeable blocs of parties.

	1978 %	1981 %
Traditional parties	79.7	73.0
Traditional parties (+ PCB)	83.0	75.3
Community parties	15.5	15.1
'New parties'	1.5	9.6

Figures from the late 1960s[97] — the most recent available at the time of writing — showed that PSC voters would as an alternative vote for the PRL (28.3 per cent) and saw themselves as furthest from the PCB and RW. CVP voters preferred as an alternative the VU (24.3 per cent) and saw themselves as farthest from the KPB and SP. Liberals preferred the CVP (30.3), PSC or FDF as an alternative. Socialists in Wallonia preferred equally as an alternative the PSC and RW, and SP voters preferred the CVP (20.0 per cent). The Community parties preferred, for the RW-FDF, the PS (RW) and PRL (FDF) — and, for the VU, the CVP (47.3 per cent). This clearly excludes the 'new parties', a major new factor in the equation. These figures also show strong Community antipathies, e.g. PVV voters (unitary) were opposed to the VU. They do however suggest that, in terms of distance theory, the parties might be placed on a continuum (left-right) in the following manner (with the total Flemish spectrum more to the right):

For Wallonia
LEFT   PCB-PS-RW-PSC-PRL-UDRT   RIGHT

For Flanders
LEFT   KPB-BP-CVP-PVV-RAD   RIGHT
                            AGALEV-VU

It is now doubtful whether any 'national' continuum makes much sense, given the importance of the Community parties, except to note that the Flemish wings of the former 'national' parties are on the whole more to the right.

The party system and sub-systems

Until the arrival of the Community parties on the parliamentary scene, there was a clear national party system, with limited possibilities for interaction between the parties. Before 1900 the system was essentially one of two parties with Catholics and Liberals in contention for power. Up to the First World War, Socialists and Liberals co-operated as a 'progressive' and anti-clerical opposition. Then, after 1920, a three-party system developed, in which four basic coalition possibilities were available, all of which were in fact applied before 1940: Liberal-Catholic or Socialist-Catholic; or Liberal-Socialist or tripartite crisis coalitions. The Liberals were faced with difficult choices: they favoured alliances with Socialists on traditional grounds, but increasingly tended, on socio-economic grounds, to prefer alliances with the Catholic Party and these were in fact more frequent. After 1947, when the Communists were excluded from government, the old three-party system reappeared. Indeed in the 1950–4 period, with an absolute PSC-CVP majority, the pre-1914 situation of a Liberal-Socialist rapprochement intervened and a period — the last — of PS/SP-PRL/PVV coalition followed, as the 'school war' (see pp. 49–50) hotted up again (1954–8). When the school *Pacte* of 1958 restored peace, Liberal-

Socialist coalitions were excluded. From then until 1974, despite the importance of Community parties, the possibilities were restricted to CVP/PSC-PS/SP or CVP/PSC-PRL/PVV or tripartite coalitions, all of which were in fact tried.

Between 1974 and 1980, new interactions became possible with the entry into the coalition game of the Community parties. During this period, the need for the so-called special majorities, both to amend the constitution and apply its article 107 *quater*, and the political desire to associate 'a significant majority' in each region with the decisions relating to the Reform of the State, especially required the participation of the FDF (which in turn also required at times the participation of the VU). It was these considerations which led to the participation of the Community parties in power, in order to carry out the various *Pactes Communautaires*. First, the RW entered a CVP/PSC-PRL/PVV Cabinet, but this was inadequate for full implementation of article 107 *quater* of the constitution. There then followed the 'Egmont Pact' majority, which associated the FDF and the VU, and later only the VU, with the PSC/CVP and the Socialists. When this approach failed, the parties fell back on the traditional tripartite coalition to carry through the 1980 Reform of the State, which excluded Brussels.

On economic and social questions the Socialists and Liberals became increasingly incompatible and tended to try to exclude each other from coalitions with the PSC/CVP, whereas at the same time tensions over the choice of coalition partners grew within the PSC in particular. Well before the 1981 elections the CVP and the CEPIC wing of the PSC were working for the reversal of alliances which occured in 1981, whereas the Christian Democratic wing of the PSC feared such a change. Coalition possibilities now seem to have been reduced on the national level to less frequent tripartite coalitions, CVP/PSC-PRL/PVV coalitions as at the time of writing (1981–) or CVP/PSC-PS/SP coalitions. Ideas (probably unrealistic) for the exclusion of the 'weaker' wing of the CVP/PSC or PS/SP from a coalition, perhaps 'topped up' with a Community party, have occasionally been ventilated.

Gradually, after 1974, sub-systems have developed in anticipation of full regionalisation[98] — which will occur after the next election, when the principle of proportional representation in the executives will be dropped. In Wallonia the centre of political gravity is more to the left, and the key issue is whether there is a 'progressive majority' which would enable — for that is the real issue — the exclusion not of the Liberals but also the PSC from the Regional (and possibly the Community) executive. This is indeed the sense of the new policy of the '*Ouverture*' proposed by Mr Spitaels (PS). At present the progressives are the PCB, PS, RW and *Ecolo*. The PSC uneasily straddles the centre, with its Christian Democratic wing under pressure from the MOC and CSC. The PRL and UDRT have moved to the right. In 1981 and in 1978 (if it had been constituted as at the time of writing), the Regional Council was constituted as per Table A.[99]

Table A

	1978			1981		
Party	Senators directly elected	Deputies	TOTAL	Senators directly elected	Deputies	TOTAL
PCB	1	3	4	1	2	3
PS	16	28	44	17	31	48
Ecolo	0	0	0	1	2	3
RW	3	4	7	0	2	2
'Progressives'	20	35	55	19	37	56
PSC	10	21	31	7	15	22
PRL	5	14	19	9	19	28
UDRT	0	0	0	0	0	0
Centre/Right	15	35	50	16	34	50
Total	35	70	105*	35	71	106

* + 1 PVV

Thus, despite the gains of the PRL and the UDRT, there is a *Majorité de progrès* in the Walloon Regional council.

In the Flemish council, which includes the Flemish-speaking Deputies and Senators from Brussels, the composition for 1978 and 1981 was as shown in Table B.[100]

Table B

	1978			1981		
	Senators (elected)	Deputies	Total	Senators	Deputies	Total
KPB	—	1	1	—	—	—
SP	13	26	39	13	26	39
AGALEV	—	—	—	1	2	3
CVP	29	57	86	22	43	65
PVV	11	22	33	14	28	42
VU	7	14	21	10	20	30
RAD	—	—	—	—	1	1
Vl. Blok	—	1	1	—	1	1
Total	60	120	180	60	121	181

The position of the CVP as the dominant party — with almost an absolute majority in 1978 - has been whittled away, and it is less dominant than the PS in Wallonia. However, there is a strong right-of-centre majority and the CVP/PVV have a dominant position (110 seats).

In Brussels, the dominance of the FDF has been considerably reduced, but it remains the strongest single party. However, it is now smaller than the PSC/CVP family or the PVV/PRL family. The 'progressive' parties (PS/SP, FDF, *Ecolo*) are in a minority with nineteen Deputies and Senators against thirty-three PSC/CVP, PRL/PVV, UDRT/RAD, VU Deputies and Senators. Following the 1981 election, the PSC/CVP, PRL/PVV alone had twenty-five Deputies and Senators.

The main conclusion of this analysis of the Belgian party system must be that there is a permanent state of tension between stability and violent upheaval. Periods of stability alternate with periods of upheaval. The late 1950s and early 1960s were key periods of change, when the last remnants of the old anti-clerical Socialist-Liberal alliance disappeared and the Community parties achieved their breakthrough. The changes of the early 1980s with the appearance of autonomous regional sub-systems, potentially in conflict with the national party system, and the arrival of 'new' parties on the scene may indicate that the relative stability of the era of Community politics 1968–80 is ending, and a new more variegated and even more complex system is emerging. However, it is too early to offer any confident prognosis on this point.

NOTES

1. On the role of the Mechelen Congresses, see Luykx, op. cit., 124–5.
2. For a brief history of the origins of the Catholic Party, see Luykx, op. cit., 123–7 and *Dossiers du CRISP*, no. 10, 'Les Partis Politiques en Belgique' (hereafter CRD 10), 3.
3. CRD 10, 14 and 39.
4. CRD 10, 11–14, for the structure of the PSC.
5. On the MOC, see G. Spitaels, *Le Mouvement Syndical en Belgique*, Editions de l'Université de Bruxelles 1975, 59–61. On its recent moves see *Le Soir*, 10 April 1982, p. 2.
6. On the CEPIC, see *Courrier Hebdomadaire du CRISP* (hereafter 'CH'), no. 787. 'Le centre politique des cadres Chrétiens (CEPIC)'.
7. The CEPIC structure is described in CH 787, 9–14.
8. CEPIC ideology is described in CH 787, 19–32.
9. CH 787, 18.

10. For all election results in this chapter, see CH 826, 'Les elections législatives du 17 décembre 1978'; and for 1981 *La Libre Belgique*, 10-11 November 1981, p. 3. Walloon area: CH 826, 18; Flemish area: ibid., 4; Brussels area: ibid., 32 and 33.
11. The data on the electorates of the various parties is taken from N. Delruelle, R. Evalenko, W. Fraeys, *Le Comportement Politique des Electeurs Belges*, Editions de l'Institut de Sociologie de l'Université Libre de Bruxelles, 1970, tables V and VI, and analysis, 48-91, for 'statistically valid' determinants of voting preferences. For the Flemish parties later (September 1979), figures are taken from a poll cited in R. Van Malderghem's 'Welke zijn de nieuwe publiek en volksgroepen die de Socialistische Beweging aanspreekt?', *Socialistische Standpunten*, 2/81, 87-95. Poll data, 94-5.
12. *Le Soir* 10-11 Nov. 1981, 2.
13. On PSC policy, see CRD 10, 9-10.
14. See note 10 for source.
15. See note II for source.
16. 'Verkiezingsprogramma van de CVP', published in *Tele-Zeg*, 3-4.
16a.'Verkiezingsprogramma 1981', 5-21.
17. Ibid., 55-6. See also Van den Broude Bill on the five national sectors.
18. See CVP Statutes (1974, 1977, 1979), published in *Tele-Zeg* (1980), especially articles 17, 18 and 19 for the *Arrondissement* structure, and articles 28-35 for the national structure.
19. CVP Statutes, article 37 and poll regulation.
20. CH 820, 'Le Renouvellement des Candidatures en vue des législations du 17 décembre 1978', 11-17.
21. CVP Statutes, articles 35 (1), (2), (3) and (4).
22. For a brief history of the POB, see R. Abs, *Histoire du Parti Socialiste Belge*, Eds. Fondation Louis de Brouckère, Brussels, 1979, 17-46.
23. CRD 10, annexe, p. 1.
24. See Statutes of the PS adopted at Namur, 26 Nov. 1978, for the organisation of the PS.
25. PS Statutes, articles 17-28 on the congress.
26. CH 821, 2-7, on polls held in 1978.
27. CRD 10, 14 and 34. For 1979, see Keesing's *Political Parties of the World*, Longman, Harlow, England, 1980.
28. See note 11 for source.
29. See note 10 for source.
30. For an examination of the election of Mr Spitaels and the changes he has brought about, see an article published in three parts in *Le Soir* of 11, 12 and 13 Jan. 1982 (p. 2 each day), entitled 'Le PS dans un drôle de cure d'opposition'.
31. *Le Programme du Parti Socialiste: elections legislatives*, 1981.
32. *Programme. . . .*, chapter I: 'Le riposte socio-économique du Parti Socialiste' for the Economic Programme.
33. *Le Soir*, 28 March 1982, and Document 'Renover et Agir'.

34. See note 10 for source.
35. See note 11 for source.
36. 'Statuten van de SP' adopted 8 and 9 March 1980.
37. Ibid., paras 5 and 6.
38. Ibid., paras 7 and 10.
39. Ibid., paras 2–38 on the various national bodies.
40. Article 50 for the age limit and article 53 on the *'cumul'*.
41. CH 820 (I), 17–21.
42. CRD 10, 14 and 34. and Keesing's *Political Parties of the World*, op. cit.
43. Statutes, article 1.
44. See Van Malderghem, op. cit. (note 11).
45. For the early history of the Liberal party, see Luykx, op. cit., 94–7 and 181–3.
46. R. Willemyns, 'Politieke ideologie en vrijzinnigheid', *Socialistische standpunten*, 5/81, 264–79.
47. For the problem of the Brussels Liberals, see Luykx, op. cit., 586–8 and CRD 10, 2–3 and annexe, 3–4.
48. CRD 10, 27 and annexe, 3–4.
49. CRD 10, 11–14.
50. On Jean Gol and the changes he introduced, see *Le Soir* 15 and 16 May 1981, 'Voyage au Parti Réformateur Libéral' (each day on p. 3).
51. See note 10.
52. See note 11.
53. *Le Soir*, 'Voyage au Parti Réformateur Libéral'.
54. On policy, see CRD 10, 10–11, and J. Moden and J. Sloover, *Le Patronat Belge*, CRISP 1980, 284–91.
55. See note 10.
56. See note 11.
57. CRD 10, 11–14.
58. Quoted in *Le Patronat Belge*, op. cit., 291.
59. See 'Handvest van het Moderne Liberalisme', Kortrijk 1979.
60. The origins and early history of the PCB are set out in R. Lewin (ed.), *Le Parti Communiste de Belgique (1921–44)*, CHEMA 1980, 17–27, and in the inter-war period, 41–53.
61. See Statutes of the PCB (XX Congress, Charleroi 1971) and the resolution adopted by the Central Committee on 27 Oct. 1980: 'Fonctionnement démocratique du Parti', which seeks to create both more open political debate and some regionalised structures.
62. See note 10.
63. See note 11.
64. A good resumé of party doctrine is given in 'Introduction Politique' to the XXIII Congress 1979, by President Van Geyt, published in the PCB bulletin *Faits et arguments*, no. 48, June 1979, especially on regionalisation, 3–9; on economic policy, 9–16, on international relations, 16–23, and on the concept of a 'Union des Progressistes', 37–8.

65. See an article on the XXIV Congress, 'L'Eurocommunisme', by Claude Renard (PCB Vice President) in *Le Soir*, 14 April 1982, pp. 1–2.

66. See CRD 10, 5–6, for the origins of the RW.

67. See note 10.

68. See note 11.

69. CRD 10, 11–14.

70. For an account of the RW in power, see CH 786: 'L'évolution du Rassemblement Wallon d'avril 1974 à mars 1977'.

71. CH 786, 32–3.

72. For the origins and character of the FDF, see CRD 10, 3–4, 10–11 and 24.

73. Statutes of the FDF (1977, amended 1981), article 1.

74. FDF 1981: 'Maitre chez soi', 5–15.

75. Ibid., 21–40.

76. Ibid., 47–8.

77. CRD 10, 34.

78. See note 11.

79. See Statutes, esp. articles 5–6 (congress); 7–10 (*conseil général*); and 23 (*commission electorale*).

80. *Volksunie: Identity, history and programme*, published in English by the Volksunie, 1979, 4–5 and CRD 10, 4.

81. See note 10.

82. See note 11.

83. Statuten van de Volksunie, esp. articles 48–73 for the Party's national organisation.

84. Volksunie: Identity, history and programme, op. cit., 4.

85. M. Van Haegendoren, 'De Volksunie ziet het zo', *Vlaams Nationaal Standpunten*, 6/7 1980, 8–10.

86. 'Vlaamse Staatshervorming: Blauwdruk voor en Konfederaal Model' (June 1981).

87. Details of policies in *Werk en Zekerheid in een Vlaamse Staat* (1981 election manifesto).

88. CH 924 UDRT-RAD (I), 3–5 for origins and 13–16 for structure of the UDRT-RAD.

89. *Le Soir*, 15 June 1981, 'Descente au coeur de l'UDRT', 3.

90. CH 924, 11–13, for election results.

91. On UDRT-RAD policy, see CH 941 and 942, 'L'UDRT-RAD' (2 parts), esp. 2–11 for its 'anti-system' analysis and 17–40 for its programme.

92. See note 10.

93. *Le Soir*, 8–9 Nov. 1981, 3.

94. See the *Ecolo* programme '90 Propositions des Ecologistes: une autre manière de faire la politique'. This is a detailed programme of 74 pages.

95. *La Libre Belgique*, 10 Nov. 1981, 3.

96. Delruelle, Evalenko and Fraeys, op. cit., 12, and CH 820, 'Les Elections Legislatives du 17 décembre', 1978 (II).

97. Delruelle *et al.*, op. cit., tables XLVIII and XLIV.
98. For a regional analysis, see CH 864, 'Le Système des Partis dans la Belgique post-unitaire', esp. 19–22.
99. Figures taken from CH 957, 'La Formation des Premiers Executifs hors-gouvernement', 11.
100. CH 937, 7.

6

OTHER POLITICAL ACTORS

In a complex modern democracy such as Belgium, political parties are not the only political actors. Indeed, if there has been a tendency for power to be displaced from the formal political institutions towards the parties, there has also been a tendency for both economic and political power to be displaced towards a whole interlocking network of interest groups which make up the *'Partenaires sociaux'* (social partners) and *'Interlocuteurs'* (literally partners, but applied to those in any kind of official consultation) in a whole series of 'dialogues' or *'Concertations'* between government and interest groups. Some have seen in this tendency a dangerous semi-corporatist tendency threatening the parliamentary system. The Liberal/Christian Social government which took power in 1981 imposed major changes in the indexation of wages by way of the Special Powers Act without any *Concertation*, particularly not with the unions. Indeed, it has elevated this refusal to an ideological standpoint. Others, such as the left wing of the Socialist Party and the ecologists, see the active involvement of what is called the *'vie associative'* and the trade unions in protest and local planning battles as an extension rather than a limitation to democracy. Both viewpoints have merit, but both contain contradictions. The one suggests that consultative organisations are 'unrepresentative', while the other makes a similar suggestion regarding the official political bodies.

Here we shall look at some of the more important interest groups and their links to political parties, and the whole system of parapolitical organisations. We shall also look at the media — press and television — as a major force in shaping political opinion.

A key phenomenon concerning interest groups is that of *'Verzuiling'*,[1] a notion of a pluralist society, split into ideological sub-societies, gravitating around the three major 'political families' and, to a less extent, around the Regional parties. In this way almost all interest groups are closely linked to a political party, and jostle with other competing interest groups in their own sector; sometimes they co-operate with these competitors. This holds true of trade unions (Socialist, Christian, Liberal), farmers (PSC/CVP, VU or neutral), *Mutualités* (Socialist, Christian, neutral) and even in the field of employers and self-employed (*Indépendants* or *Classes moyennes*), which are Liberal or PSC/CVP. Thus, as we shall see, it is possible to speak of a '*Monde Chrétien*' a '*Monde Socialiste*' or a '*Monde Libéral*' composed of interest groups and associations of one type or another gravitating around the parent political party, and a *Mouvement Flamand* and *Mouvement Wallon* made up of cultural and political organisations.

The trade unions

Despite the country's early industrialisation, trade unionism developed late in Belgium. The Socialist leader, Hendrik De Man, ascribed this to the widespread co-operative movement which hindered union activity. Now, however, the level of unionisation is high. In the whole country it is 67 per cent, being over 80 per cent in the northern Flemish Provinces, 59 in Hainaut and 52 in Liège.[2] Although there were some isolated craft bodies as early as 1806, it is generally accepted that Belgian trade unionism was born in Ghent with the formation of, first, the Weavers' Association of Ghent in 1857 and then the *Werkers Bond* in 1860, which grouped several organisations. There was only limited progress at first because of the inertia of the developing working-class and bourgeois opposition. The first clearly Catholic union (of cotton workers also in Ghent) was formed in 1886.[3]

Trade unionism until the Second World War

Trade unionism in Belgium soon developed along pluralist, ideological lines.

Socialist trade unions. From 1880 a large number of national *Fédérations* was formed (*Fédération Nationale des Travailleurs de Bois* 1883), to be followed in the early twentieth century by *Centrales Industrielles* (industrial unions) which by 1914 represented 58 per cent of affiliated members, a proportion which had risen rapidly from 11.5 per cent in 1911.[4] The *Parti Ouvrier Belge* (POB) brought the movement under direct Party control: article 9 of its statutes (1892) provided for only national *Fédérations* and later national *Centrales Industrielles* joining the Party. In 1898 it established the first centralised union organisation under a committee appointed by the Party's *Conseil général*, called the *Commission Syndicale*, which had no independent policy line. In 1907, the Commission obtained its own statutes and organised congresses.[5] At the same time 'independent' (non-party) unions were admitted, provided they accepted the basic tenets of POB ideology. The *Commission Syndicale* was renamed the *Commission Syndicale du POB et des*

Syndicats Indépendents. Party and unions developed a degree of mutual independence, and the unions even publicly regretted the refusal of the POB to join the 1939 Pierlot government. The *Commission Syndicale* also reinforced its authority over the *Fédérations* and *Centrales*, jealous of their right to call strikes and call them off. The year 1922 saw the first proposals to give these powers to the central body; at the time the proposals were rejected. In 1937 the *Commission* was transformed into the quite independent (at least formally) *Confédération Générale du Travail de Belgique* (CGTB), which was accorded these vital powers; it also had control over the *Caisse Nationale de Résistance* (strike funds) first set up in 1909.[6] At the same time the structures of the *Fédérations* and *Centrales* had been greatly simplified by numerous amalgamations.

Christian unions. The first Christian union, as already mentioned, was the Cotton Workers', founded in Ghent in 1886. It was 'anti-Socialist', but nevertheless met opposition in Catholic circles. The 1893 papal encyclical *Rerum Novarum* gave the movement new impetus. The same process of initial diversification followed by amalgamation and consolidation occurred as in the Socialist unions. By 1906, there were thirteen *Fédérations*, mostly in Flanders, and only in 1908 were the first Walloon unions set up — the *Fédération nationale des Francs Mineurs*.

Moves began in 1904 for the creation of centralised organs. Thus the *Secrétariat Général des Unions professionnelles Chrétiennes* was set up, but it had no power over the *Fédérations*. This weakness led to the creation of two separate Flemish (1909) and Walloon (1909) confederations, based respectively in Ghent and La Louvière. These were fused in 1912 to form the *Confédération Générale des Syndicats Chrétiens et libres de Belgique* (CSC).[7] The next period saw the CSC considerably reinforce its powers. In 1922 it gained control over the strike fund (*Caisse de Réassurance*), and in 1930 it obtained powers over decisions on industrial action; the *Fédérations* could still launch strikes, but only if the CSC did not object. In the CSC the *Fédérations* were weak and the organisation as a whole was largely Flemish-dominated.

Liberal Trade Unions. The Confédération Générale des Syndicats Libéraux de Belgique was founded in 1930. It is the smallest of the three *Confédérations*, but the most centralised. It has no *Fédérations*, but is based on geographical sections. Its influence at the grassroots level is slight, but is greater at the national level.[8]

Independent Unions. These are found in the public service, and in
some very specialised sectors (taxis, trams, docks). Before the
Second World War, the most important was the *Confédération
Nationale Indépendante des Travailleurs* (1938).[9] The independent
unions formed the *Cartel des Syndicats Libres de Belgique* in 1959
with private and public sector affiliates of respectively 62,000 and
52,000 members.

The trade unions and the War

The Nazi occupation put an end for five years to traditional trade
unionism, and left scars which were later to provoke changes in
structure for the Socialists and at least in policies if not structures for
the other confederations. The occupation led to a radicalisation.
Unions were faced with the choice of underground resistance or
joining (as proposed by the then leader of the POB, Hendrik De
Man) the *Union des Travailleurs Manuels et Intellectuels* (UTMI),
set up in 1940 by Dr Voos to federate the three organisations and
the Nazi *Arbeitsorde* in an overtly collaborationist body. Neither
workers nor employers ever supported UTMI. The traditional
unions ceased to exist, and factory committees, often left-inclined
(anarcho-syndicalists), led impressive resistance and strike activities,
especially in the Liège steel industry, exacting wage rises from the
occupying power in a massive strike in 1941. From the co-ordination
body of these committees (*Mouvement Métallurgiste* — MMU) and
the Communist organisation *Comité de Lutte Syndicale* (CLS) came
the *Mouvement Syndical Unifié* (MSU), formed in early 1944. Its
manifesto '*Pour une révolution constructive*' was a left-wing radical
statement which, in the new climate, would inevitably represent a
challenge to the old CGTB after the liberation. The Communist CLS
also created the *Confédération Belge des Syndicats Unifiés* (CBSU),
and in the public service the *Syndicat Général des Services Publics*
(SGSP) was formed in 1942.[10]

Post-War developments

The Christian and Liberal unions faced no major difficulties in re-
establishing themselves after 1945. The same cannot be said for the
CGTB, which was threatened by three new and dynamic organisations on its left. On 8 September 1944 it called for an '*Assemblée de
réunification*', to include the CSC, but the latter withdrew after an
inaugural meeting. After many difficulties, a Unification Congress
was held in Brussels on 28 and 29 April 1945, which led to the formation of a new organisation, uniting the four previous ones (CGTB,

MSU, SGSP and SBSU) into the *Fédération Générale de Travail de Belgique* (FGTB). The balance of power was established in the way shown in the table. This gave the Communists (CBSU) a far from negligible influence in the new body. A new declaration of principles was adopted which was to the left of previous positions, and which made the FGTB independent of all political parties. For some time, internal problems continued. Communist *Centrales* continued to act semi-independently, and the '*tendances*' continued to show up in Congress votes. After the 'Prague coup' in February 1948, the Bureau excluded the Communist secretaries, and in April all Communists in the National Committee resigned, but many Communist members stayed on as individuals. After 1950, the movement maintained its unity, aided by the *Question royale*, over which the FGTB launched a general strike against Leopold III.[11]

	Membership	*Seats in the secretariat*
CGTB	248,259	3
CBSU	165,968	2
MSU	59,535	1
SGSP	51,789	1

The structure of Belgian trade unions

The Socialists. The régime set up in 1945 lasted until the strikes of 1960–1 and was then replaced by a 'transitional régime', (1963–78). In 1978, the statutes were modified to ensure a regionalised structure for the FGTB in line with the moves towards political federalism. In 1965, a structure was adopted which gave two-thirds of the representation at the Congress to the *Centrales Professionnelles* and one-third to the *Régionales Interprofessionnelles*. The *Régionales* are weaker than the *Centrales* and do nothing but reflect the make-up of the *Centrales* in that Region, being composed as they are of delegates of the *Centrales*. The *Centrale* is made up of *Centrales Professionnelles Régionales* and the *Sections d'Entreprises* (workplace Sections).[12]

The FGTB faced a major crisis which split it on community lines at the time of the 1960–1 strikes. The *Comité National* met on 16 December 1960 to consider two motions: the Smets motion (for a national day of action and a campaign against the *Loi unique*) and the Renard motion (for a general strike). Smets and Renard were the two key leaders of the FGTB. Smets was a moderate, whereas

Renard was a radical and a federalist, who contributed greatly to the FGTB's (and later the PS's) policy of major structural reforms in the economy. The Renard motion was lost by 475,823 votes to 496,487 (mostly Flemish) and 53,112 abstentions (mostly from Brussels).[13] The Movement was strongest in Wallonia, and its *de facto* leadership came from the unofficial Walloon Co-ordination Committee. Out of this came pressure, led by André Renard, for a degree of federalism inside the FGTB. This pressure was most evident in Liège and on the political level in the new *Mouvement Populaire Wallon* (MPW). The internal debate led to an agreement on a 'transitional régime' in June 1963. The agreement did not institute federalism, but provided for linguistic parity in the FGTB *Bureau* and secretariat, but not in the Congress. It provided for a sort of '*Sonnette d'alarme*' (alarm-bell) procedure on any matter where there was a '*Rupture*', either between the *Centrales* and *Régionales* or between Walloons and Flemish.[14] In such a case, a compromise was to be sought which would be approved by a majority of Walloon and Flemish Regions and *Centrales*. There were rules on the right to establish '*Tendances*' and for regionalised publicity activities.[15] These procedures were never invoked, but they certainly incited mutual searches for compromise. In 1966, the first purely Walloon position emerged and led to the creation of an *Assemblée Générale des Régions Wallonnes*. In 1966, a '*comité des sages*' thus proposed an addition to the 1963 agreement, which permitted the creation of inter-regional organisations on Community lines and created a *Conseil National de Politique Economique* of twenty-three members to work out general economic policy, co-ordinate the programmes of the Regions and *Inter-régionales* and make proposals for action. It met on twenty-nine occasions between 1968 and 1975.[16] This body was the first to incorporate the principle — strongly supported by the Liègeois and the public sector workers — that the *Centrales* and *Régionales* should have equal representation in all organs.

Each *Inter-régionale* (IR) then set up its own machinery and statutes. Each reflected its traditions and preoccupations both as to its structure and issues treated. In the Flemish IR both the *Centrales* and *Régionales* are represented, but in the Walloon IR[17] only the *Régionales* are represented. Both have a secretariat (four members in each), a *Bureau* composed of representatives of the *Régionales* (and *Centrales* for the Flemish IR), and an *Assemblée Générale* composed (in the Walloon IR) of the Executive Committee of the *Régionales* and, on the Flemish side, of the *Bureau* plus representatives of the *Régionales*.[18]

The Walloon IR has concerned itself with the 1971–5 and 1976–80 plan options, the public sector and the implementation of article 107 *quater* (regionalisation) of the constitution. It has worked actively in the *Conseil Economique Wallon* (CEW), an advisory body set up under two 1970 laws.[19] The Flemish IR has concentrated on seaports policy, energy policy and the policy of the BRT (Flemish TV network), on which it has created joint working parties with the SP.[20]

The 1978 Reform simply legalised these arrangements, harmonised the structures of the IR's to include both *Centrales* and *Régionales* and established a third Brussels *Inter-régionale*.[21]

The Christian trade unions. The national organisation, as laid down in 1947, of the CSC is not dissimilar to that of the FGTB. Its Congress is its supreme body, which meets at least every two years. Otherwise the most powerful body is the Committee which, meeting every two months, defines policy between Congresses. The Committee is the true decision-making body of the CSC. It is made up of the *Bureau journalier*, one representative of each *Régionale* and *Centrale* and a representative of the Catholic Church. The *Bureau* (twenty-four members: twelve representatives of the *Centrales*, seven Provincial representatives and five members of the *Bureau journalier*) and the *Bureau journalier* (President, General Secretary and members appointed by the Committee) run the day-to-day administration of the CSC.[22]

The CSC, despite its 'Christian' appellation, is relatively open. In it, the *Centrales* have less power than in the FGTB. The President, elected by the Committee, has a considerable position. Walloon members are, at all levels, officially in the minority according to the statutes.

Later, and less directly, the CSC faced the same federalising pressures as the FGTB.[23] Also, as in the FGTB, pressure came from Wallonia. The response was more pragmatic and slower. The first signs came at the 1966 Congress, and in 1967 a Committee was set up to look at the problem. One response was to 'regionalise' the existing *Commission pour les Problèmes Régionaux et Sectoriels* into two Regional Committees. On the Walloon side, pressures were accelerating, and manifested themselves above all in the Liège area. They showed strongly at the 1971 Congress on the Democratisation of the Firm. A *'Groupe des 40'*, including all CSC Walloon leaders, was set up in 1975. Motions were passed in various *Régionales* in favour of a more advanced policy, co-operation with the FGTB workers, and a separate Walloon economic strategy against the economic crisis.

In 1978, the '*Groupe des 40*' reported in the form of a 'Walloon Action Programme'.[24]

In the face of these developments, the CSC *Bureau* decided on 10 October 1978 to set up three Regional Committees each with 50–100 members, drawn equally from the *Centrales* and *Régionales* and the CSC *Bureau*. There was a clear determination of 'national matters', for which the Regional Committees were not to be competent. It was now, however, fully accepted that there should be regionally differentiated approaches. The Flemish Committee was much less active than the Walloon Committee; meeting first in March 1979, it then only discussed formal organisational matters. The Walloon Committee continued its work on the 'Walloon Action Programme'.[25]

Liberal trade unions. The Liberal *Confédération* includes a public-sector and private-sector section. Otherwise the structure is very unitary. The sections and sub-sections are directly linked to the *Centrale générale* for the region irrespective of profession or trade. The Liberal trade union's main distinguishing feature is its belief in solidarity between employers and workers in respect of liberal principles as the basis of 'justice and social peace' (article 3 of the 1962 statutes). It favours German-type participation in management, and conciliation at the national level in appropriate bodies.[26]

Relative membership

We shall now look at the relative membership of the different confederations and the structure of each membership.

The FGTB was the largest union before 1939, but despite steady increases in membership, it was overtaken in 1959 by the CSC. Membership of the FGTB was stable until 1965 and then began to increase again. Some figures are significant:

1910	69,370	1965	750,318
1945	447,992	1975	962,506
1959	731,281	1979	1,112,757
1962	685,862		

The largest *Centrale* is the *Centrale générale*, followed by the metal-working industries and the public services. These big three represented 63 per cent of all members in 1961, 67 per cent in 1965 and 58.5 per cent in 1979. Otherwise textiles (7.6 per cent), transport

(3.5), food processing (3.5) were the only other *Centrales* of any size. Flanders had 47 per cent of members, Wallonia 41 per cent and Brussels 12 per cent (1965 figures).[27]

The membership of the CSC has shown a dramatic rise in the post-war period:

1910	49,478	1965	844,410
1945	342,099	1976	1,100,000
1959	737,286	1979	1,273,000
1962	772,208		

This exceptional progress perhaps results from its greater image of unity, its links with a Catholic recruitment network, its younger activist element, its greater attention to youth and family policy and perhaps, lastly, on its greater openness since 1945 to non-Catholics. The main *Centrales* are woodwork and construction (18.9 per cent), metal workers (15.6), textiles (14.6), office workers (9.7), teachers (8.4), food processing (6.8), public services (6.2) and railways (4.4).[28] This gives a much more even spread than in the FGTB. The 'big three' (the three largest *Centrales*) have only 43.8 per cent of membership (1976). The textile *Centrale* is now running down and the greatest growth is in the office workers' *Centrale* (+ 42 per cent over the last six years). The regional structure of membership brings out the Flemish dominance: Flanders 74.5 per cent, Wallonia 17.6, and Brussels 7.7 in 1965. In absolute terms, the CSC had 146,306 members in Wallonia against 293,557 for the FGTB, and in Flanders 810,918 members against 358,478 for the FGTB. In Brussels, the FGTB had 87,067 against 63,447 CSC members. Thus the CSC is dominated by its Flemish wing and offers no statutory guarantees to its Walloon wing.

The Liberals had 30,000 members in 1930, 100,000 in 1940 and 122,000 in 1972. The only areas — taking trade union elections as a guide — where the Liberals have real influence are non-ferrous metals (9.7 per cent of votes in elections for the *Comités d'Entreprise*) and buses (12.4).[29] The *Indépendants* had 114,000 members in 1972.

Policy and doctrine

The FGTB has clear origins in the Socialist movement, and its first doctrinal statement was that of the POB. It cherishes the ideal of a socialist transformation of society, and in practice too it has emphasised its residual attachment to notions of class struggle by its reluctance to be 'co-opted into the system'. It seeks to maintain a different economic logic from the capitalist system, in that its social demands are not subordinated to the economic performance of the enterprise. The practical policies of the union have been to favour expansion by neo-Keynesian methods and above all in more recent years by structural reforms which would make greater use of the public sector. These would represent 'breaks in the capitalist wall'. This policy, though first developed in 1954–5, has remained unchanged, subject only to increasing radicalisation and autonomist pressures in Wallonia.[30]

The CSC has a much less clear doctrine. It does favour dialogue rather than the notion of class struggle. Its main aim is the wellbeing of the workers, but achieved in a much more *ad hoc* manner. It has favoured participation, and above all it holds the view, different in essence from the FGTB, that union power involves responsibility. Its Walloon wing is, as we shall see, much more radical and has found common ground with the FGTB in Wallonia.[31]

The Liberals, as we have seen, seek — even more than the CSC — non-conflictual class-co-operative solutions to disputes and naturally oppose collectivist or interventionist strategies.

Links with parties

Both the FGTB and CSC (and Liberal CGSLB) are in theory — according to their statutes — independent of any one political party. Article 4 of the FGTB statute pledges the Union to co-operate with parties which support its goals but without giving the Party the right to become involved in the Union's affairs.[32] The Union also, in 1964, limited the '*Cumul*' (addition) of political and trade union posts, but did not eliminate it. Recent attempts to tie the FGTB more explicitly to the PS have not found favour. The Union and Party have and desire considerable autonomy, but are linked in bodies such as the *Action Commune Socialiste* (PS, FGTB, *Mutualités Socialistes* and *Coopératives*). The level of activity of the *Action Commune* is very variable. Relations between the FGTB and the SP in Flanders have been the closest. In Wallonia the issue has been clouded by the FGTB's links with the MPW (at the origin of the *Inter-régionale*) and later with the RW.[33]

The CSC (article 3) is 'independent'. Its 1953 Congress decided that it would have no organic link with the PSC/CVP; however, CSC leaders are often active in CVP/PSC policy committees. The *Cumul* is forbidden (Deputies, Senators, mayors or *Echevins* in *Communes* with over 10,000 inhabitants). However, the CSC belongs to the *Mouvement Ouvrier Chrétien* (MOC), or ACW in Flanders, founded in 1945. Originally, the MOC (or ACW) was independent of the CVP/PSC; from its 21st Congress in 1964 it moved closer to it, inviting its members to join the PSC, but it is now moving away from it again in seeking to form a new political move-ment, involving non-Catholics and non-Socialists. Thus the MOC forms a link between the CSC and the PSC. The CSC also plays an important role in the PSC research centre's Agenda Committee. The pressure of the CSC and MOC is more marked on the PSC (Wallonia) than on the CVP, where the '*Aile démocrate chrétienne*' is weaker.[34] Problems have arisen when the PS is in opposition (as it has been since 1981), creating competitive militancy between the FGTB and the CSC.

Co-operation between the unions

The weakness resulting from the division of the union movement has led to co-operation and common action (even strikes) through the tactic of the '*Front commun*'. This has been an almost exclusively Walloon phenomenon, as the CSC in Flanders is so dominant, close to the CVP and too far in position from the FGTB.

One consequence of the fact that CSC is in the minority in Wallonia and of the radicalisation of Walloon opinion since the onset of the crisis, has been co-operation between CSC and the FGTB in Wallonia. Work began in 1978, in the so-called Sabic-Yerna group, to draw up a common Walloon programme. This programme[35] went through successive drafts and was eventually issued by both bodies under different names, illustrating their pre-occupations: *Priorités pour les responsables politiques régionaux de Wallonie* (CSC) and *Les axes d'une politique progressiste Wallonne* (FGTB). Contacts continued and a first joint action in a *Front commun* in Wallonia took place on 29 March 1979. On 16 March 1979, a '*Proclamation commune*' of the *Front commun* (Wallon) to which the two national *Bureaux* did not agree, was issued. Common action, however does not exclude competition.

Employers' organisations

The development of employers' organisations cannot be dissociated from the growth of the industrial proletariat and their trade unions. Early '*Intérêts des producteurs*' were largely directed against producers' clients,[36] and only in the 1880s was the need felt for a defensive organisation. Initial attempts were not successful. Thus it was only in 1895 that the *Comité Central du Travail Industriel* (CCTI) was formed and this was as much involved in lobbying for industrial interests with government ·as with confronting union power. It was transformed in 1913 into the *Comité Central Industriel* and in the war it began, with severe misgivings, to participate with the unions in bi-partite or corporate (with government) bodies such as the *Conférences nationales du travail*. By 1935, the CCI grouped together firms employing 100,000 workers. In 1946, the *Fédération des Industries de Belgique* (FIB) was formed.[37] It was made up of *Fédérations*, on the basis of one per industrial sector, which greatly homogenised the structure of the various organisations. Its most important component *Fédérations* were *Fabrimétal, Fédération des Industries Chimiques de Belgique, Confédération Nationale de la Construction* and *Groupement des Hauts Fourneaux*, all of which had their own organisation and considerable influence in their own right. In parallel, the tertiary sector was organising itself. In 1953, the *Fédération du Commerce, des Banques et des Assurances* was set up and was transformed into the *Fédération des Entreprises non-industrielles* (FENIB). In 1973, FENIB and FIB merged to form the blanket body, the *Fédération des Entreprises Belges* (FEB).[38]

The main aims of such bodies are to provide and centralise services and information for its members on business and tax law, marketing information and suchlike; to deal with the trade union *Confédérations*; to negotiate with government on issues of concern to industry, and to present the concerns of industry to public opinion and improve its image.

At the same time, business organisation has been regionalised. The earliest regional organisation was the *Vlaams Economisch Verbond* (VEV), founded in 1926 as part of the drive to increase the Flemish role in national economic life. Its present Walloon counterpart, the *Union Wallone des Entreprises* (1967) took over from the earlier *Union Industrielle Wallone* (1954), and the *Union des Entreprises de Bruxelles* was set up in 1971. On a more local level, the traditional *Chambres de Commerce* remain active, and they too have their own national organisation.[39]

There has been a tendency for employers' organisations to develop an autonomy, to become actors on the political scene distinct from the firms which make them up, but at the same time there is a close identity, in terms of the leadership élites, between the leadership of the employers' organisations (FEB and individual sectoral *Fédérations*) and the managers or owners of large companies.[40] Nor should it be forgotten that the small group of holdings which exercise a dominant position in the Belgian economy, together with several large multinationals, represent a political force in their own right quite independant of the official organisations. They can and do exercise a major, but often hidden, influence on decision-making.

Employers' organisations have, especially since the onset of the economic crisis in the 1970s, been developing a more offensive ideological line[41] in the face of what they see as 'the constant denigration of profit and the free market' not only by what they characterise as 'active minorities' — which include the consumer movement, Ecologists and the left-wing press — but also by official media such as the RTBF (the French-speaking television network). In this new 'crisis of values and authority', the *Patronat* (= employers or employers' organisations) sees a threat to established procedures of *Concertation* between the two sides of industry, since the authority of trade union leaderships is also under threat, and must therefore react more radically. That is not to say that the *Patronat* has ever liked *Concertation* as such, but it has come to accept it as a stabilising element, as the devil it knows, which has made possible a certain consensus, an accomodation with union power.[42] The new situation has created uncertainties and faces the *Patronat* with new and 'unrealistic' demands — 'unrealistic' in the sense that they deliberately ignore the 'laws of the market' and the need, as seen by the employers, to control costs, which to them largely means wage costs. These phenomena are noted especially in Wallonia — 'the spirit of class struggle and a doctrinal and unrealistic attitude'[43] is said to characterise the Walloon trade unions. Trade union power is now being abused, according to the employers. There has also been an attempt to present the unions, with their mass membership, finances and political influence as inevitably more powerful than the employers' bodies, which are often divided among themselves.

The reaction to this perceived situation has been to seek to influence public opinion, to show the superiority of free enterprise against state interventionism and abuse of power by the unions. The FEB has sought to improve its structure and its coherence, co-operating with other groups (*Fédérations*, 'middle-class' organisations and the regional '*Patronat*' such as the VEV). A counter-offensive has thus been lauched.

In relation to the trade unions, this has involved since 1976 the notion of a re-invigorated system of *Concertation* based on a consensus around defined and agreed objectives, expressed solemnly in a '*pacte social*' (social contract). Such an approach would have made possible — as one of its main promoters, *Fabrimétal*, argued — class co-operation within the firm, permitting wage moderation and restructuring in response to the economic crisis, and accepting the logic of market forces — in a concerted fashion, enabling the shocks to be attenuated. As to the state, it would be limited to giving general orientations in economic policy, creating favourable conditions for firms by reducing taxation and welfare insurance costs and indeed reducing the 'work disincentive aspects' of the welfare state. It should only enter the *Concertation* arena as an arbiter of last resort. It should also severely reduce public expenditure, and limit public aid to industry in difficulty (on this some sectoral *Fédérations* such as *Febeltex* [textiles] dissent). These doctrines have become more radical from the beginning of the 1980s. Many employers' leaders and managers have forsaken their more traditional allegiance to the CVP/PSC and have increasingly turned to the less divided and more dynamic PVV under Willy De Clercq, and the revitalised PRL under Jean Gol since 1979. Among the smaller businessmen, the self-employed, café owners *et al.*, the more radical defence of the free enterprise system offered by the Liberals and even the UDRT, especially in Brussels, has caught on and explains to a large extent the poor results of the PSC/CVP at the 1981 elections.

This new philosophy is openly anti-trade union, aggressively for free enterprise and against state interventionism. It may differ very little in substance from the earlier more prudent employers' ideology, but it is more intransigent and unconditional and certainly less defensive. It is this trend which has led the Martens-Gol-De Clercq government, formed in late 1981, to abandon the traditional *Concertation* approach. Earlier, even governments containing Liberal ministers sought consensus with the social partners as preferable to legislation on incomes, as in 1979–80. The Martens V (1981–) government brought in special powers and unilaterally imposed measures affecting the automatic indexation of wages, and placed conditions (salary reductions) on state aid to companies in difficulty, by *Arrêté royal*, without *Concertation*. This is entirely consistent with the view that government and Parliament must resume their 'rightful place' and govern, even against the social partners. As Jean Gol put it in 1979, 'The country is no longer governed.' There is in short a reaction in the early 1980s against the traditional system of *Concertation*, consensus and compromise, this has already led to a hardening of trade union positions, but it has caused profound internal difficulties for the CSC, which is split between support for a PSC/CVP ministry and the pressure from the grassroots, especially in Wallonia.

Middle-class organisations

Middle-class organisations, in Belgian terminology, means independent tradesmen and very small businessmen. These constitute a large bloc which, although it has declined, remains a considerable influence. Their organisations include the *Fédération nationale des*

Chambres de Commerce de Belgique, the *Nationaal Christelijk Middenstandsverbond* in Flanders, close to the CVP and the more neutral *Fédération des Unions Syndicales de Classes Moyennes* in Wallonia. There is also the *Entente Wallone des Associations de Classes Moyennes* and the *Inter-syndicale des Indépendents de la Région Bruxelloise*, which 'regionalise' these organisations. The main concerns of these bodies have been restrictions on opening hours for supermarkets, taxation rates, rigidities in labour law and their unfair pension situation. On all these items they have had some success, notably via a special ministry for middle class affairs.[44]

Organisations representing the liberal professions, in particular doctors, are very powerful.[45] Several strikes by doctors have occurred since the early 1970s both to obtain increases in the fees they may charge and to combat any creeping socialisation of medicine. The *Ordre des Médecins* (Medical Association) has also attempted to play a part in influencing opinion in such sensitive ethical issues as abortion.

Farmers' organisations

The most powerful farmers' organisation has always been the *Boerenbond* in Flanders and, from 1931, the *Alliance Agricole* in Wallonia.[46] These bodies formed one of the '*Standen*' in the old Catholic Party before 1945. They remain close to the CVP/PSC, and many Deputies from these parties — Dupont (PSC), Héger (PSC) Martens (CVP) and De Keersmaeker (CVP) — have been close to these farmers organisations. There is also the much less important, politically neutral *Fédération Nationale des Unions Professionelles Agricoles Belges*. These organisations are active on the national level, but since vital price and other decisions on agriculture are now taken by the EEC, they have had to increase their sphere of activity to the European level. They have in any event been fairly successful in keeping the Belgian government to a high-price position in EEC negotiations.[47]

The Walloon and Flemish movements

As well as socio-economic bodies, which have themselves, as we have seen, become regionalised over the course of time, there is what is called the 'Flemish movement' and, as a later development, the 'Walloon movement'.[48] These 'movements' consist of a series of cultural, social and political organisations seeking to promote a regional or national (Flemish) identity. These organisations have been influential in exercising pressure on the political parties and creating a new climate of Flemish and Walloon consciousness.

In Flanders, there are the three 'political' cultural foundations: the *Davidsfonds* (Catholic), *Willemsfonds* (Liberal), and the *Vermeylensfonds* (Socialist). There are also 'patriotic' groups such as the *Ijzerbedevaart* committee (the Ijzer Pilgrimage Committee), which organises an annual pilgrimage to the Ijzer Tower to commemorate the 1914–18 dead of the Ijzerfront, which is an occasion for nationalist speeches, and a federalist pressure group, the *Vlaamse Volksbeweging* (VVB). These diverse groups are coordinated by the *Overlegcentrum der Vlaamse Verenigingen*. There are also less respectable extremist and extreme right-wing organisations such as the *Taal Aktiekomitee* (TAK), which mounts demonstrations and protests on language questions, and the semi-Fascist *Vlaams Militanten Orde* (VMO). These latter are rejected by the mainstream Flemish movement.

In the early 1960s, the Walloon movement began to develop with such organisations as *Wallonie Libre*, *Rénovation Wallone* and, above all, the *Mouvement Populaire Wallon* (MPW), which grew out of the 1960–1 strikes. The Walloon movement is in general overtly left-of-centre in both its cultural and economic approaches, which broadly distinguishes it from the Flemish movement, which has been more politically conservative.

The role of pressure groups

Despite their widely differing objectives, ideologies and structures, all the groups we have discussed have at least one aim in common, and that is to influence public opinion and decision-makers. They seek to 'lobby' as effectively as possible. As in all modern states, there is in the Belgium a degree of mutual interest — which of course has its limits — between the government and pressure groups. Pressure groups favour participation in a whole system of consultative committees, because of the leverage this gives them and the information which they can thereby gain, but seek to avoid becoming too compromised in the eyes of their membership. The government too gains much useful information and prior warning of opposition in its consultations. It may also hope to 'co-opt' interest groups into the system, to disarm them by making them appear to accept joint responsibility with government for agreed compromises.

Interest groups have been involved not only in a network of consultative committees of a permanent and an *ad hoc* nature, but have also been co-opted into bodies exercising powers of decision in certain matters.[49] The most important consultative bodies deal with economic and social policy, such as the *Conseil Centrale de l'Economie* and tri-partite councils for each sector and firm, involving both sides of industry, the *Conseil Supérieur des Classes Moyennes* (1949), the *Conseil National de la Politique Scientifique* (1952) and the *Conseil de la Consommation* (1964). In addition, there are the occasional *Conférences Nationales du Travail* for national *Concertation* on such problems as the cost-of-living indexation of wages. Since 1968, collective bargaining can also take place in these '*Concertation* bodies' at firm, industry and national level. A whole range of sectoral committees and informal direct consultations between government, parties and interest groups completes the picture.

In several areas such as energy, steel, banking and credit, social welfare administration and price control, interest groups sit in committees which have decision-making or administrative functions, such as the *Comité du Contrôle de l'Electricité et du Gaz*, the *Comité de Concertation et de Contrôle du Pétrole* (1974), the *Comité de Concertation de la Politique Sidérurgique*, and the *Conseils Economiques Regionaux*. They also nominate members of the boards of '*Parastataux*' (semi-state bodies or, the British parlance, QUANGOS), which operate many social and economic services.

The major characteristics of the Belgian interest groups are their diversity, their pluralism and their regionalisation. There is an extremely wide range of interest groups, covering the whole field of economic and social activity: trade unions, various employer and middle-class organisations, 'family organisations', Flemish and Walloon cultural and political pressure groups, powerful professional bodies. Alongside them are powerful holdings, banks and multinationals, which are important political actors in their own right. Nor should the influence of the Catholic Church be underestimated, especially in matters such as education, social policy, abortion, etc., though it tends to work indirectly through the CSC and the CVP/PSC.

Each 'political family' (Christian, Liberal and Socialist) forms its own 'sub-society' of organisations, centred around the Party.[50] The FGTB, the *Mutualités Socialistes*, the co-operatives, cultural bodies like the Flemish *Vermeylenfonds*, and the women's organisation *Femmes Prévoyantes Socialistes* form the Socialist movement. The 'Christian world' is composed of the CSC; the *Alliance Nationale des Mutualités Chrétiennes*; the *Fédération Nationale des Coopératives Chrétiennes*; the *Mouvement Ouvrier Chrétien* (MOC), which does not give its sole allegiance to the PSC, and the Flemish equivalent, the ACW, which is very close to the CVP: the CEPIC and the *Nationaal Christelijk Middenstandsverbond* for employers and the *Indépendants*. The *Patronat's* politically 'neutral' bodies such as the FEB and the VEV, the *Boerenbond* and the *Alliance Agricole* also have strong links with the Christian organisations. As will be seen, links of the 'Christian movement' are wider and more contradictory, but in large part duplicate those of the Socialists. The Liberals have a less developed sub-society. There are the Liberal unions and *mutualités* and a *Centre National des Indépendants et Cadres* for small businessmen and managers.

As well as their ideological differentiation, the various pressure groups have also, as we have seen, become regionalised. The different regional wings often face different situations and therefore take up different attitudes. This is true of the CSC, the MOC and the ACW. As to the *Patronat*, the more ambivalent PSC is less appealing than the Liberals and the tougher CVP; however, this has not always been so, for as a '*Standen Partij*' the CVP as a whole had to remain more moderate than the CEPIC wing of the PSC.

Despite the important social changes of the last thirty years, including the decline of both religious observance and ideology, these '*Mondes*' have retained their structure and at least some of their vitality. They are however increasingly being contested as too powerful, too ossified and unresponsive to changing conditions. The polarisation of opinion in Wallonia is causing particular strain in the Catholic world, with its large working-class support.

The press

The press remains, despite TV and radio, an important actor on the political scene. It shares with TV both an agenda-setting and opinion-forming or opinion reinforcing role. A nationwide poll, now very old but the most recent of its kind, found that while more voters regarded television as the more important influence on their political behaviour, the press retained an important place in the formation of political views.[51]

There are few genuine party newspapers. There were until 1979–80 Socialist papers such as *Le Peuple* in Wallonia (1973 circulation 60,000) and two Flemish Socialist papers *De Volksgazet* (78,000) and *Vooruit* (= 'forward' or 'progress' — 32,000). These have all been forced to close. There are now only the daily *De Morgen* and weekly *L'Eglantine*, which are 'close' to the Socialist parties (PS/SP). There is also a Communist Party paper, the *Drapeau Rouge*, or *Rode Vaan*, which has been a daily since 1974.[52] Many voters therefore read papers which are 'close' to parties for which they do not vote. In Wallonia it was found that 36.4 per cent of PS voters read Socialist papers, 14.1 per cent Liberal papers and 11.7 per cent PSC papers. In Flanders, only 28 per cent of SP voters read Socialist papers against 32.8 who read CVP papers. Even in Flanders, only 52.8 per cent of CVP voters read CVP papers, but in Wallonia 60.8 per cent of PSC voters read PSC papers. Of Liberals in Wallonia, 40.9 per cent read neutral papers, and only 24.2 per cent Liberal papers against 36.4 per cent PSC papers.[53]

There has been a tendency for the number of papers to decline over the years and the pluralism of the press has also been reduced. The figures in the adjoining table are eloquent.[54] There have been further closures since 1978. No doubt the economic crisis has had its effects, but the conclusion is clear: fewer daily papers and above all, fewer political papers. In 1971, there were 2,032 weeklies (ninety-six political and fifteen economic or financial), and in 1978 this had fallen to 1,632 (eighty political and three financial and economic publications). There had been a slight rise in periodicals (monthly or less frequent).

Type of daily paper	1971	1972	1973	1974	1975	1976	1977	1978
Political	47	46	45	41	40	40	39	39
Economic and financial	2	2	1	1	1	1	6	6
Agriculture, commerce, industry	2	2	2	2	2	3	2	2
Arts, literary, scientific	—	—	—	—	—	—	—	—
Other	24	26	22	14	15	13	14	17
Total	75	76	70	58	58	57	61	64

The main papers (those of above 100,000 circulation), with their 'political tendencies' and circulation are, for each region, those shown in the accompanying table.[55] Only *Le Soir* and *De Standard* have a certain 'national' or 'inter-regional' readership; otherwise the press is entirely regionalised.

Flanders	*Wallonia*	*Brussels + Brabant*
Het Volk (689,000, CVP)	*La Libre Belgique* (170,000, Catholic)	*Le Soir* (270,000, Ind/Lib)
Gazet van Antwerpen (576,800, CVP/Flemish)	*La Dernière Heure* (256,400, Ind/PRL)	
Het Laatste Nieuws (397,909, Ind/Liberal)		
De Standaard (390,148, CVP, Flemish)		

These figures are in fact only limited indications of the degree of concentration of the Belgian press and the implied threat to

pluralism and open reporting. An analysis of the ownership structure of the press is even more revealing. Despite its special importance and status in a democracy, the press is in reality, as near as
makes no difference, a business enterprise like any other, subject to
the same market pressures towards concentration and often forming
part, among other activities, of the diversified portfolios of large
holding companies. Indeed, the commercial and industrial activities
may come into conflict with critical freedom for the press side of a
company's activities; for example, it may be difficult for pollution,
the arms trade or 'economic restructuring', to name but a few issues,
to be discussed critically in the Belgian press.

There are no strict laws controlling press mergers and concen-
trations. In Flanders, four groups control 86.9 per cent of the daily
press market. One group, *Vlaamse Uitgevers Maatschappij* (VUM),
controls 27.6 per cent with 864,300 readers. In Wallonia, four
groups control 90.1 per cent, and just one of them, Rossel, controls
48.4 per cent (1,215,900) of the market (including *Le Soir* and *La
Meuse*).[56] When one looks at the ownership structure of the various
groups, matters become extremely complicated. In VUM, for
example, 23.65 per cent of the capital is owned, directly and
indirectly, by the *Kredietbank*, the *Société Générale* holds 15 per
cent and *Paribas* (the *Banque de Paris et des Pays-Bas*) directly
controls about 25 per cent of VUM's capital. The Brébart group (*La
Dernière Heure* and *La Libre Belgique*) have a large injection of
Société Générale capital. The Luxembourg TV, RTL, is 54.6 per cent
owned by the Brussels-Lambert Bank. 51.65 per cent of VUM's
capital is in the hands of the Antwerp shipping industry via various
complex holdings. Roularta, which publishes the magazines *Knack*
and *Trends* (economic and financial periodicals), is owned by several
property groups. The Belgian Press Agency is directed by the
Belgian press, the RTBF and the BRT. However, several banks
(*Kredietbank*) and large companies (GB-Inno-BM) have shares in
the Agency.[57]

Radio and television in Belgium is a public service, without
advertising. It is now regionalised into two distinct and independent
public corporations: for Wallonia the *Radio-Télévision de Belgique
Française* (RTBF) and for Flanders the *Belgische Radio en Televisie*
(BRT). These corporations have normal public service obligations
under their parent legislation, such as neutrality, impartiality,
balance in news and reporting and the right of reply (very rarely
invoked or accorded). They are financed by a TV and radio license,
as in Britain. The RTBF and the government are now considering the
adoption of advertising. Each corporation's statutes, the appointment of its board, and the political, administrative and political

'*Tutelle*' (supervision) are devolved to the Community councils (article 4[6] of the Special Law of 8 August 1980). Only decisions on license fees and on advertising are excepted. There has been a constant tendency to politicise the RTBF and BRT by '*Dosages*' (balance) in appointments not only to the board, but of administrative staff and journalists. Indeed, the boards are elected by the Community councils by proportional representation, the candidates being proposed by the political groups in the council. The *Patronat* (FEB), for example, tends to see an excessive left-wing influence in the RTBF-BRT, especially the RTBF.

NOTES

1. For an examination of this concept, see X. Mabille and V. Lorwin, 'Belgium' in Henig (ed.), *Political Parties in the European Community*, PSI/Allen & Unwin 1979, 8–10.
2. G. Spitaels, *Le Mouvement Syndical en Belgique*, Editions de l'Université de Bruxelles 1974, 74.
3. Ibid., 9–13, for the early history of Belgian trade unionism.
4. Ibid., 13.
5. Ibid., 15.
6. Ibid., 15–16.
7. Ibid., 19.
8. Ibid., 20–1.
9. Ibid., 21.
10. On the unions in the war, see ibid., 21–3.
11. Ibid., 24.
12. Ibid., 29–31.
13. *Courrier Hebdomadaire du CRISP* ('CH') 866, '*Evolution aux Structures Internes de la FGTB et de la CSC*', 1980, 3.
14. Ibid., 4.
15. For details, ibid., 4–8.
16. Ibid., 8.
17. Ibid., 9–10.
18. Ibid., 11–12.
19. Ibid., 9–10.
20. Ibid., 12.
21. Ibid., 13–15.
22. Spitaels, op. cit., 45–7.
23. CH 866, 16.
24. Ibid., 17–19.
25. Ibid., 20.
26. Spitaels, op. cit., 64–7.
27. Figures from ibid., 32–5. For more recent figures, see A.P. Coldrick and P. Jones, *International Directory of the Trade Union Movement*, Macmillan, London & Basingstoke, 1979.
28. Figures from Spitaels, op. cit., 48–52; Coldrick and Jones, op. cit.

29. Spitaels, op. cit., 65.
30. On the FGTB doctrine, see ibid., 36–40.
31. On the CSC doctrine, see ibid., 53–8.
32. Ibid., 40–1.
33. *Dossier du CRISP* no. 10 'Les Parties Politiques en Belgique'.
34. Spitaels, op. cit., 58–61.
35. See CH 866, 22–4 and 26–30.
36. J. Moden and J. Sloover, *Le Patronat Belge* (CRISP — 1981), 10.
37. Ibid., 11.
38. Ibid.
39. Ibid., 11–12.
40. Ibid., 13–14.
41. The discussion of the ideology of the *Patronat* is taken from ibid., esp. 21–41 (analysis of the offensive against business); 42–61 (on industrial relations) and 71–149 (for the riposte).
42. However, in an interview to *Libre Belgique* (27 April 1979), Mr J. de Staercke of the FEB considered 'concertation to be now impossible, at least in the short term'. This was already a sign of later attitudes.
43. Report to the 2nd Congress of Walloon industrialists (1973), 3.
44. *Dossier du CRISP* no. 11, '*La Décision Politique en Belgique*', 17.
45. Ibid., 17.
46. Ibid., 17.
47. Ibid., 17–18.
48. For details, see ibid., 17–19.
49. For details, see ibid., 12–13.
50. Details in *Dossier du CRISP* no. 10, '*Les Partis Politiques en Belgique*, 23–5.
51. Delruelle, Evalenko and Fraeys, op. cit., 147.
52. *Dossier du CRISP* no. 10, 16–17.
53. Figures from Delruelle, Evalenko and Fraeys, op. cit., table XXXIX (p. 147).
54. Figures from the *Annuaire Statistique* (1979), 369.
55. Figures from R. Campé, M. Dumon and J.J. Jespers, *Radioscopie de la Presse Belge*, Marabout, Verviers 1975.
56. H. Verstraeten, *Pers en Macht*, Kritak, Leuven, Table 1 (p. 14).
57. For these details, see Verstraeten, op. cit., 22–4.

7

FOREIGN AND SECURITY POLICY

Like many small nations, Belgium has been largely at the mercy of outside events, rather than ever being able to shape them. Her foreign policy options have usually been very few and in any case dictated by the great powers. She has rarely been in a position to exercise any real choice in the matter.

The foreign policy-making process

Several articles of the constitution refer to foreign and defence policy. Article 68 lays down that the King commands the armed forces. He did in fact do so personally in both world wars, but that is now inconceivable. However, articles 118 and 119 provide that the organisation of the armed forces must be fixed by law and their size voted annually. The King (the government) declares war and makes peace (article 68), but no cession, addition or exchange of territory may be made other than by law. The King concludes all treaties, but trade treaties and those imposing a charge on the state, imposing obligations on Belgian citizens, or dealing with matters already regulated by law, must be approved by Parliament. Other treaties must be communicated to Parliament. These provisions taken together place the conduct of foreign and defence policy in the hands of the Crown, but with certain limitations imposed by the need for parliamentary approval and the enactment of implementing provisions.[1]

Modern diplomacy has created far simpler forms of agreements than in the past, often called 'Executive Agreements'. These are accepted in Belgium and are concluded by officials or ministers, without the formality of a treaty. Nevertheless, if they involve measures which would, under article 68, require parliamentary approval, such agreements do not by their form alone escape this requirement, as the *Cour de Cassation* and the *Conseil d'Etat* have made clear in several decisions.[2]

Article 59 *bis* of the constitution has created a novel situation. Under this article, the Community councils are competent to conduct international co-operation in relation to cultural matters and '*personalisable*' matters (health, social, etc.). This means that treaties in these fields must, according to article 16 (1) of the Special Law of 8 August 1980, be approved not by the national Parliament but by the Community council.[3] Such treaties are presented by the

Executive of the Community. The doctrine seems to suppose that because the King concludes treaties, hence even those under article 59 *bis* must be negotiated by the central government. This seems a limitation on the rights of the Executives which is not self-evident from article 59 *bis* of the constitution, although the Executives would, as a minimum, have the right to be consulted on the negotiations. However, in an important keynote speech on Walloon external relations delivered on 2 April 1982 in Liège, M. Moureaux (PS), President of the Francophone Community Executive, set out a much more radical view, to the effect that the conduct of external relations in the 'devolved areas' fell entirely to the Community Executives and not to the National Government and that included the conclusion of Agreements. He went on to outline the measures which the Executive had taken or intended to take in order to give effect to this viewpoint, which included the creation of a Commissariat for External Relations, a proposal for Community Observers in a wide range of International Organisations and the conclusion of Agreements in the newly devolved field of '*personalisable*' matters. We see here an almost unique arrangement, however cautiously undertaken: a lower level of government in a semi-federal system involved in international relations. The French-speaking community has already made some use of these provisions, even before the 1980 Reform, to conclude agreements with foreign states or sub-states such as Québec on cultural and educational matters.

Parliament (or the councils) usually give their approval in the form of a law (or decree) with a single article stating approval of the treaty, which *does not* form part of the law and therefore may not be amended. Article 68 implies that for all treaties other than territorial ones Parliament may give its agreement by a method simpler than that of a law. However, a provision in a finance act to spend money on the execution of an international delegation does not suffice.[4]

Once approved, treaties are normally ratified, but the constitution does not require this. A more difficult question is that of promulgation. Laws must be promulgated to be binding (article 129 of the constitution), and the *Cour de Cassation* has ruled that to bind, individual treaties must be promulgated too. The law of 31 May 1961 (article 8) covering treaties is not clear on the manner of promulgation.[5]

Problems have arisen in relation to treaties and internal laws and norms. EEC regulations (or directives under the ECSC Treaty) are directly applicable and binding, and some EEC treaty provisions have been held to be directly applicable. In 1970 the constitution partly caught up with the development of European and international law, with the addition of article 25 *bis* which regularises the transfer of sovereignty to international bodies (such as the EEC). The ECSC Treaty had involved a very broad interpretation of the constitution; the European Defence Community (EDC), it was accepted by the government, would have required an amendment, as was probably the case for the EEC Treaty.[6] Article 25 *bis* has some limitations; it does not permit the permanent transfer of powers with no possible reversal nor does it permit the transfer of unlimited powers. The 1968–71 *Constituant* parliament was unable to deal with the issue of the relationship between treaties and derived international norms (such as EEC legislation) and domestic law, which has caused some problems in the doctrine (though few in practice). The courts have accepted the primacy of EEC law, though this interpretation went the other way from a 1926 decision of the *Cour de Cassation*, which was generally accepted until some years ago. The 1968 *Déclaration de Révision* included article 68, but no final action was taken. The Senate proposed to modernise the article and solve the problem of 'primacy' and impose a stricter condition for the approval of treaties under article 25 *bis*. The 1978 and 1981 *Révisions Déclarations* also include article 68.

The practical conduct of foreign policy

From the earliest days of the Belgian state, foreign policy-making has been a central concern of governments. The Foreign Ministry, earlier called the Department of Foreign Affairs, was one of the original five departments of state, together with the War Department and in 1908 a Department for the Colonies.[7] The Foreign Ministry was always an important department sometimes taken by the Prime Minister or in earlier times *Formateur* — 1831, 1832, 1836–40, 1847–52, 1852–5, 1870–1, 1878–84, 1917–18, 1935–6, 1938–9 (Spaak), 1939 (Pierlot), 1946 (Spaak) and 1947–9 (Spaak). In more recent times the post has usually not gone to a vice prime minister, but it does represent a senior Cabinet position, often going to a representative of a different party from the prime minister, but not always. On the one hand, for example, Spaak was Foreign Minister in various governments headed by P. Van Zeeland (Catholic) or Pierlot (Catholic), and Simonet (PS) was Foreign Minister in the Tindemans II and Martens I and II governments, but now for example Mr Tindemans (CVP) is Foreign Minister in the Martens V (CVP) government.[8]

Though the Ministry has remained a single administrative unit, its name has successively altered. In 1958 it added Foreign Trade and in 1961 Technical Assistance (to developing countries), renamed

Development in 1968.[9] Sometimes the various components —
Foreign Affairs and Foreign Trade and Development — had
separate full ministers in 1968–71 and 1977–8, for example, whereas
on other occasions one component would be covered only by a state
secretary. In the 1960s there were not very successful experiments
with deputy foreign ministers or state secretaries for European
affairs (e.g. H. Fayat, 1965–6) and a full Minister for European
Affairs in the 1966–8 government (R. Van Eslande [CVP]).

Prime ministers have come increasingly to play a major rôle in
foreign affairs, not least in EEC matters due to the regular European
Council meetings. This is particularly true of a figure like Leo
Tindemans, one of Belgium's few internationally known politicians.
The King, too, has a rôle to play in foreign policy; he is kept well
informed of events by the Ministry and may from time to time
directly advance Belgian interests.[10] Major decisions in foreign
policy will require discussion in Cabinet, and may create serious
divisions in the government coalition, such as SP opposition to the
NATO Council's decision in 1979 on Theatre Nuclear Forces (TNF).
Other more routine or urgent matters will be examined in the
Cabinet's External Policy Committee. Where co-ordination is
important, as between various departmental viewpoints, (this is
especially marked in connection with EEC affairs, which touch areas
well beyond those normally affected by foreign affairs, such as
agriculture, social policy, etc.), the *Comité Ministériel de Coordina-
tion Economique et Sociale* (CMCES), backed by the Civil Servants'
Committee, the *Commission Economique Internationale* is the
responsible central body. This was not without difficulties, since the
CMCES was overloaded with domestic policy issues and the
External Policy Committee was not ideal for many of the economically oriented foreign policy issues which had been in the forefront of
attention in the 1950s and 1960s. The issue was solved at least for
European issues by the creation — under Vicomte Davignon, the
long-term *Chef de Cabinet* of successive Ministers — of *ad hoc*
groups of officials. Ministers concerned with EEC affairs also met.
Under the first government of Leo Tindemans, the CMCES made a
comeback and became a powerful co-ordinating and centralising
body, with more sub-committees — at least nine of the CEI being
set up to support the CMCES. The Foreign Affairs Committee was
virtually abolished.[11]

The Ministry itself, like all ministries, is headed by the Secretary
General, but the Political Department, especially under Davignon,
has always played a dominant rôle. The Ministry employs 1,675 full-
time staff (1,298 in 1970) and 1,903 technical personnel (1,687 in

1970), making it one of the smaller ministries, at least as regards its central Brussels-based personnel.[12]

Under the General Secretary is a legal service, a department for European policy co-ordination, and a 'think tank'. There are Directorates-General for Administration; for External Economic Relations (area directorates), supported by a *Comité Consultatif du Commerce extérieur*; for Chancery matters; for Political Affairs with seventeen area and Regional services; and for Information and Cultural matters. Finally, there is an Administration for Development Co-operation, assisted by a consultative '*Conseil de Coopération au Développement*'.[13]

The role of Parliament

Here we shall consider the rôle of the Central Parliament though, as we have seen, the Community Councils can be involved in foreign policy making and both the *Vlaamse Raad* and the *Conseil de la Communauté française* have set up foreign policy (or co-operation) committees. As we have seen, article 46 of the constitution authorises Parliament's two Houses to organise their work as they think fit. Initially, the standing orders of both Houses provided for one committee per department (the Senate in 1850 and the Chamber in 1936). As we have seen, this strict parallelism has been abandoned. After a period of multiplication of committees dealing with foreign affairs in both Houses during the 1960s — with separate committees for development policy, foreign trade, foreign affairs and, in the Chamber, European affairs (1963–79) — there has been a concentration in both Houses, leaving only a single committee in each House: *Affaires étrangeres* (the Chamber) and *Rélations extérieures et Défense* (the Senate).[14] In general, the Senate has shown less interest than the Chamber in foreign policy. Other committees deal with foreign affairs issues from time to time.[15] Such issues involving constitutional revision (articles 25 *bis* and 68) are always made the responsibility of a special committee. Some major treaties such as the Council of Europe Statute, Marshall Aid Treaties, and the ECSC and EEC Treaties were examined in special committees.

Most treaties are examined in the foreign affairs committees. In the Senate only thirty-two out of 455 were sent to other committees (twenty-one to the Finance Committee). In the Chamber, of those treaties not approved without report, 90 per cent went to the FAC (foreign affairs committee).[16] Some treaties with special technical characteristics such as ILO conventions, maritime pollution conventions, double taxation agreements and bilateral transport agreements have gone to the appropriate specialist committees. Few other bills come to the FAC, since the Foreign Ministry sponsors few bills. Foreign related bills — aliens legislation, extradition legislation, matrimonial and other family private international law bills — mostly go to the Legal Committee.[17]

The FAC has made little use of the provisions of the Chamber's standing orders which allow other committees to be consulted for an opinion. There seem to be only five cases since 1955, but *rapporteurs* do ask for information from other committees and from ministries other than the sponsoring ministry.[18] The FAC itself has been asked for opinions on the two direct election bills.

The Chamber and Senate rules permit joint committee meetings and even joint Chamber-Senate committee sessions, but usually only for information sessions. The Senate Defence and FAC, for example, met in joint session on 29 November 1973 to hear an exposé on a reform plan for the army; the same committees held three joint meetings in November/December 1979 to discuss the TNF issue. The Chamber's committees met in July 1979 to discuss the military situation in Zaire.[19] Joint committee meetings on bills are very rare and, except for the Direct Elections Bill in 1977/78 and the Lomé Conventions, have all taken place a long time ago (ECSC Treaty, EDC Treaty).

Joint Chamber-Senate meetings have usually been held to hear an exposé from ministers or other personalities on a topical and urgent issue.[20] Kurt Waldheim addressed the two Foreign Affairs Committees in February 1975; Claude Cheysson (later French Foreign Minister but then EEC Commission Member responsible for Development Policy and the EEC Budget) in April 1975, and Leo Tindemans (on European union) in February 1978. There were joint meetings on the European Council (1979), Afghanistan (1981) and African policy (March 1981).

As in all committees, the composition of the Chamber (twenty-three members) and Senate (twenty-seven members) committees are microcosms of the Houses as a whole. At present there are ten PSC/CVP, seven PS/SP, four PRL/PVV, one FDF and one VU in the Chamber committee and nine CVP/PSC, seven SP/PS, three PRL/PVV, six FDF and two VU in the Senate Committee. Over the past twenty years this has varied but little; the lowest PRL/PVV representation was two, the highest PS/SP representation ten.[21] Until 1979 it was traditional for the President of each House to chair the Foreign Affairs Committee, hence the Chairman often (as now) came from the opposition.[22] There is one Vice Chairman. All Deputies have been able to attend committee meetings since 1973 in the Chamber and all Senators since 1945, without the right to vote or speak, unless the Committee decides otherwise, as has happened, but not recently except for government statements, especially on defence matters. Staff of the political groups and party research institutes (Chamber only) may also attend. Groups too small to be represented in the committees (e.g. Communists) may send one representative. Since direct elections, provision has been made to permit Belgian MEPs who are not Deputies to attend the Foreign Affairs Committee in the House.[23] The committees are attended by ministers: not merely by the Foreign Minister, but by whichever minister may be competent to deal with a specific issue. They are accompanied by officials.[24] In both Houses there are ten senior officials responsible for the secretariat of *all* committees.[25]

There is considerable continuity in membership in the Chamber and Senate committees. Over the last twenty years, 104 members have belonged to the Chamber Committee and 113 in the Senate. The average length of membership is 5.3 sessions in the Chamber and six sessions in the Senate. The record is twenty-two sessions in the Chamber FAC (Mr Glinne). Two Senators have been members for twenty-one sessions. Few members have been members for less than three sessions (twenty-eight in the Senate and thirty in the Chamber). The committees have numbered among their members many past and future ministers in the Chamber (Larock, Spaak, Fayat, Petry, Nothomb, Van Eslande, Van Aal) and in the Senate (Harmel, Eyskens and Calewaert).[26]

As to procedure, the committees may deal with bills (rarely) referred by the President of their House, hear reports from ministers, and discuss reports. The Chairman calls the meetings and fixes the agenda. Priority is given to the budget of the Foreign Affairs Ministry and government bills. As in other committees — with even more emphasis — reports do not identify the speakers who expressed particular views and the committee minutes are confidential. As a general rule members' statements in the committee cannot be referred to in plenary, but ministers' and officials' statements may be mentioned. Committees may hold hearings — since 1973 this power has been considered to cover any issue before the committee. The majority of the committee must agree to the hearing. With the assent of the Bureau of the House, contradictory hearings can take place, but the FAC's have held almost no such hearings. Likewise few Enquiry Missions have been sent (only Ruanda in 1971).

Looking at the balance sheet of activity of the FAC in the Chamber, it has held about twenty meetings in an average session (seventeen in 1975/6 and twenty-four each in 1977/8 and 1979/80) as against 242 meetings of all thirteen committees in 1979/80. It is only behind the Finance Committee (sixty-two meetings in 1979/80) and Legal Affairs (thirty-two).[27] In the Chamber, since 1962, treaties may be dealt with (as other matters) without report, where there are no amendments or important comments. This happened with 296 out of 491 treaties presented for ratification between 1961 and 1981.[28]

Between 1963 and 1979 there was, as we have seen, a special European Affairs Committee (EAC)[29] in the Chamber, established by article 83 of the rules as revised in 1962. The idea of such a committee had already arisen in the debate on the ratification of the Rome Treaties in 1957, especially in relation to the law of ratification (article 2), which requires the government to present an annual EEC report. The committee was to examine 'the consequences and application of the treaties', but was not to develop in the direction of Denmark's Market Relations Committee, exercising control: '[It] shall exercise a power not of control, but of information and contact.' The committee was quite active before 1970, though hardly dynamic or effective; thereafter it faded out. In all it held ninety-five meetings, but only twenty-three have been held since 1970, mostly on the Direct Elections bill. It has only examined two bills and has only presented six reports to the whole House, the last in 1970. These reports were mostly of a purely factual nature. The committee has mostly met to hear ministerial statements: forty in all (only nine since 1970). On the other tasks laid down in the old article 83 of the Chamber's Rules, the balance sheet is also thin:

— Reports from the government: 3 in all; 2 debated (1962 and 1972).
— Reports from Belgian delegations to international assemblies:
  European Parliament   7
  Council of Europe   4
  Benelux   6
  WEU Assembly   5

Parliament can also consider foreign affairs in plenary session. As we have seen, in the case of treaty ratification, the plenary Chamber and Senate devote little time or interest to such matters. Indeed, with only rare exceptions such as the purchase of the F-16, the controversy over the NATO TNF decision, the Schelde River Treaties and earlier the European Defence Community, and the Congolese events, foreign policy issues are rarely controversial on the floor of either House. Foreign affairs debates are organised from time to time with an exposé by the Minister as well as occasional statements and short debates on some issues. There are few parliamentary questions on foreign affairs.[30]

In sum, Parliament has never, with the possible exception of EEC affairs, shown a marked interest in or influence on foreign affairs, which remains almost exclusively within the domain of the Executive.

Belgian foreign policy

From Independence till the Second World War

Belgium's lack of options has not in any way diminished the importance of international relations; which have been and remain vital for the survival and prosperity of a small virtually indefensible trading nation with an open economy. Indeed, it should be recalled that the very existence of Belgium is due to the support of certain great powers at the crucial moment after the Revolution of September 1830 had obtained an initial success. Britain and France combined to ensure the survival of the fledgling state. Other powers, such as Russia and Prussia, supported the Dutch cause but were unable to impose this 'legitimist' viewpoint in the face of the Franco-British front.[31] Belgium therefore lived from 1830 till 1914 under an International Statute, which imposed neutrality upon her in perpetuity. This was the price — a small price — which had to be paid to ensure her survival and the withdrawal of the Dutch armies from her territory. Belgian independence and territorial integrity were guaranteed by the major powers such as Britain, France and Prussia (later Germany).

The fundamental options of Belgium's foreign policy were thus defined by her International Statute.[32] She had in effect to refrain from participation in alliances or other combinations of powers which made up the fabric of nineteenth- and early twentieth-century international relations. Her concerns were therefore essentially localised or economic: to foster good relations with her immediate neighbours France, Germany and the Netherlands (to repair the damage caused by the Revolution), to maintain good relations with her main guarantor Britain, and to develop freer trade by a number of commercial treaties. As a liberal and neutral state, she became the haven for opponents of repressive regimes such as the Second Empire and Bismarck's Germany, which caused pressure to be brought to bear on her — which she could not always resist — to curb their activities. These, however, were mere incidents of little fundamental longer-term importance, despite the controversy generated inside and outside Belgium by such events. Likewise, the

severing of diplomatic relations with the Vatican in 1880, controversial though it was, had few genuine international consequences,
representing in reality more a symbolic gesture in the internal
struggle between the temporarily ascendent anti-clerical Liberals
and the Catholic Church.

The only matters of substantive importance in foreign policy in
the period up to 1914 were colonial policy, at first the personal
venture of Leopold II and after 1908 of the state, and the difficult
question of military policy.

There was initially a great reluctance on the part of the Belgian
state to become a colonial power. The expense and military obligations involved and above all the dangers of conflict in Africa with
other major colonial powers, some of which were vital for Belgian
security in Europe, were factors in this negative attitude. The King
however pursued the policy of colonisation in the Congo as a private
policy. Gradually, first by giving him the necessary constitutional
waiver to become head of a second state and then from 1900 by
providing loans and guarantees, the Belgian state became progressively involved, until in 1908 a take-over became both necessary and
unavoidable. Thus Belgium joined the ranks of the major colonial
powers.[33]

Military policy became an issue in the later nineteenth century
both in regard to the fortification of Antwerp, the level of military
expenditure, and the injustice of the conscription system which
allowed richer young men to escape their obligations by purchasing a
replacement. There was always a strong body of opinion, led by
Leopold II and Albert I, who sought a stronger defence policy:
Belgium should be able to defend her neutrality effectively. But
others were sceptical, believing such a rôle to be impossible in a
modern war. The debate concentrated in the 1870s on the new
defence concept of a withdrawal from the old 'barrier' fortresses
dating from 1715 to a redoubt at Antwerp to serve as the base from
which foreign allies could launch a counter-attack. This provoked
tension between the Communities and the strong opposition of the
progressive local, particularist and anti-militarist Antwerp *Meeting
Partij* (the English word was used — they began by holding
meetings). The real value of such a defence policy was in any case
doubtful, but this internal opposition showed the limits to which any
government could go.[34]

However, the dangers facing the new nation were real enough: the
Dutch threat, until the Five Treaties of London of 1839 whereby
reasonable relations were restored with the Netherlands; Prussian
opposition to Belgian military measures; and the ambitions of
Napoleon III, who sought to reverse the order established at the

Congress of Vienna. After the fall of Napoleon III in the Franco-Prussian war, the rise of Germany as the leading continental power was the chief menace to Belgium.

As early as 1866, Napoleon III and Bismarck, had discussed a partition of Belgium; Bismarck's aim then was to buy off France without offending Britain. However, Germany had no need of any such compromise in order to complete its unification, since she easily defeated France in 1870. Britain firmly opposed any action by France to involve Belgium in that war; nevertheless, Belgium mobilised 83,000 men in great haste, but the rapid defeat of France at Sedan avoided any use of Belgian territory by either side.[35]

The period 1871-1914 was one of alliance-building, from which Belgium was excluded by her Statute. The *Entente Cordiale* (1904) became the Triple *Entente* with the inclusion of Russia in 1907. The central powers of Germany, Austria, Turkey and Italy constituted the opposing bloc. The 1899 disarmament Congress at The Hague failed, and the period to 1914 was marked by an arms race, and competitive colonial expansion (the division of Africa took place at the Berlin Conference of 1885), punctuated by periodic crisis which might as easily have led to a generalised European war as did the fatal shots at Sarajevo in July 1914. It became ominously clear in the period before 1914 that German military plans probably involved the use of Belgian territory in their enveloping attack against France — the famous Schlieffen plan. For example, the question of the Belgian attitude to such a passage was raised during the visit of King Leopold II to Potsdam in January 1904 and again during a visit by King Albert in November 1913.[36]

Belgium was committed to defending her neutrality against attack from *any* quarter. That was the dilemma: all knew where the attack would come from, but no alliances could be prepared to counter the threat in order to preserve a fictive 'neutrality'. In 1887 new fortified positions were built on the Meuse at Liège and Namur. At the same time partisans of a field army capable of a more active defence joined supporters of personal military service in the interests of equity. However, an early attempt at such a reform failed in the Chamber by 69-62 in July 1887. Leopold II personally entered the battle for a stronger and fairer army as did his successor Albert. The law of 1902, increasing the army strength from 130,000 to 187,000, likewise failed to grasp this nettle, which was only grasped in 1909 together with other measures reinforcing the defensive triangle Antwerp-Liège-Namur. Finally, with international tension mounting, Parliament approved an increase in the length of military service from fifteen months to two years.

All these efforts were inadequate. Germany issued her ultimatum to Belgium on 2 August 1914, entering Belgian territory two days later. By 20 August Brussels had fallen, and by October Belgian forces only held, despite the efforts of her allies in the Mons area, a small strip of territory on the River Ijzer in the north-west, a salient with Ypres, Dixmude and Nieuwpoort on the coast as its outer extremities. So it was to remain until the end of the war, with the government sitting in Sainte-Adresse near Le Havre in France.

The key diplomatic issue had been the belligerent status of Belgium. She had fought to defend her independence and neutrality, but she was not *ipso facto* a member of the *Entente*, in spite of having fought alongside the *Entente* powers. She declined to sign the Treaty of London of September 1914, by which the those powers pledged themselves not to conclude a separate peace. She did, however, obtain in 1916 the 'Declaration of Ste Adresse' by which the *Entente* powers declared that they would conclude no peace which did not restore Belgium to full independence.[37]

Some sought to push Belgium fully into the Allied camp and increase her peace demands, for instance over the matter of the River Schelde. King Albert rejected such an approach and even refused an integrated military command. He continued to conduct his independent diplomacy, following up President Wilson's 1916 Peace Appeal; he later supported an active Belgian rôle in the first, abortive Franco-German contacts in July 1917. These failures led eventually to Paul Hymans becoming Foreign Minister and de Brocqueville's resignation as Prime Minister in July 1918. Indeed, continued German demands on Belgium made compromise impossible.

At the Versailles Peace Conference, Belgium appeared as a power 'with limited interests'. However, she had formulated wide-ranging demands in a series of notes, the first of which was sent to the Allied powers on 18 September 1918 — before the end of the war. These demands involved the ending of her compulsory neutrality, the return of areas ceded to the Netherlands in 1831 and 1839, resolution of the Schelde question, the return by Germany of the *Cantons de l'Est* (Eupen-Malmedy); colonial acquisitions in Africa and reparations for war damage. But Belgium was not an Allied power — by her own choice — and so had no seat in the inner circles of the conference such as the Council of Ten (the leaders of the five major Allied powers: the United States, Britain, France, Japan and Italy) or the 'Big Three' meetings (the United States, Britain and France). Also, Belgian demands either to a great extent affected the neutral Netherlands which President Wilson rejected, or, in the case of Luxembourg, which she sought to annexe, clashed with the goals of a larger power, France. Belgium had therefore to be content with reparations spread over thirty years and with $2\frac{1}{2}$ billion gold francs as an immediate payment; a commission on the Schelde, which achieved little; League mandates over Rwanda and Burundi in Africa; gaining Eupen-Malmedy; and the ending of her imposed neutrality. Later, in 1921, an economic union with Luxembourg was achieved.[38]

Belgium, between the world wars,[39] followed three basic lines of foreign policies and sometimes two of them in parallel. She joined the League of Nations and worked actively within the League for effective collective security policies and disarmament. Thus she signed the Kellogg-Briand Pact of 1926, condemning recourse to war and offering disarmament negotiations. She also sought closer economic relations with the small Nordic democracies and the Netherlands. This policy led to the Oslo Covention (1930) and the aborted Ouchy Convention (1931). These attempts, which could also have had political effects, were blocked by Britain for economic reasons. It is no accident that these were also the countries which sought most keenly to give the League some value in terms of collective security. Belgium also signed the Locarno Pact of 1925 by which several powers, including Germany, France and Britain, exchanged mutual guarantees and obligations to assist other contracting parties against aggression.

In the period before 1930, Belgium was a hard liner in respect to Germany and sought — without much success — to maintain a vigorous *Entente* relationship between Britain and France. Thus she signed a military pact with France in 1920, but failed to achieve a similar agreement with Britain. When Germany defaulted on reparations in 1923, Belgium joined France in occupying the Ruhr. The Dawes (1924) and Young (1929) Plans limited reparations, but did ensure some payments, until the powers accepted an end to reparations at the 1932 Lausanne Conference. Belgian toughness — while other powers vacillated — was without effect. Belgium did not understand — any more than France — the need to allow the Weimar democracy in Germany to breathe and live, little realising that the Third Reich under Adolf Hitler was at least in part the consequence of their attitude.

After 1933 — when reparations had been ended, the League became ineffectual and France and Britain showed in successive crises that they lacked the will to oppose the Nazi dictator — Belgium returned to voluntary neutrality, backed by greater military effort. Like France, she sought to preserve the '*acquis*' of Locarno, but a different spirit was abroad, exemplified by the total failure of the 1932–3 Disarmament Conference and Mussolini's proposal for a four-power 'directorate' in Europe, which would have involved the tearing up of both the Versailles and Locarno Treaties. Belgium sought to moderate what she still saw as French 'extremism' in relation to Germany, and sought international agreement to limit German rearmament. Such appeasement and weakness (but not total weakness!) were the muddled elements of Belgian policy in the face of increasing international tension in this period. Her policy — both military and diplomatic — was and remained contradictory, without any clear line.

Attempts at greater military strength alternated with periods of reduction. The room for manoeuvre was limited by the combined opposition of Socialists and the Flemish Movement (suspicious of a foreign policy too closely linked to France) to greater military efforts. Thus, in line with the tough policy in the Ruhr question, national service was increased to fourteen months in 1923, but it was later cut to ten months again, and the size of the army was reduced in the optimism of the spirit of Locarno in 1926. Pressure for six months' service led to a new compromise in 1928: a 43,000-man army, with 23,000 on eight months' service and 21,000 on 12–14 months. In 1936 when Hitler remilitarised the Rhineland, service was increased to seventeen months, but the 1920 pact with France was rescinded.

In the face of the worsening situation, the only apparent policy was that of avoiding conflict with Germany. Some Flemish opinion also saw in such a policy the opportunity to break with the *Entente* policy, which was based inevitably on a close relationship with France. Therefore in 1936 the government defined a new policy. P.-H. Spaak spoke variously of a policy 'exclusively and wholly Belgian' or of one 'which does not imply a return to neutrality, but which is merely independent'. Leopold III said that the country's military policy 'should serve only to preserve us from war, wherever it comes from'. Despite the words, this *was* neutrality, and Britain, France and Germany (!) gave guarantees to respect her neutrality in 1937. Each crisis thereafter was met with declarations of neutrality and mobilisation of the army — as occurred in the 1938 Sudetenland crisis, 'solved' by the Munich agreement, and when war did break out in September 1939.

Post-War foreign policy[40]

In the war against Hitler, Belgium became a fully-fledged Ally. Her government-in-exile spent the war in London, and the country became a founder-member of the United Nations in San Francisco in 1945. Like most nations, she hoped that the wartime alliance would continue into the post-war world, enabling the United Nations to function effectively to keep the peace as the League had so singularly failed to do. Despite not inconsiderable Communist influ ·nce in the Resistance, which caused some local problems, Belgium was liberated by the Western Allies, and by her own choice belonged to the Western alliance which formed with the onset of the Cold War. Opinion had matured in the face of the bitter realities of being a small country confronted by major aggressive powers. It was clear that Germany no longer represented a threat, but that with the onset of the Cold War, which paralysed the collective security mechanisms of the UN, a new threat had appeared in Europe: Soviet power, which stood on the Elbe. Despite assurances, one by one all the states of Eastern Europe had Soviet Communist-style regimes imposed upon them. The greatest impact was made by the last to fall: Czechoslovakia, which until 1948 had maintained enough external independence to, at first, accept Marshall aid and a degree of internal democracy. The 'Prague coup' in which the Communist Party seized power was a clear sign that Stalin had abandoned his cautious efforts to avoid conflict with the Western powers while making stealthy advances. Everywhere in Western Europe the threat was perceived — it would work either through military pressure or by an internal collapse provoked by the severe economic problems which arose from post-war recovery. Reaction was rapid and healthy: Belgium no longer sought refuge in the escapism of 'neutrality'.[41]

The reaction to the needs of post-war recovery and the later perceived threats from the Soviet Union as the Cold War deepened led to a series of initiatives in international co-operation, which profoundly modified Belgium's foreign policy. From being a traditional 'loner', reluctantly accepting aid in each crisis, she became an active and enthusiastic member of a series of interlocking European and Atlantic alliances. She was indeed one of the fi ·t to see the need for co-operation between Europ an states and to act on that viewpoint with the formation of the Benelux Union in 1944.

The three small 'Benelux' nations (Belgium, the Netherlands and Luxembourg) were all heavily dependent on trade, had suffered from the inter-war protectionism and 'beggar my neighbour' policies, and foresaw bleak prospects in a post-war Europe in ruins and with trade flows interrupted. To provide an enlarged market, they formed a customs union under a treaty signed in London on 5 September 1944. Despite some difficulties — safeguard clauses were agreed in 1953 and there was failure to move towards monetary union and supranational institutions as prefigured in 1949 — the Benelux was a success in itself and a model for later European integration.

Belgium was an active founder-member of the various European organisations formed in the late 1940s and early 1950s. Some of her statesmen, most notably P.-H. Spaak, became powerful advocates of European integration, which grew out of the Congresses of the European Movement (The Hague, 1948; Brussels and London, 1949). Belgium joined the Council of Europe (1950), but largely though not exclusively due to British opposition, it failed to meet the federalist aspirations of its founders, and was thus a disappointment.

There has always been a certain and perhaps deliberate ambiguity over the relationship between European integration and Atlantic co-operation. For some they were complementary approaches — this, at least initially, was undoubtedly the view of the United States. But for others they were at least potentially contradictory, with European integration seeking to create Europe as a 'Third Force', standing independently, but in an equal (or more than equal) alliance with the United States. No doubt this was one reason why Britain has always been so reserved about 'Europe', but Belgium never saw any such contradiction, but rather complementarity. She joined the European Coal and Steel Community set up following the Schuman declaration in 1950 — the basis of the 'Europe of the Six'. When the European Defence Community (EDC) — to which we shall return — failed to win approval in the French National Assembly, the Benelux states were among the most concerned at the loss of momentum, and worked tirelessly for the '*relance*' of European integration, spurred on by Jean Monnet when President of the ECSC's High Authority. It was the Benelux memorandum, in fact drafted by Mr Beyen (the Netherlands Foreign Minister) and P.-H. Spaak, which formed the basis of the *relance* of Messina in June 1955. Spaak presided over the ministerial committee which drafted the two Rome Treaties, setting up Euratom and the EEC, which were signed in 1957, both of which obtained ratification in the Belgian Parliament without any difficulty.

At the same time, there had been important developments in Atlantic co-operation. With the hardening of the Cold War, the US Secretary of State unveiled the Marshall Plan in July 1947 from which Belgium obtained US\$ 113 million in the following ten years. A European organisation of sixteen nations — the OEEC — was set up to co-ordinate recovery and the use of Marshall aid; the European Payments Union was set up as well to facilitate trade where currencies were often not convertible. Belgium joined both these bodies, a timely initial reaction to the dangers of collapse of the European economies which could have posed as great a threat as direct Soviet military intervention or pressure.

On the military level, Belgium joined, with Britain and France and

her Benelux partners, the Western European Union (1948) and
NATO (1949), which initially involved twelve countries. To meet her
obligations under the new integrated NATO command structure,
Belgium was required to increase her armed forces from 69,000 men
in 1950 to 169,000 in 1953, and to introduce twenty-four months
national service. These measures, taken by a homogeneous
PSC/CVP government, met severe opposition in Parliament from
the Communists, Socialists (despite P.-H. Spaak) and even Liberals,
and in street demonstrations, which forced ᴠ 1e government *de facto*
to reduce service to twenty-one months.

Whether it was liked or not, the key issue had now become, especially under American pressure, the rearming of Germany. Efforts
were made as early as 1951 to include her in NATO but these failed.
This was the genesis of the Pleven Plan, which surfaced in 1952 for a
European Defence Community (EDC), in which a German force
would be part of a supranationally controlled European army,
linked to NATO. An early problem was the refusal of Britain to join
the scheme. No doubt many 'European' activists saw this initiative
as part of the general drive towards European integration. Geo-
political hindsight, as well as the fact that, despite the failure of the
EDC, Europe was able to move ahead with the Messina *relance*,
shows us that the EDC was much more closely linked with the
German rearmament problem than with European integration. The
plan therefore was much more strongly opposed in Belgium than
either the ECSC or the later EEC and Euratom Treaties. The EDC
was ratified in the Chamber in 1953 by 148–49 (there were only seven
Communists) and by 125–40 in the Senate (three Communists),
showing considerable Socialist and even Liberal opposition. When
the plan fell in the French National Assembly, time had moved on
sufficiently to allow the direct integration of Germany and Italy into
both the WEU and NATO, under the Paris Agreement of October
1954 with only nine votes against in the Belgian Chamber.

For Belgium the following period was marked — apart from the
colonial problems considered separately — by EEC issues, NATO
and related military questions, and an active Belgian policy for
détente. She supported all efforts to speed up European integration,
and indeed it was her Commissioner (later EEC President), Jean
Rey, who gave the EEC its first real appearance on the world stage as
negotiator in the 1962 Kennedy Round trade talks. Belgium strongly
supported British entry to the EEC and opposed Gaullist attempts to
weaken the supranational nature of the community. However,
Belgian policy was always prudent and conciliatory. In the 1965–6
empty chair crisis, Spaak as Foreign Minister worked to act as bridge
between the 'Five' and Gaullist France, an approach which was

effective in bringing France back into the Community Councils.

Also, Belgium actually worked for a new impulse towards a stronger and more integrated Community. Her Prime Minister Tindemans was the author of a report, requested by the European Council and delivered on 29 December 1975, on European Union, which supported the notion of a common 'decision centre' on foreign policy and a common foreign policy, following up in a sense the initiative of the Davignon Report (1970) which formed the basis of political co-operation in the Community. The second central theme of the Tindemans report was support for more powers for Parliament and the Commission. She also enthusiastically pressed for direct elections, although public opinion was not particularly favourable to this initiative, showing stronger opposition (16 per cent) than all except Denmark and Britain.[42]

This last point is not without significance. Belgian public opinion — which is not unfamiliar with Europe, since the major Community institutions are in Brussels — has been merely passively supportive despite the strong support given by political leaders. The EEC has rarely been an internal political issue, and then almost always in a negative sense: protests by farmers over inadequate price increases; protests by small traders in 1970–1, against the introduction of VAT; Walloon reaction in 1980 and 1981 to Commission reservations about state aid to the Walloon steel industry; and reaction to a Commission recommendation to Belgium in 1981 on the level of public spending. However, Belgian opinion does remain conscious of the need for an effective community.

NATO was transferred from Paris to Brussels (civil organisation) and Le Casteau near Mons (military HQ) in 1967 following its expulsion by President de Gaulle. In the 1970s support for NATO policies and the military obligations arising from them became less automatic. In 1973 there were serious demonstrations against attempts to deprive students of the right to postpone their military service; these demonstrations at times took on an anti-NATO colouring. The government was forced to temporise and make concessions, looking more towards a differentiated army with a core of full-time professionals and a six-month national service period. The 'sale of the century' to replace the outdated Lockheed F-104 fighter, which involved costs of BF 30 billion over ten years, caused serious political repercussions. There was a prolonged campaign of demonstrations against the purchase, and objections were raised by Walloon Federalists in the FDF-RW against the choice of the American F-16 in preference to the French (hence European) 'Mirage'. The RW ministers were instructed to veto the deal in the Cabinet by their party executive, but did not do so. The government was lucky (the attitude of the RW Deputies being in doubt) to have its policy approved by the Chamber on 12, June 1975 by 113–92 with three abstentions.[43]

The issue of the regional distribution of employment arising from this deal, and the conflict over the three Belgo-Dutch Treaties on Schelde navigation and water flow rate on the Meuse/Scheldt which were opposed in Wallonia (1975), highlighted the increasing tendency for all issues, even those of foreign policy, to become involved in regional controversy.

At the same time these military debates were the precursor of a new trend, which became evident in the controversy surrounding the decision of NATO in December 1979 to install theatre nuclear weapons in Europe, in principle in Belgium, Germany and Italy to meet the alledged superiority of the Soviet tactical nuclear forces equipped with the SS-20. Despite some reactions to specific military decisions from the Socialists, foreign policy in Belgium had hitherto been a matter of broad consensus, barely worthy of debate. This consensus has broken down and both sides have taken up more trenchant positions. The SP (Flemish Socialists), under the impulsion of Chairman K. Van Miert and its defence spokesman Tobback, have become increasingly hostile to the NATO decision and insisted on the need to open serious discussions with the Soviet Union *before* any installation takes place. However, it is likely that the SP, would oppose any such installation in Belgium, especially while it is in opposition. This attitude finds support from some sections of the PS, the *Volksunie*, the Ecologists and Church groups, which are influential on the left wing of the PSC. This was evident in the massive demonstration in Brussels (200,000 people) on 25 October 1981 as part of the Europe-wide campaign against the NATO decision. The defenders of a strong defence posture, such as General Close, retired for making public statements attacking the weakness of government defence policy, have also become more active and less defensive. General Close has now become an active protagonist of the NATO case on many platforms, published a book on the issue and entered politics as a PRL Deputy.

Belgium had begun to explore the possibilities of détente at an early stage; in 1966–7 the Foreign Minister, Pierre Harmel, began a series of contacts with East European leaders (Romanian, Polish, Yugoslav), which were broken off by the Soviet invasion of Czechoslovakia in August 1968 but then resumed when he became, from 1970, the EEC's unofficial spokesman in the discussions preparatory to the opening of the CSCE Conference in Helsinki.

Pragmatism, bridge building and prudence have been the hallmarks of Belgian foreign policy since the Second World War. Her options and possibilities for action have always been narrow, but her activism and concillatory approach have enabled her to play a rôle beyond her size and power.

Colonial issues

As we saw in Chapter 1, from the mid 1950s internal pressures towards decolonisation, both in Belgium and the Congo, and external pressures in the United Nations and from the 'neutralist' block (later Group of 77), increased sharply. Matters came rapidly to a head after bloody riots in Leopoldville in January 1959. In January 1960 a 'Round table' of Congolese and Belgian leaders was held, which led to independence on 30 June 1960, after elections which were won by the partisans of Patrice Lumumba.[44] The new state had a disastrous beginning, when tribal warfare and an army mutiny broke out on 6 July. The threat to the large remaining Belgian colony and to Belgian interests led the government to intervene militarily in her former colony. This action was condemned by the UN Security Council, and Belgian troops were replaced by UN forces. Belgium also showed considerable sympathy, stopping short of recognition, for the breakaway Katanga régime led by Tshombe. These events, coupled with the murder of Lumumba, who had been dismissed as premier because of his move to the left and to a more 'neutralist' foreign policy, caused a violent anti-Belgian reaction both in the Congo, renamed Zaire, and in the Eastern bloc and Third World states.[45] Diplomatic relations were only restored with Zaire in 1963 after the Katangese separatist state had been defeated by UN troops. Further unrest led to a new armed intervention in 1964 but difficulties between Belgium and the United Nations were by this time less acute, as the Belgian aim was clearly to rescue white residents in danger. Financial and other problems between Belgium and Zaire were provisionally resolved in a 1965 Agreement, but the *coup d'état* by General Mobutu in November 1965 was to create new problems. Tension continued from time to time over financial and economic issues. The internal situation remained unstable and led to revolts in Katanga, which forced the Belgian government to withdraw technicians. The virtual nationalisation of the *Union Minière* company of Katanga in 1966 also provoked difficulties. From 1969 relations improved, with the visit of an economic mission to Zaire, a state visit to Belgium by Mobutu in 1969 and a visit to Zaire by King Baudouin in 1970 for the tenth anniversary of the country's independence.

Problems continued to arise sporadically, not least due to the activities of Mobutu's political opponents in Belgium and the

Franco-Belgian intervention in the Shaba province in 1978 to rescue white residents. It is difficult to avoid the conclusion that Belgium had not adequately prepared its colony for independence, and that in consequence of the important interests in mineral extraction (uranium, copper) of such companies as the *Union Minière*, she attempted to maintain at best a paternalistic and at worst a neo-colonialist interest in the internal affairs of Zaire well into the 1960s.

NOTES

1. For discussion of these constitutional requirements see Mast, op. cit., 320–6.
2. Ibid., 322 and fn. 57.
3. Ibid., 324.
4. See Ruling of the *Cour de Cassation*, 25 Nov. 1955, published in PASSIS (Law Reports), 1956, 285.
5. Mast, op. cit., 329–30.
6. See W.J. Ganshoff Van der Meersch, *Organisations Européennes*, vol. 1, Bruylant, Brussels, 1963, and P. Hayoit de Termincourt, 'Conflict Tussen het Verdrag en de interne Wet' (speech of the Procureur-Général, 20 Sept. 1963), *Rechtskundig Weekblad*, 1963/4, cols 73–94.
7. Luykx, op. cit., 407–8.
8. Ibid., 409–18 *passim* and 710–20 *passim*.
9. J.J.A. Salmon, 'Les Commissions des affaires étrangères du Parlement Belge', unpublished paper for the Colloquium on Parliamentary Foreign Affairs Committees held in Florence, April 1981, 8–9.
10. A. Molitor, *La fonction Royale en Belgique*, CRISP (1978) 51–9.
11. C. Sasse, *Regierungen, Parlamente, Ministerrat*, Europa Union Verlag, Bonn, 1975, 52–6.
12. *Annuaire Statistique*, 1979, 500.
13. *Annuaire Administratif et Judiciaire*, 1981/2.
14. Salmon, op. cit., 9–10.
15. For details, ibid., 18–22.
16. Figures in ibid., 24–5.
17. Ibid., 25–6.
18. P.F. Smets, *Les Traités Internationaux devant le Parlement*, Bruylant, Brussels 1978 and Salmon, op. cit., 26, fn. 39, for detailed cases; also 27.
19. Salmon, op. cit., 28, for rules, and 29–31 for more cases.
20. Ibid., 31–3.
21. Ibid., 34 and 35.
22. Ibid., 35.
23. For these rules, ibid., 40–2 and 45–7.
24. Ibid., 43–4.
25. Ibid., 42.
26. Ibid., 26–40, for data on membership.

27. Ibid., 51.
28. Ibid., 54.
29. For details on EAC, ibid 10–18.
30. Information provided by the Research and Documentation Services of the C.R. and Senate.
31. Frans Van Kalken *Histoire de la Belgique*, Office de Publicité, Brussels 1959, 565–9 and 574–5.
32. Ibid., 579–81.
33. Ibid., 641–52 and Luykx, op. cit., 239–42.
34. Van Kalken, op. cit., 594–6 and Luykx, op. cit., 186, 187 and 320–1.
35. Van Kalken, op. cit., 591–3.
36. Luykx, op. cit., 260.
37. Ibid., 266–9, for diplomatic developments during the war.
38. Van Kalken, op. cit., 703–6.
39. For a summary of her policy between the wars, ibid., 718–20; and Luykx, op. cit., 300–1 (Franco-Belgian military agreement), 344–5, 353–4, 365–7 (neutrality in 1936), and 379–81. For a more detailed account, see H. Jaspar, 'Locarno et la Belgique', *Revue Belge*, 1925, and Ministry of Foreign Affairs, 'La position Internationale de la Belgique 1934–39'.
40. For post-war foreign policy (on which this section is based), see Luykx, op. cit., 460–4, 471, 478 (EDC), 483–4, 545–7, 668–9 and 671.
41. Ibid., 460–4.
42. See D. Hearl, 'Belgium: Two into three will go' in Herman and Hagger (eds), *The Legislation of Direct Elections to the European Parliament*, Gower Press 1980.
43. Luykx, op. cit., 568–70.
44. Ibid., 498–501, and W.J. Ganshoff Van der Meersch,, *Fin de la Souveraineté belge au Congo*, Brussels 1963.
45. Luykx, op. cit., 516–19 and 547–8.

8
CONCLUSION: THE PRESENT AND THE FUTURE

Belgium, like other Western industrialised democracies, has been undergoing extremely rapid economic and political changes since the Second World War, and these have created considerable problems of governability and a certain crisis of credibility in her traditional institutions. As we have seen throughout this book, change has always been a painful and complicated process in Belgium, not least because of the complexity of the structure of the country's institutions, made necessary by her cultural and political pluralism. Our aim in this concluding section will be to bring together some of the threads which have run through our excursion into Belgian political life, and seek to see Belgium as she is now — a relatively young state, but an old nation, with many question-marks about her future stability. If, as would seem to be the case, the likely effect of these has been somewhat exaggerated, that is not to say that the country does not face serious and demanding problems. The points causing the greatest anguish today are relations between the country's two communities, the effects of economic and industrial decline, and the top-heaviness of decision-making structures.

It should never be forgotten that Belgium is two communities, or even nations, with a divergent, or at least different, historical experience and a different religious, cultural and economic history. It is, of course, true that a common allegiance to the Catholic religion in the seventeenth century war of liberation from Spain led to the Southern provinces remaining separate as the Spanish and later the Austrian Netherlands, but the Belgian state of 1830 was born of great-power interests and expediency as much as of a genuine 'national' feeling. The Revolution of 1830 was a Walloon or Francophone phenomenon, in which the Flemish provinces were passive bystanders, whereas they had been active and even leading actors in the previous dramas of the history of the Southern low countries. Thus not only was the state born in 1831 as in part an external and relatively artificial creation, but its internal basis was effectively only one of the two national communities. This fact alone does much to explain the difficult course of subsequent relations between the two communities. With the passage of time, a Belgian national interest or consciousness developed, but it did so unevenly and for mixed motives. For many economic interests, Flemish as well as Walloon, the national dimension was central to prosperity. For others on the

Flemish side, the future lay not in the restrictive nationalism of part of the Flemish movement, but rather in the dominance of Flanders and — through the dominance of Flanders within the Belgian State, which population trends and economic developments made inevitable — the eventual dominance of a wider space. This has been the logic of the long PVV and especially CVP attachment to the unitary state and wariness about federalism. It is indeed the logic of the '*CVP-Staat.*' (This means the process whereby the CVP, as the dominant party in the major region [Flanders], in effect dominated the whole of the unitary Belgian state. Although the term itself has been used by opponents of the CVP, the concept itself was — right up to 1980 if not still today — central to CVP thinking).

At the same time, if this development has provoked the Walloon movement into existence, broken the unitarism of the Socialist movement, and brought the PS to its present Walloon autonomist stance, it should be remembered that this is merely the same route which was travelled by the nineteenth and early twentieth-century Flemish movement. The political and economic history of Belgium is one of perpetual flux between the two communities, with predominance shifting from one to the other over time.

Although by the early 1960s a series of events had made the existing unitary state untenable, it was to take twenty years longer for the compromise of the 1980 Reform of the State to be reached, with the landmarks of the 1971 reform of the constitution and the 1977 Egmont Pact along the way. The 1980 solution was far from ideal, leaving too many overlapping competences and too few regional competences, failing to resolve the fiscal and administrative implications of the reform, and above all excluding Brussels. In an earlier period before the economic crisis, it is hardly imaginable that public opinion would have settled for a solution which, at least in respect of Brussels, the *Conseil d'Etat* itself regarded as of dubious constitutionality. However, the long years of attrition in the debate about 'Reform of the State' have no doubt wearied public opinion and led to a lowering of expectations. The collapse of the FDF vote in the 1981 elections seems to indicate this.

The Reform is indeed already under attack from both sides. The Liberals, always unitarists in spirit, have begun to ask themselves, despite their support for the 1980 package, whether devolution has not gone too far. Some Flemish opinion is also concerned that the regionalisation may have given the Walloon Regional Council complete freedom to spend Flemish money, and insists that regional autonomy and financial responsibility must be linked together. Other opinion, above all in Wallonia but also in Flanders, is looking to deepen the degree of regionalisation to be given to major crisis-hit industrial sectors, including steel, textiles and ship-building. The expressions of opinion from the CVP Congress of 13 and 14 March 1982 and the PS Congress of 26 and 27 March 1982, which tended in essentially the same direction, are most interesting in this respect.

Indeed, far from abating, as might have been expected, in order to allow the Reform of 1980 to settle down, these considerations have led to a renewed debate about regionalisation. The CVP now appears close to concluding that its old Belgicist concept, on which the CVP-*Staat* doctrine was based, is now played out, with regionalisation having reached the point of no return. It therefore now argues — *vide* the Van den Brande Bill (1983) for the Regionalisation of the Five 'National Sectors' — for a much more radical regionalisation, especially of responsibility for Walloon 'lameducks' such as steel, which would no longer benefit from Flemish financial strength. There is, in any case, a consciousness on all sides that the 1980 Reform is an inadequate patchwork and that a new, global initiative is needed. However, there is no consensus on its content.

Given the difficulties in pushing through even the relatively modest reforms of 1980, the persistent administrative and financial problems in making them operative and the continued criticism as to their utility, although few doubt their necessity, it might seem that a degree of consolidation was more appropriate as an immediate goal. The reforms must and most certainly can work, if given a fair wind. It would be wrong to under-estimate the degree of autonomy to be given to each region, especially after the next election, when the Regional Executive will be the pure expression of the majority of each community as expressed in the Community Council. When the final piece of the jigsaw-puzzle — the reform of the Senate — is in place, the life of the regional authorities will have acquired a permanence, untroubled by the vicissitudes of national political life and by the periodic dissolutions of Parliament. The reforms will in time give each community the opportunity to develop its own approach to its problems, freed from the heavy incubus of consensus-building at the national level. If that should turn out to be a more radical progressive approach in Wallonia and a more neo-Liberal approach in Flanders, so be it. Nevertheless, such development will require a degree of new thinking, a degree of flexibility at the national level, which will test the national genius for compromise. However, it is not impossible.

Brussels, paradoxically both the apple of discord and the last cement which holds the country together, must be given a proper status in this new regionalised Belgium. It would be hazardous to venture to guess as to what might be an appropriate solution. In the tradition of compromise, it must lie between the rival concepts of a '*region à part entière*' (a full regional status) demanded by the FDF and, with less conviction, by most of the Francophone parties, and on the other hand, the concept of a '*rijksgebied*' (national capital zone) under central government tutelage, such as is proposed with variants by most of the Flemish parties. In 1982 and 1983 talks have been held under the auspices of the FDF, between all Brussels Francophone parties in order to define a common position. Such a restructured Belgium can work; it can be the receptacle for more devolved powers as and when the necessity for such greater devolution is felt; and it can bring citizens closer to decision-making and enable them to give a more direct orientation to policy by their votes, since in each region the regional majority will not be counteracted by the majority in the other region or regions (if Brussels becomes a region). The reforms may enable some of the criticisms of immobilism, to which we shall return, to be met. Much depends on the economic climate, on a degree of patience in allowing the new institutions to prove themselves, and on a degree of give and take in political and inter-institutional (national/regional and inter-regional) relations.

The continued deterioration of the economic climate and its disproportionately heavy impact on Wallonia are matters for serious concern in themselves, as are the strains which they may impose on the political system. We have examined in Chapter 2 the Belgian economy, its underlying problems and inter-regional comparisons, and it is sufficient here to recall some of the most recent facets of those problems. Despite apparently strong action both on the unemployment front (the Spitaels plan from 1977 for job creation; public subsidies to promote investment amounting to 0.7 per cent of GDP) and on the cost-inflation front (reductions in public spending equivalent to 1 per cent of GDP in 1981, the freezing of salaries above 35,000 FB per month in January 1981 except for index-linked rises, increases in VAT), the Public Sector deficit has continued to rise, reaching 13 per cent of GDP in 1981 (target of 6.4 per cent) as against 9.1 per cent in 1980, and unemployment remains at 11 per cent. This situation has led to the unprecedented step of a strong EEC Commission Recommendation to Belgium in July 1981 to reduce its deficit and to look at the system of automatic indexation of wages and salaries, and to the subsequent microscopic scrutiny by the EEC of state subsidies to the ailing Charleroi and Liège steel industries. The Martens V government moved to introduce special powers in January 1982 for one year, which enabled it to moderate the indexation of wages by *Arrêté Royal* as a preparation for the 8.5 per cent devaluation of the Belgian franc (the first since 1949) on 21 February 1982. Given that 70 per cent of Belgium's raw materials, energy and foods are imported, such a devaluation (and the government wanted 12 per cent) inevitably led in time to inflationary pressures of considerable magnitude, which were contained initially by a price freeze until June 1982, and then by limitations on automatic wage indexation. The 1982/3 budget cuts were substantial.

In the end the issue is a political one: how long can the economic and political structure stand the successive shocks imposed upon it without reaction? Naturally those — the neo-Liberal PSC/CVP-PRL/PVV coalition — who have the task of administering the medicine argue that the shock is salutory and long overdue and will lead to a revitalisation of the ailing economy via greater profitability and a new incentive to invest and produce, whereas the opposition argue that not only are these measures socially inequitable, but they are bound to fail since they will not obtain the support of the working class and will depress still further an economy that is already depressed. Both sides in this permanent argument tend to agree on one point: the political structures of the country and of its interest groups ('social partners') contain excessive rigidities which make a rapid and constructive reaction to the present crisis — in one direction or the other — extremely difficult to achieve and carry through with consistency over a long enough period to ensure success. Therefore, it is to these rigidities that we should look to see where the country's main problems lie, and what are the chances of resolving or at least limiting them. Naturally, there are many and varied diagnoses, prognoses and proposed treatments for the '*mal belge*' (to borrow the title of a well known book, *Le mal français*). Yet it is striking that there is a great deal of common ground in all this analysis and self-analysis.

Belgium has seen the general scepticism and questioning of all institutions, which is a feature of our times in all Western societies, but she has seen it take particular forms. The loosening of religious and ideological references — with people becoming more free-thinking in every sense, with the Liberals actively seeking Catholic voters, the Catholic and Socialist sub-societies which cocooned their members losing their exclusive appeal — have contributed to the discrediting of the traditional structures of political parties and of bodies like the trade unions and the *Patronat*. At the same time, the rise of regional parties and sentiment, cutting across traditional confessional and ideological lines (the front of Francophone parties and the *de facto* common Flemish positions on community issues being but one example), have contributed to the weakening of traditional structures. The combination of confessional, ideological and community changes in both political parties and interest groups has greatly increased the complexity of decision-making on any issue which has community or ideological overtones — as most issues do. The fragmentation of society has also multiplied the need for formal or informal guarantees: linguistic parity in the Cabinet, coalition

majorities in both communities, the need for special majorities for
community matters, the need to associate Catholic and Socialist
trade unions with decisions and to take into account both the
Walloon and Flemish wings of interest groups — these have created
a multiplicity of institutional checks and balances — formal and
informal — and a total politicisation of all decisions.

The loosening of ties to traditional organisations — parties, the
Church, the unions at the grassroots level — has meant additional
complication, which may have its good side in that the character of
these traditional organisations may in time change, but in the short
term merely makes it more difficult for decisions taken by compromise and consensus methods to be made to 'stick'.

It is in the political parties that these tensions are felt most acutely,
and where criticism has been the most severe. It is often forgotten
that political parties are necessary in a modern complex democracy,
in order to give any meaning to individual votes and to permit collective action. The charge, however, is that the parties have become
ossified and bureaucratic, insensitive to change, machines dedicated
less to ideology than to the defence of their privileges and to the
exercise of power. This charge lies heaviest against the two parties
which have played a dominant role in their Community, both in
national and regional politics: the CVP and the PS. The PS has often
seemed over-reluctant to go into opposition; its local administration
has been called '*socialisme alimentaire*' (best translated as 'self-
interest socialism'), based on procuring advantages for its members
at communal and provincial levels. In such a situation, its ideological aims appear to have become watered down and its desire for
change tepid. Likewise, the CVP has been accused of using its
dominance to immobilise any reform of the unitary state until it was
virtually too late. The PS is also attacked from the standpoint of
Walloon activists as being ossified, still unitarist at gut level and
lacking in genuine pluralism or *ouverture*. Some, on the more radical
left, ask whether the PS represents 'more than a degraded version of
social democracy . . . so degraded that even its reformist nature
must be open to doubt.[1] These critics argue that the notion of
'structural reform', first espoused by the FGTB in 1954 and later by
the Party, as well as the apparently more radical analysis of the
development of the capitalist economy which emerged from the
doctrinal congress of 1974, is quite ineffective both theoretically and
practically. It is precisely to meet these organisational and doctrinal
weaknesses that the Party President, Spitaels, called the two congresses '*Renover et Agir*' in March and October 1982 in order to
modernise and dynamise the Party.

Parties have also been immobilised by internal tensions, which
have created ambiguity about their doctrines. The emergence of

'*Tendances*' in the PS (the left-wing *Tribune Socialiste* led by Ernest Glinne and the Social Democratic *Alternative Socialiste* identified with Mr Leburton)[2] have on the whole been fruitful, although the Charleroi-Liège rivalries in the Party have been less so. On the other hand, for the PSC the internecine struggles between the CEPIC and the *Democratie Chrétienne* have been disastrous to the Party's image and the clarity of its profile: the CVP too has been seen to become too much a party of notables and no longer a 'broad Movement'.

Many of these tendencies which alienate voters, especially young voters, from the traditional parties and even from the community parties can be subsumed under the term '*Particratie*', coined by former minister Marcel Grégoire as early as 1965 to explain the excessive power of the party apparatus, to the detriment of Parliament which, as, for example, Mr Périn shows in a recent book, has been reduced to a rubber stamp. Without going as far as the UDRT, which sometimes calls Deputies party functionaries, many statesmen — even those who have been Party Presidents such as Messrs Nothomb, Tindemans, Martens (PSC/CVP) and Gol (PRL) — denounce the *Particratie*. The CVP in its 1981 programme called for power of decision to be returned to Parliament and the Cabinet. Mr Nothomb has denounced the 'junta of Party Presidents',[3] which replaced the Cabinet as the real source of power. Of course, there are two sides to every question, and while it may be true that parties have in fact reduced the power of the Cabinet, it has not been unknown for the Cabinet and even the King to appeal to the Party Presidents of the coalition as if they were an arbitral institution, and especially on community questions, they have indeed been able to resolve situations which had become a total impasse.

As we have seen, the criticism of the CVP/PSC and PRL/PVV leaders seems directed more against the corporatism which has immobilised not only government and Parliament, than against the parties. This corporatism is seen to reside chiefly in trade union power, with which those centre-right parties have to deal even when the PS/SP is in opposition. Governments are faced with the need to obtain a consensus with the 'social partners' since there is in Belgium little tradition — given the ambiguities of the PSC/CVP, how could there be? — of government imposing its will on refractory interest groups. Compromise and consensus are the key.

This question should probably be seen in a wider context, especially in view of the widespread disillusionment among the electorate with the traditional parties and institutions. The multiplicity of layers of government, the need for consensus between regionally and ideologically divided unions and employers, the unwieldly and incoherent coalition formula which has been required to meet the pluralism and diversity of the country, has made government almost totally unresponsive to change and has made the time between a stimulus from the electorate and its working through the system, so long as to appear meaningless to the elector. The creation of coalitions rarely seems to spring from the will of the electorate. The Belgian polity can be compared to a massive oil tanker: a hefty pull on the tiller produces an infinitesmal change in course after about five miles of travel. Here the potentially more responsive regional governments, closer as they are to the people, can offer some hope — that is if their competences, though substantial, are not too diffused, too incoherent and too easily subordinated to the demands of national policy. If the regional path does offer some hope, it can only do so if it is allowed to operate as it should, with increased competences being added over time.

If this is not the path, or if it is made too hard and long, then it is possible that the alienation of the electorate will increase and a block of Deputies will emerge — certainly disparate but all equally opposed to the *status quo* — which will not be as easy to assimilate into the mainstream of traditional politics as the community parties in fact proved to be. However, the system as such has considerable resilience and the parties have an ability to move — which, combined together, will perhaps make such visions seem excessive. The evolution of the economy is central to such hopes, and this must be of concern to us outside Belgium, both because of the lessons that can be learned from the Belgian situation and for the possible impact on Belgian foreign policy, which could manifest itself in considerably less enthusiasm for European integration and in a further lessening of support for NATO policies at least in some sectors of public opinion. The key is that the continued success of the 1980 Reform of the State should be assured, and that there should be a degree of revitalisation in the economy as the 1980s proceed. A considerable evolution in attitudes must take place. Given Belgian pragmatism and realism, this is not impossible.

NOTES

1. M. Liebman, '*La Sociale-démocratie belge et l'héritage réformiste*', part 2 in *Contradictions*, no. 7, 1975, devoted to 'Le Réformisme Social-démocrate' in several countries (Belgium, 7–112).
2. *Dossiers du CRISP* no. 10, Annexe, 1.
3. *Le Soir*, 7 May 1981, 2, 'M. Nothomb brûle ce qu'il a adoré'.

BELGIAN MONARCHS

Leopold I	1831–1865
Leopold II	1865–1909
Albert	1909–1934
Leopold III	1934–1951
Baudouin	1951–

BELGIAN GOVERNMENTS SINCE THE LIBERATION (1944)

Prime Minister	Period of office	Party composition
1. Pierlot V (PSC)	1944-5	CVP/PSC — PLP/PVV — PSB/BSP — PCB —
2. Van Acker I (PSB)	1945 (Feb. — Aug.)	CVP/PSC — PLP/PVV — PSB/BSP — PCB
3. Van Acker II (PSB)	1945-6	BSP/PSB — PVV/PLP — PCB — UDB
4. Spaak II (PSB)	1946 (Mar.)	BSP/PSB
5. Van Acker III (PSB)	1946 (Mar. — July)	BSP/PSB — PCB — PLP/PVV
6. Huysmans I (PSB)	1946-7	BSP/PSB — PCB — PLP/PVV
7. Spaak III (PSB)	1947-9	PSC/CVP — PSB/BSP
8. Eyskens I (CVP)	1949-50	CVP/PSC — PLP/PVV
9. Duvieusart (CVP)	1950 (June — Aug.)	CVP/PCC
10. Pholien (PSC)	1950-2	CVP/PSC
11. Van Houtte (CVP)	1952-4	CVP/PSC
12. Van Acker IV (BSP)	1954-8	BSP/PSB — PLP/PVV
13. Eyskens II (CVP)	1958 (June — Nov.)	CVP
14. Eyskens III (CVP)	1958-61	PSC/CVP — PLP/PVV
15. Lefèvre (CVP)	1961-5	PSC/CVP — BSP/PSB
16. Harmel (PSC)	1965-6	PSC/CVP — BSP/PSB

17.	Vanden Boeynants I (PSC)	1966-8	PSC/CVP — PSB/BSP —
18.	Eyskens IV	1968-71	PSC/CVP — PSB/BSP
19.	Eyskens V	1972 (Jan. — Nov.)	PSC/CVP — PSB/BSP
20.	Leburton (PSB)	1972-3	PSC/CVP — BSP/PSB — PLP/PVV
21.	Tindemans I (CVP)	1974 (Apr. — June)	CVP/PSC — PLP/PVV
22.	Tindemans II	1974-7	CVP/PSC — PLP/PVV — RW
23.	Tindemans III	1977-8	CVP/PSC — PSB/BSP — FDF — VU
24.	Vanden Boeynants II	1978-9	PSC/CVP — PSB/BSP — FDF — VU
25.	Martens I (CVP)	1979-80	CVP/PSC — PS/SP — FDF
26.	Martens II	1980 (Jan. — Apr.)	CVP/PSC — PS/SP —
27.	Martens III	1980 (May — Oct.)	CVP/PSC — PS/SP — PRL/PVV
28.	Martens IV	1980-1	CVP/PSC — PS/SP
29.	Eyskens VI (CVP)	1981 (Apr. — Nov.)	CVP/PSC — PS/SP
30.	Martens V	1981 (Dec. —)	CVP/PSC — PRL/PVV

APPENDIX C

COMPOSITION OF THE CHAMBER OF REPRESENTATIVES (212 Seats)
(% of national vote and no. of seats held)

	1946 % Seats	1949 % Seats	1950 % Seats	1954 % Seats	1958 % Seats	1961 % Seats	1965 % Seats	1968 % Seats	1971 % Seats	1974 % Seats	1977 % Seats	1978 % Seats	1981* % Seats
PSC/CVP	42.5 92	13.6 105	47.7 108	41.1 95	46.5 104	41.5 96	34.4 77	31.8 69 (2)	30.1 67	32.3 72	36.0 80	36.3 82	(7.1) 26.4 61 (19.3)
PS/SP	31.6 69	29.8 66	34.5 77	37.3 86	35.8 84	36.7 84	28.8 64	28.0 59	26.4 61	26.7 59	27.1 62	25.4 58	(12.7) 25.1 61 (12.4)
PRL/PVV	8.92 17	15.25 29	11.25 20	12.1 25	11.1 21	12.3 20	21.6 48	20.9 47	15.9 34	15.2 30	15.5 33	16.4 37	(8.6) 21.5 52 (12.9)
FDF/RW	—	—	—	—	—	—	2.3 5	5.9 12	11.2 24	10.9 25	7.1 15	7.1 15	4.2 8
VU	—	2.1 0	—	2.2 1	1.9 1	3.5 5	6.7 12	9.8 20	11.1 21	10.2 22	10.0 20	7.0 14	9.7 20
PCB	12.7 23	7.5 12	4.7 7	3.6 4	1.9 2	3.1 5	4.6 6	3.3 5	3.1 5	3.2 4	2.1 2	3.2 4	2.3 2
UDB	2.2 1	—	—	—	—	—	—	—	—	—	—	—	—
Ecolo	—	—	—	—	—	—	—	—	—	—	—	0.8 0	4.8 4
UDRT	—	—	—	—	—	—	—	—	—	—	—	0.9 1	2.7 3
Vlaams blok	—	—	—	—	—	—	—	—	—	—	—	1.4 1	1.1 1
Others	—	—	—	—	—	2.9 2	2.1 0	—	—	—	—	—	1.1 1

The total size of the Chamber in 1946 was 202 seats. It was increased to 212 seats at the 1949 election.
* Figures in brackets give the PSC, CVP, the PS, SP and the PRL and PVV percentages of the vote separately.

INDEX

Index